THE WAR NEXT TIME:
Countering Rogue States and Terrorists Armed with Chemical and Biological Weapons

Edited by

Barry R. Schneider

and

Jim A. Davis

USAF Counterproliferation Center

325 Chennault Circle

Maxwell Air Force Base, Alabama 36112-6427

November 2003

Disclaimer

The views expressed in this publication are those of the authors and do not necessarily reflect the official policy or position of the U.S. Government, Department of Defense, or the USAF Counterproliferation Center.

ISBN 0-9747403-1-4

Contents

Acknowledgments

This volume is the product of many sponsors, authors, editors, and support staff of the USAF Counterproliferation Center (CPC). Special appreciation is due to the Chemical Biological Division of the Defense Threat Reduction Agency (DTRA/CB), now under the direction of Dr. Charles Galloway, who funded the printing and distribution of this book. Additional thanks to the office of the U.S. Air Force Surgeon General who provided the salary of Col Jim A. Davis, co-editor of this project, and to the U.S. Air War College, under the direction of Major General Bentley Rayburn, that did the same for Dr. Barry Schneider. Further appreciation is to be given to HQ USAF/XONP under the direction of Col Frank Wolf and to the Defense Threat Reduction Agency whose generosity provided the support to pay our staff and provide necessary resources to complete this book.

With regard to the authors, we thank each of the seventeen individuals whose combined scholarship we bring to you in this book. We, the editors, thank Mr. R. James Woolsey for permission to reprint a speech he delivered to a conference of the Foundation for the Defense of Democracies. We also appreciate that foundation for permission to reprint his words which were recorded on their internet web page.

We thank the late Dr. Burton Wright, former historian of the U.S. Army Chemical School, Fort Leonard Wood, Missouri, for supplying CANE documents that enabled Dr. Schneider to write his chapter on the effect of wearing full individual protection equipment for chemical warfare on conventional combat effectiveness. Dr. Wright was devoted to preserving the historical record of the U.S. Army Chemical Corps and is greatly missed for his valuable service.

The editors are grateful to the American Medical Association and the editor of *JAMA* for permission to reprint from their journal the chapter titled, "The Threat of Biological Weapons: Prophylaxis and Mitigation of Psychological and Social Consequences."

Similarly, we thank the CDC and journal *Emerging Infections Diseases* for its work in originally publishing the chapter we reprint here which is titled "The Economic Impact of a Bioterrorist Attack: Are Prevention and Post-Attack Intervention Programs Justifiable?" This study was brought to our attention during a visit of the Air War College elective class on "NBC Threats and Counterproliferation Issues."

Further, the editors owe a special debt of gratitude to Ms. Jo Ann Eddy and the other CPC support staff and consultants who devoted many hours to this project. Ms. Eddy's work was especially vital as she was primarily responsible for overseeing the typing, copyediting, production and printing of this volume including the taxing job of getting author and journal permissions, and securing ISBN numbers. We give our thanks to Jo Ann for her constantly outstanding work. Additional thanks are due to Ms. Brenda Alexander, Ms. Ruby Luther, and Ms. Abbey Plant for outstanding word-processing assistance. Ms. Plant was also responsible for developing the index of this book with the editor's guidance.

In addition, we give a special thanks to one of the world's best copyeditors, Mr. Armin Reitz. Each chapter of this book was improved as a result of having been "Arminized."

Finally, the editors are grateful for the loving support of our wives, Judith Keegan (Schneider) and Brenda Davis who encouraged us and gave us the freedom to devote many extra work hours to this book while they did more than their share on the home front.

Barry R. Schneider
Jim A. Davis

vi

Preface

This volume, The War Next Time, was begun before the initiation of "the war last time," namely Operation Iraqi Freedom (OIF). Most of the book has been updated to reflect that OIF experience. However, some of the chapters were reprints of journal articles or published speeches that took place prior to Operation Iraqi Freedom. Therefore, this is something the reader should keep in mind, especially when reading chapters 2, 8, and 9.

It is a central hypothesis of this book that the future conflicts of the United States are highly likely to be unconventional wars where the adversary uses unconventional means to try to level the playing field against the world's foremost military power.

Further, the editors and authors share the premise that this "war next time" very likely may take the form of biological and/or chemical warfare or terrorism. Therefore, that is the focus of this book.

As we say at the USAF Counterproliferation Center, "We cannot afford to be the unready confronting the unthinkable." To this end, this volume is aimed at educating the future U.S. policy-makers, airmen, soldiers, sailors, and marines who will be called upon to deal with the menace of adversaries armed with chemical and biological capabilities.

CHAPTER 1

Asymmetrical Rivals: The Enemy Next Time

Barry R. Schneider

Isaiah Berlin, in a famous essay, once wrote that thinkers could be classified either as foxes or hedgehogs. He wrote, "the fox knows many things, but the hedgehog knows one big thing.[1]" After watching the U.S. military demolish the Iraqi armed forces in the 1991 Gulf War over the occupation of Kuwait, one such hedgehog, the Chief of Staff of India's Air Force, concluded that the lesson of Operation Desert Storm for future U.S. opponents was "do not fight the United States without nuclear weapons." His conclusion was that no state, particularly no Third World state, could hope to defeat the U.S. military in a straight force-on-force conventional war.

Perhaps the Indian general was too specific in his advice since a more general formulation would gain a greater consensus from other strategists, namely, "don't fight the United States by conventional means; use an asymmetrical strategy and unconventional weapons to offset U.S. conventional military superiority."

In the twelve years between Operation Desert Storm and Operation Iraqi Freedom, little has changed to cause a strategist to alter this advice. Challengers are well advised not to take the U.S. armed forces on in conventional battle. One reason this is so is the massive investment that America puts into organizing, training and equipping its armed forces. The United States has fewer than five percent of the world's population but consumes and produces twenty-five percent of the world's GNP. With such riches, the U.S. Government is able to outspend all rivals in the area of military capabilities.

For example, the administration of President George W. Bush in February 2003 "requested $399.1 billion for the U.S. military in Fiscal Year 2004, $379.9 billion for the Defense Department and $19.3 billion for the nuclear weapons functions of the Department of Energy."[2] This figure does not count the additional $37 billion for the Homeland Security Department or the tens of billions in supplemental funding for Operation Iraqi Freedom. Put another way, the United States defense budget expenditures in 2001 were more than the combined expenditures of the next 12 states in the worldwide defense spending pecking order. Note the comparisons in 2001 in Table 1 below:[3]

Table 1
Military Expenditures in 2001 (in U.S. dollars)

Russia	63.7 B
China	46.0 B
Japan	39.5 B
United Kingdom	35.7 B
France	32.9 B
Germany	26.9 B
Italy	20.9 B
India	14.1 B
S. Korea	11.2 B
Brazil	10.5 B
Taiwan	10.4 B
Israel	10.4 B
	Total $322.2 B
United States	$322.4 B

The U.S. military budget increased to $379 billion in FY2003 before the multi-billion dollar supplement was voted for Operation Iraqi Freedom. The $48 billion <u>increase,</u> in the regular U.S. military expenditures between FY2002 and FY2003, was larger than the <u>total annual</u> military expenditures of any other state except Russia. Such disparities in resources mean that the outcome of Operation Iraqi Freedom was never in doubt from the outset.

The United States has become the world's military superpower, and its decisive victories against Iraq in 1991 and 2003, Serbia in 1999, and the Taliban in Afghanistan in 2002 all serve notice to its opponents that to take the United States head on in a conventional war is regime suicide. Enemies of the United States thus are driven to seek asymmetric means of preparing to fight or in attempting to deter United States use of force against them in the future.

For this reason, the enemy in the war next time likely will employ unconventional warfare strategies rather than suffer the same fate as the regimes of Saddam Hussein, Slobodan Milosevic and Mullah Omar.

A number of asymmetrical strategies are likely to be employed by the next enemy to emerge. Hit-and-run terrorist tactics will likely be emphasized even more by those who oppose and are determined to inflict damage on the United States. Cells of Al-Qaeda terrorists will continue to attack Americans, and U.S. and allied targets of opportunity until the U.S.-led Global War on Terrorism destroys their leadership, along with the state sponsors of such terrorists.

Dealing effectively with such shadowy adversaries could be the work of many years as the sources of their discontent cannot be fully addressed short of decades of re-education, economic development, settlement of outstanding international issues such as the Arab-Israeli conflict, and a persistent and global counter-terror campaign involving most of the countries of the world.

When rooting out the terrorist cells and groups allied with Al-Qaeda, the United States and its allies must pursue a careful strategy that preserves and expands its allies in the Muslim world and one that is careful not to galvanize a worldwide anti-U.S. reaction in the 45 countries that contain Muslim majorities or large pluralities. One-sixth of the world's population follow Islam as their religion and care must be made to separate the few jihadists from the vast majority of peaceful Muslims when combating terrorists. Otherwise, in the worst case, the U.S.-led war against terrorism could polarize into a war pitting the United States against a large fraction of the billion plus people who make up the Islamic world, a Herculean task that could have no good ending.[4]

It may have been the underlying strategy of Osama bin Laden and his Al-Qaeda followers when they planned the airline hijackings and lethal attacks on the World Trade Center and Pentagon on September 11, 2001, to do more than inflict pain on the United States. They may also have been trying to persuade it to withdraw from Muslim lands and claimed territory. Further they may have sought to spark a worldwide holy war that would mobilize Islamic fighters throughout the Muslim lands, influenced either by the 9/11 assault or, perhaps, by the anticipated draconian U.S. reactions or over-reactions.

Osama bin Laden's fatwa urging a jihad against Americans was published in *Al Quds al-Arabia* on 23 February 1998 and characterizes the conflict as one of Islam versus the Crusader-Zionist alliance. In it he clearly tries to rally Muslims worldwide by his inflammatory rhetoric. He asserts as "facts" that "the United States has been occupying the lands of Islam in the holiest places, the Arabian Peninsula, plundering its riches, dictating to its rulers, humiliating its people, terrorizing its neighbors, and turning its bases in the Peninsula into a spearhead through which to fight the neighboring Muslim peoples."[5]

The Al-Qaeda leader then attempted to mobilize the Muslim community by declaring that:

> "We with God's help call on every Muslim who believes in God and wishes to be rewarded to comply with God's order to kill the Americans and plunder their money wherever and whenever they find it. We also call on Muslim ulema, leaders, youths, and soldiers to launch the raid on Satan's U.S. troops and the devil's supporters allying with them, and to displace those who are behind them so that they may learn a lesson."[6]

Thus, the war next time might well be another clash with elements of bin Laden's radical Islamic groups, the state sponsors of such groups or other rogue states.

Out of the 192 countries that populate the international system at present there are less than 10 that stand out as actual or potential adversaries of The United States. These states have a combination of traits that mark them for special attention. First, their leaders have overtly identified the United States as their adversary. Second, they have been state sponsors of international terrorism, offering arms, financial support, and encouragement, training and/or safe haven. Third, they have a record of hostile and violent actions taken against Americans, U.S. allies, and U.S. interests. Fourth, and this makes them especially dangerous, they have either already acquired some types of mass casualty weapons or they seek such weapons. Fifth, they have record of collusion with similar states and groups of concern to augment each other's military capabilities, and plan actions against the United States and its allies. Finally, they are prone to violent solutions to disputes and endanger the peace and security of their regions and that of the United States.[7]

Such states as Iran, North Korea, Syria, Libya, Cuba, and Sudan fit this overall pattern, some more than others. Afghanistan under the Taliban and Iraq under Saddam Hussein, until their demise, also fit this mold. In addition to these rogue regimes, there are thirty-six international terrorist groups that top the U.S. watch list.[8] Al-Qaeda, an umbrella organization that connects many of them in the Islamic world, is the number one concern at present and has been seen to be behind such violent events as:

- The 1993 attack of the World Trade Center.

- The 2001 September 11th attacks on the World Trade Center and Pentagon.

- The 1998 bombing of the U.S. Embassies in Tanzania and Kenya.

- The 1996 bombing of the U.S. troop barracks at Khobar Towers in Saudi Arabia.

- The 2000 attack on the USS Cole when anchored at port in Yemen.

- Financing and planning numerous other terrorist events such as the blowing up of airliners, attempted assassinations of heads of state, and kidnappings.

These international terrorists of Islamic persuasion are imbedded in groups and cells of groups scattered throughout over 60 countries in the world, especially drawn from the disaffected in the 22 Arab states and other 29 non-Arab states with large Muslim populations.[9]

Indeed, elements within official U.S. allies, such as Saudi Arabia, are often the chief financial and ideological contributors to such radical terrorist groups. Note that 15 of the 19 participants in the September 11th hijackings, and subsequent attacks, were citizens of Saudi Arabia, as was Osama bin Laden, leader of Al-Qaeda.

Added to this mix of potential adversaries are the People's Republic of China (PRC) and the Russian Republic. At present, these states appear to be partners of the United States in some projects, trade rivals in others, and possible future peer competitors in other situations. China is ruled by a Communist Party that still identifies the United States as its most likely military opponent in its military literature and war games. Also, the U.S. protection and friendly association with Taiwan points toward a possible future crisis with the People's Republic of China, should Taiwan too openly declare its independence or should the PRC act too boldly to force its subjection. Clearly, there remain many hostile elements within the Chinese Communist Party (CCP), the Chinese government and Chinese military that predispose China to regard the United States as a future military opponent despite an enormous trade volume that has developed between the two states.

Chinese military writers have paid close attention to U.S. military victories in Iraq, Serbia, Kuwait, and Afghanistan and have emphasized the need both to embrace the new tools in the latest revolution in military affairs and the utility of adapting unconventional and asymmetrical methods of waging war to offset U.S. conventional capabilities.

Indeed, it would be surprising if future opponents such as these in a future military conflict did not seriously pursue asymmetrical capabilities to level the playing field against the U.S. giant. As the Chairman of the Joint Chiefs of Staff in *Joint Vision 2020* has stated:

> "In the face of such strong (U.S.) capabilities, the appeal of asymmetric approaches and the focus on the development of which capabilities will increase. By developing and using approaches that avoid U.S. strengths and exploit potential vulnerabilities using significantly different methods of operation, adversaries will attempt to create conditions that effectively delay, deter, or counter the application of U.S. military capabilities."[10]

In defeating Saddam Hussein's Iraq in the Spring of 2003, the United States National Security team planned against a number of possible Iraqi unconventional war scenarios. There was the worry about the possible use of Iraqi chemical and biological weapons. There were a number of possible times in the conflict that Iraqi forces might have plausibly used chemical and or biological weapons to disrupt the allied attack.

First, Iraq might have used such weapons on coalition forces as they massed in neighboring countries such as Kuwait or as the U.S.-U.K. forces poured personnel, equipment and supplies through regional seaports of debarkation. While this was a possibility, Saddam Hussein was unlikely to use his WMD in this preemptory fashion since his best hope of survival was to prevent the war from happening and such an attack would bring on the conflict. Using chemical and biological weapons, which he had denied having, would have lost him the last international support he had. International pressure against the war, in turn, was his last best hope of preventing the U.S.-U.K. invasion in a war he probably realized he could not win once it began.

A second place and time when some feared an Iraqi use of chemical and biological weapons was when the allied army approached and massed before the bridges crossing the Tigris and Euphrates Rivers on the march to Baghdad. Indeed, a number of Iraqi Republican Guard units blocking the way had, at the ready, their individual protective equipment including protective overgarments, gloves, boots, and masks, as if they anticipated such a chemical barrage even though none materialized.

A third scenario envisioned by some was the possible Iraqi use of chemical and biological weapons in the defense of Baghdad as U.S. forces approached the outskirts of the Iraqi capital. Again, this did not happen for reasons yet to be explained. Indeed, two key divisions of the Iraqi Republican Guards (IRG) were sent South of the city to intercept and turn back the allied Army approaching rapidly. Once in the open, and without an Iraqi aircraft in the sky, these IRG divisions were destroyed by lethal precision air and ground strikes. It appears that they were sent naked into battle as a delaying tactic, a sacrifice to allow the regime leaders to escape the trap that Baghdad was becoming.

Finally, some feared possible Iraqi revenge strikes where Iraqi forces would be ordered to launch missiles with chemical and biological warheads at surrounding countries that had cooperated with U.S.-U.K. invasion forces, cities in places like Kuwait and Qatar, for example. Indeed, it might have been just such a specter that Turkish politicians feared when they voted against allowing U.S. forces to go through Turkey to attack Iraq on a second front North of Baghdad as well as from the

South through Kuwait. Fortunately, Saddam Hussein, his sons, and the other remnants of his leadership either rejected or could not execute this Samson option in the end game of Operation Iraqi Freedom.

So, the Iraqi regime of Saddam Hussein was inept in its military tactics, strategy, and operations. They chose to hide, export, or eliminate their chemical and biological weapons rather than use them. They did not use WMD to disrupt the U.S.-U.K. attacks, nor did they deter such an attack. Further, they did not use WMD in the defense of Baghdad, choosing instead to melt away and to fight a rearguard, and not very effective, hit-and-run guerrilla war that still persists at the time of this writing (in the fall of 2003).

Thus, in the last engagement fought, the United States and allied forces encountered limited effective asymmetrical resistance, mostly after main enemy forces were defeated. However, the United States would be wise to continue to prepare fully against future foes who may be far more astute strategists and practioners of the military art[11] who may employ mass casualty weapons, utilize effective urban and guerrilla warfare tactics, utilize underground hardened shelters, launch ballistic and cruise missiles from hidden and mobile launchers, and attack our command, control and communications and ISR assets either with special operations forces, air strikes, ground strikes or cyber attacks.

For example, no such easy victory, as was achieved twice versus Iraqi forces in 1991 and 2003, is likely to be duplicated were the United States to go to war in the future with a rival as formidable as North Korea.

Indeed, a war in Korea might see multiple uses of unconventional tactics and weapons. It is possible that a conflict with the Democratic People's Republic of Korea (DPRK) would involve clashes of million-man armies on each side and hundreds of thousands of artillery rounds fired across the DMZ in the first hours of combat, many into heavily populated cities like Seoul. Also, North Korea is reputed to have over 90,000 special forces that might be directed to infiltrate the ROK and operate behind allied lines in a lethal guerrilla campaign.[12]

North Korean forces might attempt to cross the DMZ through tunnels, perhaps after attempting to soften up U.S. and Republic of Korea (ROK) forces through a combination of biological and chemical attacks. For example, such a rogue state armed with both might lead with non-lethal but incapacitating biological weapons such as Staphylococcal Enterotoxin B (SEB) and follow with non-persistent nerve gas strikes using an agent such as Sarin to create weak points in the U.S. and allied defenses that their conventional combat divisions could then pour through.

North Korean nuclear weapons might be kept in reserve as a deterrent to U.S. nuclear use, or might be utilized in high altitude nuclear bursts to create electromagnetic pulse (EMP) effects to blind U.S. satellites and destroy their downlinks, thereby robbing the U.S./ROK of much of its command, control, communications and intelligence (C^3I) connectivity advantages. It could also possibly disable U.S. satellite guidance of U.S. warplanes and precision guided munitions.

North Korean chemical, biological, and radiological weapons carried by Special Operations Forces (SOF), cruise missiles, and No Dong missiles could also contaminate ports in the Republic of Korea and Japan, interfering with U.S. re-supply and reinforcement efforts by disrupting work at the airfields and ports, possibly creating panic that, in turn, could cause Japanese politicians to close Japan's seaports and airfields to U.S. ships and aircraft.

Thus, if the next conflict were to take place on the Korean Peninsula, the U.S.-ROK casualty rate likely would be very high, and the degree of difficulty in confronting a formidable asymmetric adversary like North Korea would be daunting, even for the world's only military superpower. This is especially true for a state like the United States that is also saddled with the occupation and reconstitution of Iraq as well as a worldwide campaign against Al-Qaeda and other terrorist threats, while simultaneous shouldering a host of other security responsibilities.

In addition to security challenges on the rimlands of Eurasia, the continental United States could be a battlefield in the next conflict. Indeed, the global war on terrorism presently is being fought in the 50 states as well as outside U.S. borders. If any ruler of a radical regime wishes to defeat the United States in an escalating conflict on its home turf it probably should look at what caused the U.S. retreats from Vietnam, Lebanon, and Somalia. The best means of defeating the United States is not on the military battlefield against U.S. forces, but rather by somehow affecting the U.S. political will at home. Attacks on U.S. forces abroad or on targets in the United States might, over time, raise the threshold of pain high enough so that the U.S. leadership would decide to end the conflict by bringing American forces home.

Saddam Hussein once declared that the United States was so casualty adverse that it would not pay the price of more than 5,000 combat deaths in a regional conflict before it would withdraw.[13] He based this on his perceptions of the U.S. withdrawals from Vietnam and Lebanon, and the decline of U.S. political support for those military force deployments after U.S. forces got sufficiently bloodied. Saddam never got to test his 5,000 threshold theory in either Desert Storm or Operation Iraqi Freedom because he miscalculated the capabilities of his large, but ineffective, Iraqi Revolutionary Guard divisions. U.S. casualties in both wars combined, at this writing, are less than 500 total killed in action.

Striking the U.S. homeland is likely to be a losing strategy for a rival. It is far more likely to stir up a hornet's nest, rather than to coerce a U.S. peace initiative. Adversaries who attack the United States on its own territory in an attempt to destroy U.S. popular support for the war next time, however, will be playing with fire and are more likely to be burned badly by their own actions. While desiring the Mogadishu effect, they may be unleashing, instead, the Pearl Harbor or Post-9/11 effect of galvanizing fierce U.S. popular support for military retaliation. Rather than tie the U.S. President's hands, they may loose a tsunami of support for all-out war against the attacker.

As we consider what adversaries we might confront in future conflicts, additional care needs to be taken in planning war termination end games in order to prepare better to win the peace after winning the main military phase of the war. Critics of both Operation Iraqi Freedom in the Spring of 2003 and Operation Enduring Freedom in Afghanistan in 2002 argue that the primary military engagement phase of operations was better planned and executed than the subsequent phase of mopping up resistance, establishing a new regime and getting the Iraqi society back up and running again.

The parties to a war may choose to terminate a conflict for a number of reasons. One analyst of conflict end games identifies four theories of war termination:[14]

- Winners and Losers Theory: This "theory of termination would predict that when a state's forces were decisively defeated and the state's leaders realized that they lost the war, they would be compelled to seek an end to the war."[15]

- Cost Benefit Theory: This is "the idea that the decision to terminate a war is a rational cost benefit calculation."[16] Here the explanation is that decision-makers are predicted to only pursue their war aims through military engagement until the "marginal costs of continuing the war are not worth the objective, then the State's leaders will decide to terminate the war."[17]

- Political Leadership Shift Theory: Another explanation of why some wars are terminated is that, while leaders who plunge their states into war may be too committed to change their direction, they may be replaced in mid-course by others who are less invested in their course, who will seek peace if the war costs mount and victory seems elusive.[18]

- Second Order Change Theory: A fourth partial theory of how wars may be terminated is that, in some cases, the war begins to threaten higher values than those for which the war was launched, perhaps even the existence of the state itself. Thus, the war itself, once seen as the solution to problems, becomes the major problem itself, and must be terminated.[19]

In both Afghanistan and Iraq, guerrilla and other low intensity warfare continues at the time of this writing, even though both the Taliban rulers and Saddam Hussein's Ba'athist regime have been toppled and are unlikely ever to be reconstituted. In Iraq, the United States has suffered more combat deaths in this "post war" guerrilla stage than in the "wartime" large unit engagement stage of the conflict.

Endings of wars against determined opponents may require prolonged and bloody pacification campaigns. Few wars end like athletic conflicts where at a certain moment the game is over, a winner and loser are certified, and the record book is closed. Rather, wars end when the losing side is either terminated or has been so decisively beaten it has completely lost the will to fight on further. It helps greatly if a respected adversary leader formally capitulates and orders his or her own partisans to lay down their arms and cease hostilities, such as was the case when Emperor Hirohito ordered the Japanese to surrender in August 1945, ending the Pacific phase of World War II. Few major wars end so cleanly and some drag on for years after the decisive battles have been fought.

Clearly, if the United States and its allies fight future wars such as Operation Enduring Freedom and Operation Iraqi Freedom, they should have their planners relate the military campaign plans to the post-war rebuilding plans so that success in the first does not make success extraordinarily difficult in the latter. For example, it might be wise to develop the Air Tasking Order by keeping in mind the post-war nation-building requirements to come. Effects based targeting ought to consider the immediate military effects of taking down the assets of the adversary regime as well as simultaneously considering the long-term effects of rebuilding what is being taken down.

In the realm of weapons of mass destruction (WMD) asset targeting, the United States was careful in the 2003 Iraq campaign to attack only possible WMD delivery vehicles rather than biology laboratories, pharmaceutical plants, and possible WMD storage sites, because the latter types of targets, if hit, might cause considerable downwind and site contamination of the Iraqi civilian population, and the United States and its allies might then have been accused of using such weapons themselves as the disease agents or chemical contamination spread.

In future conflicts the United States is well advised if it were to develop a sufficient WMD elimination plan complete with:

- Sufficient numbers of trained inspectors.

- Chemical and biological sensors.

- A mobile on-site laboratory for early identification of biological and chemical agents found.

- Adequate decontamination equipment and supplies.

- Sufficient transportation for inspectors, decontamination teams, laboratory technicians, and guards.

- U.S. and allied interrogators with sufficient language skills necessary to question and understand indigenous scientists who previously worked on adversary WMD projects.

- Human intelligence that could pinpoint the locations of adversary WMD laboratories, research institutes, production facilities, storage sites, and deployed or hidden weapons.

- A system of rewards for cooperative adversary state scientists who substantially cooperate with U.S. officials in locating WMD infrastructure, materials, delivery systems and weapons.

In addition to WMD inspectors and elimination teams, post-war planning will require a comprehensive blueprint of how to turn essential services back on after the society's critical infrastructure has taken a pounding during the war. For example, teams of experts will be needed to restart the electrical power grid and get the telecommunications network (telephones, internet, radio, television, etc.) back into working order.

Police Forces will have to be brought in to augment and retrain the newly constituted local police to prevent looting, lawless behavior, and thievery that could otherwise flower in the chaotic aftermath of a military occupation.

Other U.S. and allied experts should be at the ready to reconstitute the banking and financial institutions, and health experts should be primed to oversee the maintenance of health service delivery. Water supplies must be protected and transportation (road mobile, railroad, air travel, and sea travel) routes must be protected, maintained, and kept open. Food supply and distribution systems have to be reconstituted and clean water supplies provided to the population of a defeated state. Public health facilities need to be maintained, supplied, and augmented. Roads, bridges, and tunnels will need to be repaired and reopened. Emergency services need to be reconnected to prevent chaos. Mail and shipping systems would need to be put back into operation, as would the major industrial plants, farms, ranches, and retail markets. Finally, the occupying power would need to provide the whole spectrum of government services formerly provided by the defeated regime, including a new set of laws and ordinances to keep order, provide services, and reassure the population about its future. Meanwhile, during this reconstitution of the society phase, U.S. and allied forces would have to gain full military and police control within the borders of the defeated country to combat the remnants of the defeated regime still offering resistance. To get an entire country back on its feet after a wartime collapse is an immense task and would potentially require tens of thousands of specialists to restore the infrastructure and restore vital services.

In conclusion, it appears that the United States is going to win most or all of its wars in the near term. The adversary must fight asymmetrically if he is to have much of a chance at a stalemate or victory. It is likely that one of those asymmetrical strategies will involve chemical and biological warfare attacks and the use of terrorist surrogates.[20] The United States must anticipate these asymmetrical strategies and organize, train and equip to fight and win such conflicts as well as the conventional fights it is so proficient in conducting. But winning the immediate war is just part of the planning that must take place. Winning the peace after major hostilities have ended is just as important, for that is why the war would be fought in the first place. Thus, the U.S. and its allies must plan end-to-end strategies of war, war termination, and peace construction, and these strategies must be dovetailed to accomplish our ends against asymmetrical adversaries in the war next time.

Notes

1. Isaiah Berlin, The Hedgehog and the Fox (New York: Simon & Schuster, 1953). He wrote that this was a fragment from something written by the Greek poet Archilochus "which says: 'the fox knows many things, but the hedgehog knows one big thing.' Scholars have differed about the correct interpretation of these dark words, which may mean no more than that the fox, for all his cunning, is defeated by the hedgehog's one defense. But taken figuratively, the words can be made to yield a sense in which they mark one of the deepest differences which divide writers and thinkers, and, it may be, human beings in general. For there exists a great chasm between those, on one side, who relate everything to a single central vision, one system less or more coherent or articulate, in terms of which they understand, think and feel – a single, universal, organizing principle in terms of which alone all that they are and say has significance – and, on the other side, those who pursue many ends, often unrelated and even contradictory, connected, if at all, only in some de facto way, for some psychological or physiological cause, related by no moral or aesthetic principle."...The first kind of intellectual and artistic personality belongs to the hedgehogs, the second to the foxes; and without insisting on a rigid classification, we may, without too much fear of contradiction, say that , in this sense, Dante belongs in the first category, Shakespeare to the second; Plato, Lucretius, Pascal, Hegel, Dostovevsky, Nietzsche, Ibsen, Proust are, in varying degrees, hedgehogs; Herodotus, Aristotle, Montaigne, Erasmus, Moliere, Goethe, Pushkin, Balzak Joyce are foxes." See on the Internet the excerpt from Berlin's work, http://www.cc.gatech.edu/people/home/idris/Essays/Hedge_n_Fox.htm.

2. Center for Defense Information (CDI), "Fiscal Year 2004 Budget." See http://www.cdi.org/budget/2004/highlights.cfin.

3. International Institute for Strategic Studies, <u>The Military Balance, 2002-2003</u> (London: Oxford University Press, 2003), 332-336.

4. See Samuel P. Huntington, the <u>Clash of Civilizations and the Remaking of World Order</u> (New York: Simon and Schuster, 1996). Huntington argues that the world is divided into seven very different "civilizations" the Western, Islamic, Hindu, Sinic, African, Latin American, Orthodox, Buddhist, and Japanese. He suggests that the bases of future wars, at their root, will be in the clash of those holding these very different competing worldviews. See his section on "Islam and the West," 209-216.

5. See Simon Reeve, <u>The New Jackals: Ramzi Yousef, Osama Bin Laden, and The Future of Terrorism</u> (Boston: Northeastern University Press, 1999), 268.

6. Ibid., 270.

7. As stated in the U.S. National Security Strategy issued by the Administration of President George W. Bush, a small number of rogue states share a number of attributes, including the fact that these regimes: "brutalize their own people and squander their national resources for the personal gain of leaders; display no regard for international law, threaten their neighbors, and callously violate international treaties to which they are party; are determined to acquire weapons of mass destruction, along with other advanced military technology, to be used as threats or offensively to achieve the aggressive designs of their regimes; sponsor terrorism around the world; reject human values and hate the United States and everything for which it stands."

8. These Designated Foreign Terrorist Organizations can be found in the U.S. State Department's annual report *Patterns of Global Terrorism,* issued each April. In 2003, they include the following: Abu Nidal Organization, Abu Sayyaf Group, Al-Aqsa Martyrs Brigade, Armed Islamic Group, Asbat al-Ansar, Aum Shinrikyo or Aleph, Basque Fatherland and Liberty (ETA), Communist Party of the Philippines/New People's Army, Al-Gama'a al-Islammiyya, HAMAS, Harakat ul-Mujahidin, Hizballah (party of God), Islamic Movement of Uzbekistan, Jaish-e Mohammed, Jamaah Islamiya, Al-Jihad (Egyptian Islamic Jihad), Kahane Chai (Kach), Kurdistan Worker's Party (PKK), Lashkar-e Tayyiba, Lashkar I Jhanvi, Liberation Tigers of Tamil Ewelam, Mujahedin e-Khalq Organization (MEK), National Liberation Army (ELN) of Columbia, Palestine Islamic Jihad (PIJ), Palestine Liberation Front (PLF), Popular Front for the Liberation of Palestine (PFLP), Popular Front for the Liberation of Palestine-General Command (PFLP-GC), Al-Qaeda, Real IRA, Revolutionary Armed Forces of Columbia (FARC), Revolutionary Nuclei, Revolutionary Organization 17 November, Sendero Luminosos (Shining Path or SL), and the United Self Defense Forces/Group of Columbia.

9. The 22 Arab states with large Muslim majorities are Algeria, Bahrain, Comoros, Djibouti, Egypt, Iraq, Jordan, Kuwait, Lebanon, Libya, Mauritania, Morocco, Oman, Palestine, Qatar, Saudi Arabia, Somalia, Sudan, Syria, Tunisia, United Arab Emirates and

Yemen. None are yet democracies. The 29 other states with Muslim majorities or large pluralities are as follows: Indonesia, Pakistan, India, Bangladesh, Turkey, Iran, Nigeria, China, Ethiopia, Afghanistan, Uzbekistan, Tanzania, Russia, Malaysia, Mali, Senegal, Niger, Azerbaijan, Somalia, Kazakstan, Guinea, Burkina Faso, United States, Tajikistan, Congo Democratic Republic, Turkmenistan, C'ote D'Ivorie, Chad, and Cameroon.

10. General Henry W. Shelton, Chairman of the Joint Chiefs of Staff (Washington, D.C.: U.S. Government Printing Office, June 2000), 6.

11. Saddam Hussein's application to a military academy in Iraq was rejected when he was still a teenager. His lack of military training and experience handicapped him severely in his many military adventures. Perhaps the officials at the Baghdad military academy were correct about his military potential. Indeed, General Charles Horner, the U.S. Joint Air Force Commander in Desert Storm, maintains that the coalition in the 1991 Gulf War was fortunate that it missed killing Saddam since, "as General Schwarzkoft pointed out after the war, Saddam Hussein was a lousy strategist, and thus a good man to have in charge of Iraqi armed forces, under the circumstances." See Tom Clancy and Charles A. Horner, <u>Every Man A Tiger</u> (New York: J.P. Putnam, 1999), 515.

12. Kim Il Sung, the first President of the DPRK, was a Special Forces officer operating on the side of the Russian and Communist Chinese armed forces in Manchuria during WWII. His orientation toward Special Operations Forces (SOF) has had a lasting impact on the major SOF emphasis in the North Korea military forces from 1945 to the present.

13. See Avigdor Haselkorn, <u>The Continuing Storm: Iraq, Poisonous Weapons, and Deterrence</u> (New Haven, CT: Yale University Press, 1999), 53.

14. Joseph A. Englebrecht, "War Termination: Why Does A State Decide to Stop Fighting," PhD. Dissertation, Columbia University, New York, 1992, 24-25.

15. Ibid., 29.

16. Ibid., 31.

17. Ibid.

18. Ibid., 34-36.

19. Ibid., 36-45.

20. See Jim A. Davis and Barry R. Schneider, Editors, <u>The Gathering Biological Warfare Storm</u> (Maxwell AFB, AL: USAF Counterproliferation Center, 2002) in paperback. Also, this is forthcoming in hardback, published by Praeger in 2004

CHAPTER 2

The Long War of the 21st Century[*]

R. James Woolsey

Eliot Cohen is the distinguished professor at Johns Hopkins School for Advanced International Studies. He argues that we are in World War IV. The Cold War was World War III. I think Eliot's formulation fits the circumstances much better than describing this as a war on terrorism.

Let me say a few words about who our enemy is in World War IV, why they're at war with us, why we are now at war with them, and how we have to think about fighting it both at home and abroad.

Who is the enemy? There are at least three movements, all coming out of the Middle East, who have been at war with us for years. The first is the Islamist movement of Shi'a Muslims led by the ruling clerics, the Mullahs of Iran who seized our embassy personnel in Tehran in 1979. They are a minority of the Iranian Shi'ite clerics but they constitute the ruling force in Iran; they back Hezbollah, and they have been at war with us for nearly a quarter of a century. They blew up our embassy and our Marine barracks in Beirut in 1983.

The second group is the fascists. I use that word literally, not as an expletive. The Ba'athist parties of Iraq and Syria are essentially fascist parties, modeled after the fascism parties of the '30s. They're totalitarian and they are anti-Semitic.

Saddam and the Ba'athists in Iraq have been at war with us for over a decade. For them, the Gulf War never stopped. To underscore the point, Saddam tried to assassinate former President George Bush in 1993 in

[*] This chapter is a White Paper of the Foundation for the Defense of Democracies and was also the topic of a similar presentation at the USAF Counterproliferation Center's annual conference, May 2002. Re-printed by permission of the author, the former CIA Director, who is also a Distinguished Senior Adviser of the Foundation for the Defense of Democracies.

Kuwait. Saddam and the Ba'athists have ties and associations with varying terrorist organizations, including al-Qaeda.

The third group, and the one that caused us to realize that the War was continuous, is the Islamist movement of Sunni Muslims. This is probably the most virulent and long-lasting of the three groups that are at war with us. The Wahhabis, the religious movement in Saudi Arabia dating back to the 18th century, were joined in the '50s and '60s by immigration into Saudi Arabia by fundamentalist Islamists, or a more modern stripe of essentially the same ideology, many of its followers coming from Egypt. Groups of this sort were focused on attacking what they call "the near enemy," the Mubarak regime in Egypt, and to some extent, the Saudi royal family. The attack in 1979 on the great mosque in Mecca is an example of their actions. Around 1995, they decided to turn their concentration and effort against what they call "the Crusaders and the Jews" - U.S. And they have been at war with us ever since, as evidenced by several well-known terrorist incidents, including the attack on a reserve facility in Saudi Arabia that killed Americans, the East African Embassy bombings, the attack on the U.S.S. Cole, and, of course, September 11th.

I think of these three groups as analogous to different mafia families. They hate each other, they kill each other from time to time, but outsiders fare a lot worse and each group is willing and capable to assist another to get what they want.

There are two basic reasons why they went to war against us. The first, and the underlying one, was best expressed to me last year by a D.C. cab driver. Now, I resolutely refuse to read any public opinion polls. When I want to know what people think, I talk to cab drivers. This is both more enjoyable and in many ways offers a better finger on the pulse of the nation than any poll. I got into a cab last January, the day after former President Clinton gave a speech at Georgetown University in which he implied that one reason we were attacked on September 11th was because of American slavery before 1865 and because of our treatment of the American Indian.

The cab driver was an older, black American, a long-term resident of D.C., a guy about my age. The Washington Times was open in the front seat to the story of the President's speech. I noticed it and said, "Did you read that piece about President Clinton's speech yesterday?" He said yes, and I asked him what he thought about it. He said, "These people don't hate us for what we've done *wrong.* They hate us for what we do *right.*"

I can't express it better than that. We're hated because of freedom of speech, because of freedom of religion, because of our economic freedom, because of our equal treatment of women, because of all the good things that we do. This is like the war against Nazism. We are hated because of the best of what we are.

But even if we're hated, why are we attacked? Well, I would suggest that we have been essentially hanging a "Kick Me" sign on our back in the Middle East for the past quarter century. We have given substantial evidence of being what bin Laden has called a paper tiger.

My friend Tom Moorer, former Chairman of the Joint Chiefs of Staff, was a young naval officer in World War II. Just after the war he participated in the interrogations of Prince Konoye and several of the handful of Japanese leaders who were eventually hanged after war crimes trials. Moorer's interrogation team asked each of the prisoners why they did it. "Why did you attack us at Pearl Harbor?" They said, essentially, "We looked at what you were doing in the '20s and '30s. You were disarming militarily. You wouldn't fortify Wake Island. You wouldn't fortify Guam. Your army had to drill with wooden rifles. So, we attacked because we thought we would win. We had no idea that your rich, spoiled, feckless country would fight back as you did after December 7, 1941. You stunned us, and you beat us."

Flash forward some six decades. I think we offered a lot of evidence to Saddam and to the Islamist Shi'a in Tehran and Hezbollah and to the Islamist Sunni that we were, essentially, a rich, spoiled, feckless country that wouldn't fight. In 1979, they took our people hostage in Iran and what did we do? We tied yellow ribbons around trees and launched a failed effort to rescue them. In 1983, they blew up our embassy and our marine barracks in Beirut. What did we do? We walked away, just as we did in Mogadishu in 1993 when they shot our helicopters down.

Throughout much of the 1980's, many other terrorist acts were committed against us. What was our response to vicious attacks against the U.S.? We arrested a few small fry and then prosecuted them. We litigated. The one honorable exception was President Ronald Reagan's air strike against Libya in retaliation for a terrorist bombing.

In 1991, President Bush organized a magnificent coalition to reverse the seizure of Kuwait by Saddam Hussein. We fought the war superbly, and then stopped it while Saddam's Republican Guard was intact. Then, after having encouraged the Kurds and the Shi'a to rebel against Saddam, we stood back, left the bridges intact, left their elite units intact, let them fly armed and troop-carrying helicopters around, and watched the Kurds and Shi'a, who were winning in 15 of Iraq's 18 provinces, be massacred. You didn't read much about that in the press because the media didn't pay much attention. But those who knew about this said: Well, we know what the Americans value. They save their oil in Saudi Arabia and Kuwait and after that, they don't care.

Then in 1993, Saddam tried to assassinate former President Bush in Kuwait with a bomb. How did we respond? President Clinton fired a couple of dozen cruise missiles into an empty building in the middle of the night in Baghdad, retaliating quite effectively against a handful of Iraqi cleaning women and night watchmen, but not against Saddam Hussein.

Then came the attack of September 11th and President Bush's response. Our military action in Afghanistan, like our response against the Japanese after Pearl Harbor, was something that came as a great surprise to those enemies in the Middle East who attacked us. Like the Japanese in 1941, the Islamist fascists thought that what they believed was a spoiled, feckless country would not fight.

How must we fight? At home, the war is going to be difficult in two ways. Our first problem is how to deal with the lack of resilience in the infrastructure that serves our wonderful and technologically sophisticated country. Our society is comprised of hundreds of complex networks: food processing and delivery, the internet, financial transfers, the electricity grid, oil and gas pipelines, etc. None of these was put together with any thought to making them resilient against terrorism. All are open and relatively easy to access. Their vulnerable and dangerous points are highlighted for maintenance or safety, or environmental reasons. We advertise "Transformer Here," "Hazardous Chemicals Here," "Cable Crossing Here." Before September 11, we didn't worry about this openness. After all, we experienced extremely destructive intentional violence against the major civilian infrastructure in North America only twice in our history, that I can think of: Sherman's burning of Atlanta in 1864 and the British burning of Washington in 1814.

Virtually all of our infrastructure has been put together with this spirit of transparency and ease of access.

About seven years ago, one of our communication satellites had a computer chip fail. The satellite lost its attitude control. Immediately about 90% of the pagers in the country went down. The next day they were back up again because somebody had figured out how to reroute them to a different satellite. That's the kind of random failure we cope with easily. But that's not what happened a year ago September 11th.

In the preparations for the attack of September 11th, a group of intelligent and very evil terrorists said to themselves, something like: "When the foolish Americans do baggage searches at airports they ignore short knives like box cutters. Short knives can slit throats just as easily as long knives. This is good. The stupid Americans treat all airplane hijackings as if they will land safely and passengers will only be inconvenienced for a few hours. The U.S. government tells pilots and aircrews and everyone aboard to be polite and passive to hijackers. This is very good for us. And, even though about twice a year there have been crazy people who successfully get into the cockpits of civilian airliners, and passengers and crew write to the FAA and say, 'you ought to do something about this', the airlines continue to have flimsy cockpit doors on their airliners. Let's see: short knives permitted, be polite to hijackers, flimsy cockpit doors. That means we can easily take over airliners, fly them into buildings, and kill thousands of them."

Einstein used to say, "God may be sophisticated, but He's not plain mean." What Einstein meant (since for him nature and God were pretty much the same thing) was that if you're playing against nature and trying to discover a new principle of physics, it may be a tough problem, but there's nobody trying to outwit you and make it harder. In war and terrorism there is always someone who is not only trying to make it harder, but is trying to kill you.

We have developed just-in-time delivery to hold down inventories and operating costs; great, until somebody puts a dirty bomb in one of the 50,000 containers that cross U.S. borders every day and we decide that U.S. customs has to start inspecting virtually all of the containers at ports, instead of the 2% that are inspected now. Then all of that just-in-time manufacturing comes to a halt. Full hospitals? Great idea, it keeps hospital and health care costs down and moves people through hospitals rapidly, keeping them at close to 100% occupancy. This works until there's a bioterrorist attack and thousands, or hundreds of thousands, or millions of Americans need emergency health care and there are no empty beds.

Our nation's networks all have significant weak points. Many of them operate according to incentives established to promote efficiency or for other purposes that make them more vulnerable to terrorism. We must carefully examine our infrastructure and find those vulnerabilities that are the functional equivalents of flimsy cockpit doors and get them fixed. We are going to have to pull the relevant decision-makers together and examine potential weak points like electricity grids, oil and gas pipelines, and container ports, and figure out ways to change the incentives so that we build in resilience of a kind that is compatible with a market economy.

We have to fight successfully in the United States against terrorist cells and organizations that support terrorism and we have to deal with the difficult fact that some of these groups are religiously rooted in one aspect of Islam. We must understand that the vast majority of American Muslims are not terrorists and are not sympathetic to terrorists. But there are institutions and individuals in America, some of them with a great deal money, that encourage and support the hatred that underpins terrorism.

In dealing with this problem, however, we have to both remember that Americans are creatures of Madison's Constitution and his Bill of Rights and at the same time we must be aware that we are at war here in our country, now.

This poses very hard choices. My personal judgment is that none of the decisions so far made by the Administration go beyond what is Constitutionally acceptable in taking strong action domestically against terrorism. The Supreme Court has historically been extremely tolerant of the Executive, and even more tolerant of the Executive and Congress acting together, in times of severe crisis and war. In the Civil War, Lincoln suspended habeas corpus. In World War II, we had Japanese internment camps in the western part of the country. In World War I, there was some very draconian legislation, also upheld by the Supreme Court. Nothing that has been done so far by this Administration, of course, even remotely approaches any of those steps, and it should not. We have to be alert to this. We do not want our children and grandchildren to look back on decisions that were as drastic as the incarceration of the ethnic Japanese in World War II and say, "how in the world could those people have done that?" Any country is capable of poor judgment when it becomes frightened.

In the war against terrorism abroad, the most interesting situation right now exists with the Islamist Shi'a, the ruling mullahs of Iran. This small minority of Iranian Shi'ite mullahs control the state's instruments of power. They are effectively in the same position that the leaders of the Kremlin were in 1988 or the rulers in Versailles in 1788: namely, the storm isn't quite overhead, but if they look at the horizon they can see it gathering in the distance. The mullahs have great power still. They have oil money and the military, but I think there are some tectonic shifts below the surface in Iran.

The muilahs have lost the students. They have lost the women. They have lost the brave newspaper editors and professors who are in prison, some under sentence of death and being tortured. They are losing the Ayatollahs, one by one. Ayatollah Montazeri, a very brave man, has been issuing fatwas against suicide killings and has been under house arrest for five years. Early this past summer, Ayatollah Taheri, formerly a hard line supporter of the mullahs in the City of Isfahan, issued a blast against them saying that what they were doing by supporting torture and supporting terrorism was fundamentally at odds with the tenets of Islam. There are increasing student demonstrations and the Iranians are having so much trouble keeping the students down, they are importing thugs from Syria to suppress demonstrations.

I think President Bush did exactly the right thing in the early part of the summer, when after the student demonstrations surrounding Taheri's blast, he issued a statement saying that the United States was on the side of the students, not the mullahs. This drove the mullahs crazy-evidence of the shrewdness and wisdom of the President's words.

The Islamist Sunni, al-Qaeda and their fellow travelers are going to be the hardest for America to deal with. They are fueled by oil money from the Gulf, Saudi Arabia principally. They are wealthy in and of themselves. They are present in some 60 countries and they loathe us, like the Wahhabis, who are their first cousins. They are fanatically anti-Western, anti-modern, anti-Christian, anti-Jewish, and anti-most-Muslims. If you want to get a feel for the intellectual infrastructure of this Wahhabi-Islamist movement there are websites where one can go to pull in the sermons on any given Friday throughout Saudi Arabia. I looked at translations of one such set of sermons two or three weeks ago before some discussions we were having in the Defense Policy Board. The three main themes that week were: (1) that all Jews are pigs and monkeys; (2) that all Christians and Jews are the enemy and it is our obligation to hate them and destroy them; and (3) that women in the United States routinely commit incest with their fathers and brothers and this is an ordinary and accepted thing in the United States. This is the routine Wahhabi view.

One Wahhabi cleric was interviewed by an American reporter a few weeks ago in Saudi Arabia. The reporter asked him, "Tell me. I'm a Christian. Do you hate me?" And the Wahhabi Cleric said, "Well, of course, if you're a Christian, I hate you. But, I'm not going to kill you." In these circles this is the moderate view.

We need to realize that just as angry German nationalism of the 1920's and 1930's was the soil in which Nazism grew, although not all German nationalists became Nazis. Similiarly, the angry Islamism and Wahhabism in Saudi Arabia and elsewhere today is the soil in which terrorism grows, although not all Islamists or Wahhabis become terrorists.

If you look at the world a little over 85 years ago, in the spring of 1917 when this country entered World War I, there were at most about a dozen existing democracies: the United States, Canada, Australia, New Zealand, Britain, France, Switzerland, a few countries in Northern Europe (and almost all of those were only democracies for the male half of their populations). It was a world of empires, of kingdoms, of colonies, and of various types of authoritarian regimes.

Today, 120 out of the 192 countries in the world are democracies. The democratic world is divided between free nations such as the United States, and the other democracies, such as Russia, which are partly free. But there are still 120 countries with parliamentary institutions, contested elections and some elements, at least, of the rule of law. That is an amazing change, literally an order of magnitude change, within the lifetime of many individuals now living.

No dramatic systemic political change like this has ever happened in world history. Needless to say, we have had a lot to do with it. We helped win World War I, we prevailed, along with Britain, in World War II, and we prevailed in the Cold War. Along the way, a lot of people said, very cynically, "The Germans will never be able to run a democracy; the Japanese will never be able to run a democracy; the Russians will never be able to run a democracy; no nation with a Chinese culture is going to be able to run a democracy." It took some help, but the Germans and the Japanese and now, even the Russians, the Taiwanese, and many other nations and cultures have figured it out. In spite of vast cultural differences, people with backgrounds very different from the Anglo-Saxon world of Westminster and the founding fathers of the United States are on their way to democracy.

In the Muslim world, the 22 Arab states have no democracies. Some reasonably well-governed states are moderating and changing, such as Bahrain and Qatar. But still, there are no democracies among them. There are another 16 Muslim-predominant non-Arab states. Half of these are democracies. They include some of the poorest countries in the world: Bangladesh, Mali. Well over 100 million Muslims live in a democracy in India. Outside of one province, they are generally at peace with their Hindu neighbors.

The problem is not basically Islam. There is a special situation in the Middle East attributable to historical and cultural factors. Outside of Israel and Turkey, the Middle East essentially consists of no democracies. It has, rather, two types of governments — pathological predators and vulnerable autocrats. This is a bad mix. Five of those states: Iran, Iraq, Syria, Sudan and Libya sponsor and assist terrorism in one way or another; and all five are working on weapons of mass destruction.

The Middle East thus presents a serious and massive complex of problems: all financed by the revenues of two-thirds of the world's oil. I don't believe this terror war is going to go away until we change the face of the Middle East the way we have changed the face of Europe.

I say to the terrorists and the pathological predators such as Saddam Hussein, as well as to the autocrats, the Mubaraks, and the Saudi Royal family. You must realize that now, for the fourth time in 100 years, America has been awakened and our country is on the march. We didn't choose this fight, but we're in it. There's only one way we're going to be able to win. It's the way we won World War I fighting for Wilson's 14 points, the way we won World War II fighting for Churchill's and Roosevelt's Atlantic Charter, and the way we won the cold war or World War III, fighting against the Soviet Union for the noble ideas most eloquently expressed by President Reagan, and at the beginning by President Truman. We won these wars with our allies because we made it clear that these were not wars of "us against them." They were not wars between countries or civilizations. They were wars of freedom against tyranny.

We have to convince the good people of the Middle East that we are on their side, as we convinced Lech Walesa, and Vaclav Havel, and Andrei Sakharov that we were on their side. This will take time. It will be difficult. For some countries the development of lasting democracy will take many years.

CHAPTER 3

The Secret Program:
South Africa's Chemical and Biological Weapons

Stephen Burgess and Helen Purkitt

From the 1960s until the 1990s, apartheid South Africa was an isolated state that felt threatened by growing domestic unrest, as well as by a more powerful state actor, the Soviet Union, which was helping hostile regimes and liberation movements in southern Africa.

One response of the apartheid regime to changing threat perceptions outside and inside of South Africa was to develop a new and more sophisticated chemical and biological warfare (CBW) program, code-named "Project Coast," starting in 1981 or earlier, and to accelerate a nuclear weapons program. The focus here is on the especially sophisticated biological aspect of the program and how it developed. The CBW decision-making process was secretive and controlled by the military and enabled a very sophisticated program to be developed with little outside scrutiny. Military and police units used chemical and biological agents for counter-insurgency warfare, assassination, and execution of war prisoners.

As the regime felt increasingly threatened by opposition at home, top political leaders approved plans for research and development of exotic means to neutralize opponents, large-scale offensive uses of the program, and weaponization. However, the plans were not operationalized. The end of the external threat led to a decision to unilaterally dismantle the program, prior to a shift to majority rule. Lack of civilian control over military programs made the rollback difficult, rife with corruption, and left proliferation concerns in place.

Ultimately, the United States, the United Kingdom, and other countries pressured the South African government to ensure that the CBW program would be dismantled and the former project manager, Dr. Wouter

Basson, constrained. However, Basson secretly retained copies of Project Coast documents, which helped to perpetuate proliferation concerns.

Today, a divide exists between those who believe that South Africa developed the "second most sophisticated" CBW program, after the Soviet Union's, and are concerned about proliferation, and those who believe that it was "pedestrian." The former are focused on the proliferation danger, while the latter are focused on the criminality and corruption of the program.

Project Coast was not the first CBW program the South African government had developed. Between 1914-1918 and 1939-1945, South African troops fought in the two World Wars and faced the threat of CBW. Although the 1925 Geneva Convention banned the use of chemical and biological weapons in warfare, Japan and possibly the Soviet Union employed such weapons in WW II. As early as the 1930s, widespread evidence emerged of the efficacy of biological warfare (BW) based on scientific work conducted in the U.S., United Kingdom, and the Soviet Union.[1] The South African scientific and military communities kept pace with the various developments in CBW.

The literature on South Africa's WW II CBW program was maintained.[2] Also, the South African Defense Force (SADF) maintained a small military program related to CBW research and development. The government also maintained funding for a modest number of basic research projects located in the Afrikaans universities and other government supported institutions. Much of this research was conducted under the umbrella of the Council for Scientific and Industrial Research (CSIR).

In the 1940s and 1950s, South Africa's wartime connections with Britain and the United States continued. South African officers trained in Britain and the United States in chemical and biological warfare strategy and tactics.[3] Also, in the 1950s, the Eisenhower administration initiated the United States "Atoms for Peace" program, which proved to be a significant factor contributing to South Africa's later ability to produce nuclear weapons.[4]

From 1925 to 1963, South Africa was not willing to forswear CBW in combat situations. In 1963, South Africa belatedly became a party to the 1925 Geneva Convention, banning the use of chemical and biological weapons in warfare. South African accession to the Geneva Convention and ratification of the 1975 Convention on the Prohibition of the

Development, Production and Stockpiling of Bacteriological and Toxin Weapons and on their Destruction (BWC) did not deter apartheid leaders from continuing to develop a new and more sophisticated CBW program in the 1980s.

South African forces were reportedly involved in using CBW in counter-insurgency operations in southern Africa in the 1960s and 1970s, especially in Rhodesia. In 1978-1979, SADF Special Forces allegedly planted anthrax spores in grain fed to cattle in guerrilla-held areas. An anthrax epidemic afflicted nearly 10,000 cattle. South Africa had increasingly provided financial support and military hardware in the 1970s to the Rhodesian government, and SADF military intelligence was a principal source of funding for the Rhodesian counter-insurgency program, including the elite Selous Scouts. The Rhodesian defense budget was very small, and the regime had one rudimentary chemical and biological warfare plant that received outside aid from South Africa. In assisting Rhodesia, South African researchers continued work on CBW and land mine projects.

The collapse of Portuguese colonialism led, from 1974 to 1976, to the takeover of Angola and Mozambique by revolutionary communist regimes, backed by the Soviet Union and Cuba. Suddenly, South African leaders found themselves surrounded by communist forces, which were viewed as implacable and unscrupulous enemies. South African defense experts knew that the Soviet Union possessed nuclear, biological and chemical (NBC) weapons. In regard to the Soviet BW program, indications of its scale and sophistication had been gained during and after negotiations surrounding the 1972 Biological Weapons Convention (BWC).

According to former South African leaders and generals, NBC programs were developed with the intention of "countering the communist onslaught." General (retired) Georg Meiring, former SADF Chief of Staff, commented that SADF sought protection against BW in the 1970s, as biological weapons became known as the "poor man's atomic bomb," and as the possibility increased of BW operations by Soviet-trained guerrillas of the South West African Peoples Organization (SWAPO) and African National Congress/Umkhonto we Sizwe (ANC/MK).[5]

According to Magnus Malan (SADF Chief of Staff, 1975-80 and Defense Minister, 1980-91), the U.S. encouraged the SADF to enter Angola in October 1975, and then abandoned South Africa to face Cuban forces alone.[6] In addition, South Africa faced the Soviet and Cuban NBC threat alone.

In 1976, the Soweto uprisings began, bringing a wave of unrest to South Africa, after more than a decade of relative calm. The 1976 wave of rebellion continued into 1977. Unrest would persist until 1984, when an even greater uprising commenced and lasted for more than two years and reverberated until 1990. The 1976 uprisings led the apartheid regime to search for ways, including the use of chemical agents, to control or incapacitate large groups of people.

In the wake of these regime-shaking events, the Defense Minister, P.W. Botha, replaced B.J. Vorster as Prime Minister in 1978 and initiated his vision of the "total strategy." Botha differed from his predecessor in that he was oriented towards the military (and special forces), especially because of his years of service as defense minister. He initiated a range of reforms, combined with the widespread use of coercive power, to ensure the survival of the regime. Power was increasingly consolidated in the hands of the military and taken away from civilians.

In particular, Botha favored the development of advanced weapons projects and covert operations that would give South Africa additional advantages against its adversaries. South Africa initiated a series of internal and external military and paramilitary operations. These included assassinations, torture, and smuggling, as well as forgery, propaganda, and subversion. All were defined as "legitimate" weapons against the "total onslaught" of "red" and "black" forces. These practices were established at the top and legitimized deviant behavior throughout the military, police and intelligence services.[7]

Within the "any means necessary to survive" framework, preparations began to develop a chemical and biological warfare (CBW) program, called Project Coast, which would counteract and even rival the Soviet program. P.W. Botha and SADF Chief, Magnus Malan, directed the Surgeon General, Major General Nieuwoudt, to launch the program.[8] Nieuwoudt enlisted a young military doctor, Wouter Basson, to be his lieutenant and program director. In the late 1970s, they approached South African university scientists and specialists in weapons development to determine if they would be willing to participate in and even lead the different components of a CBW program.[9] They also began to make contacts in the international scientific community.

Project Coast, 1981-1993

From 1979 through 1981, the State Security Council, led by Prime Minister Botha and Malan, and the SADF discussed the principles that might apply to the CBW program. It became clear that a program to defend against a Soviet CBW attack could only be built if the Soviet offensive program was emulated and then tested.[10] As it became evident that an offensive CBW program was to be developed, discussions began concerning the possible uses for such a program. Malan proposed that signs of a chemical warfare attack in Angola would force the Cuban and Angolan forces to don suits, which would cut combat effectiveness in half. In 1981, General Constand Viljoen, SADF Chief of Staff, requested that the CBW program provide SADF with agents for crowd control in South Africa. Other possible uses considered included counter-insurgency, assassinations, and black population control. It is noteworthy that, during the process of launching the CBW program, no delegation from South Africa appeared at the 1980 review conference for the 1975 Biological Weapons Convention.

In April 1981, a top-level SADF committee finalized the principles for Project Coast.[11] One principle was that chemical and biological warfare (CBW) should be treated as a top-secret matter, because it was susceptible to deception by adversaries. Another was that, since the West had supposedly fallen behind the Soviet Union, South Africa had to fend for itself in the CBW arena. The SADF committee decided that secrecy was essential and that South Africa would use front companies to research and produce chemical and biological weapons in top-secret installations. The desire for secrecy meant secret funding for the project, the creation of front companies, and the exclusion of the state arms producer (ARMSCOR) from the initial phases of the project. ARMSCOR would only be brought in during the weaponization phase of the program.

As Malan suggested, South Africa would experiment with a strategy of forcing the enemy in Angola to don protective suits. The CBW program would also investigate means of dealing with massive demonstrations, insurrection, and insurgency, as well as black population growth. Another principle was that biological warfare (BW) had to be used with caution. BW could be devastatingly effective and, therefore, attractive. However, the regime was concerned that BW was difficult to control and that it could cause tremendous, plague-like damage.

In May 1981, the Surgeon General and head of the South African Medical Service (SAMS), Maj. Gen. Nieuwoudt, established Project Coast, and the Minister of Defense, Magnus Malan, and the Minister of Finance, Barend du Plessis, approved the Program.[12] Nieuwoudt made Dr. Wouter Basson the Project Coast director, as well as specialist adviser to the Surgeon General. Basson also became a lieutenant colonel, joined the 7th SAMS Battalion, and began making trips to Angola with the SADF. In addition, he continued making trips abroad to make contacts with scientists and to procure supplies for Project Coast.

In August 1981, the SADF launched Operation Protea in Angola. During the operation, evidence was discovered that the Cubans might be preparing for chemical warfare.[13] Although the evidence was sketchy, top SADF generals chose to take action to counter CBW anyway. Defense Minister Malan took SADF generals to Angola to examine CBW protective suits and demonstrate problems that they created during combat. Afterwards, Malan reiterated his proposal that the SADF take measures that would force the Cubans rather than the South Africans to don suits. Accordingly, the SADF developed a strategy of deception, by firing "smoke" that would achieve such a result. In addition, Malan proposed that the CBW program be developed to counteract the ANC/MK, which was in the process of escalating a revolutionary war with more than 3,000 guerrilla forces. The SADF had evidence that some of the ANC/MK troops had been trained in the Soviet Union in CBW techniques.[14]

Basson was ordered to develop Project Coast by a "kitchen cabinet," composed of Minister of Defense Malan, SADF Chief (Gen. C. Viljoen), the Commanding Officer of Strategic Intelligence and Special Forces (Gen. K. Liebenberg), South African Police (SAP) Commissioner General van der Merwe, and the Director General of the National Intelligence Service (NIS). Basson was placed in charge of managing all aspects of Project Coast, including defensive and offensive measures.[15] The annual budget for Project Coast was estimated to be $10 million, with a staff of 200 involved.[16] Members of the Project Working Group included Surgeon General Nieuwoudt and his deputy and successor, Dr. Niels Knobel. They were supposed to supervise Project Coast, but Knobel has claimed that they would rarely visit the front companies for fear of compromising their cover. Basson decided with the scientific researchers on requirements and costs. Much of Basson's efforts went into circumventing sanctions against the sale of military-related items to South Africa and into black market, sanctions-busting activities. All procurement was undertaken by Basson and signed for by Nieuwoudt and his successor, Knobel, who has claimed that he and Nieuwoudt were only told after the fact about Basson's activities.

The problem of procurement by SADF was the lack of civilian leadership and supervision. The SADF was still supplied with uniforms using 1930s regulations. A Special Defense Account was established by the SADF that precluded access by the Auditor-General.[17] Thus, while Wouter Basson was required to provide records of financial expenditures for Project Coast activities, there was no effort throughout this period to match these records with those of covert special operations.[18] The rationale of the need for secrecy for covert programs and Basson's unsupervised activities would lead Project Coast into a morass of corruption.

In 1982, the Delta G Scientific Company began work on chemical warfare agents for Project Coast. The chemicals that Delta G developed for testing were divided into lethal, incapacitating, and irritating agents. Roodeplaat Research Laboratories (RRL) then tested the biological effects of the agents from Delta G. RRL was the company that was primarily responsible for biological warfare. Protechnik Company was to develop the protective CBW equipment.

In 1983, RRL opened and started research on biological agents and on the biological effects of chemical agents. Daan Goosen became the first head of RRL and served until 1986. According to Gen. (ret.) Georg Meiring, South Africa developed a sophisticated and dispersed project. Project Coast was not just one individual and was not just RRL.[19] There were a number of different research and testing centers at universities and companies, and scientists in various parts of South Africa assisted Project Coast.

Anthrax, cholera, botulinum, and a variety of pathogens were collected and/or developed at RRL and elsewhere for testing. Apparently, a principal objective was to collect and test a range of biological agents in order to develop protection from a Soviet BW attack. In 1984, Dr. Schalk van Rensburg joined RRL and started the cholera research program. By the end of 1984, Project Coast and RRL had tested a range of BW toxins and had developed countermeasures to ricin and botulinum. Reportedly, they had acquired anthrax, Plague, cholera, E. coli, staph, necrotizing fasciitis, ricin, botulinum, gas gangrene, anti-matter bacteria, and the Ebola, Marburg, and Rift Valley viruses.[20] However, one must question if RRL had the facilities to keep Marburg, Rift Valley, and Ebola viruses.

Eventually, according to a number of sources in the U.S. and South Africa, Project Coast developed pathogens that had never before been seen. Project Coast managed to obtain the Soviet-developed flesh-eating bacteria, necrotizing fasciitis, as well as the antidote. In 1994, the South Africans surprised the Americans by revealing that they had the bacteria and then gave it to the U.S.[21] However, claims by Basson and former Surgeon General Knobel that South African espionage agents penetrated Soviet Russian programs during 1980s remain to be proven.

According to Tom Mangold in *Plague Wars*,[22] baboons, trapped up-country in Kruger National Park, were shipped by crate load to RRL for biological tests. There is evidence that some of these tests were done in the park itself. Tourists reportedly witnessed researchers using poison darts that took several hours to incapacitate or kill primates. The tourists registered their complaints and demanded that the practice be terminated. According to the Chief Warden of Kruger Park, the SADF used Kruger and other parks for military tests. However, Kruger Park officials were not told what was being tested, only what areas would be restricted and for how long. His impression is that more sensitive tests occurred on private reserves or Cape testing areas. [23]

It appears that, from the start, Project Coast was not just a defensive program.[24] In the early 1980s, fears of a "black tidal wave" drove white scientists to try to develop a variety of means that could ensure the survival of white South Africa. Plans were devised to build a large-scale anthrax production facility at RRL. The anthrax could have been used either outside or inside South Africa, particularly where guerrillas were present. According to former RRL scientist, Mike Odendaal, who testified in the Basson trial, those plans were nearly operationalized in 1985.

Also, reportedly part of Project Coast was genetic engineering research, which was being conducted to produce a "black bomb," bacteria or other biological agents that would kill or weaken blacks and not whites. The black bomb could be used to wipe out or incapacitate an entire area where an insurrection was taking place.[25] Project Coast scientists asked Basson to obtain a peptide synthesizer outside of South Africa that would assist in genetic engineering efforts.

Many aspects of Project Coast research projects, including the country's links with other states, have not and may never be uncovered. Research on birth control methods to reduce the black birth rate was one such area. Daan Goosen, the managing director of Roodeplaat Research Laboratories between 1983 and 1986, told Tom Mangold of the BBC that Project Coast supported a project to develop a contraceptive that would have been applied clandestinely to blacks.[26] Goosen claimed that Dr. Knobel knew all about this project and those scientists had been told that this was the most important research on which they could work. Goosen reported that the project had developed a vaccine for males and females and that the researchers were still searching for a means that it could be delivered to make blacks sterile without making them aware.[27] Testimony given at the Truth and Reconciliation Commission (TRC) suggested that Project Coast researchers were also looking into putting birth control substances in water supplies.[28]

Project Coast claimed its first victims at the end of 1982, when "Operation Duel" was launched, which aimed to eliminate hundreds of SWAPO prisoners and SADF informants.[29] Col. Johan Theron, Counterintelligence Officer in the Special Forces, testified at the Basson trial that he received muscle relaxant pills from Basson in December 1982 and killed approximately 200 SWAPO prisoners, then dumped their bodies from airplanes out to sea. Also in Namibia, the Soviet Union accused South Africa of using herbicides. Napalm and phosphorous were allegedly used by the SADF in Angola during the 1980s, actions that violated the 1925 Geneva Protocol.

In November 1983, Basson was allegedly involved in the use of CBW against regime opponents in Dukuduku in KwaZulu-Natal. There he instructed South African agents to tie their intended victims to trees and smear a jell-like ointment on their bodies. When that failed to kill them, they were allegedly injected with an anaesthetic drug and then a muscle relaxant. After they had died, their bodies were thrown into the sea.

In 1985, four SWAPO detainees held at Reconnaissance Regiment headquarters were allegedly given a sleeping drug in soft drinks, taken to Lanseria airport outside Johannesburg and injected with three toxic substances supplied by Basson. Their bodies were thrown into the Atlantic Ocean.

In 1986, Basson is also alleged to have supplied poisoned tea and oranges that killed Special Forces member Lance Corporal Victor de Fonseca in a military hospital in Pretoria. Fonseca is said to have started "talking" about clandestine operations after developing brain cancer. These acts were part of the 16 murder charges introduced on 26 March 1999, prior to the October 1999 opening of Basson's trial in South Africa.

In 1984, uprisings in South Africa started in the Vaal Triangle, south of Johannesburg, and spread throughout the country. The mass actions were far more widespread, violent and deadly than in 1960 or after 1976. The nationwide scope of these protests intensified concerns over crowd control and fueled ongoing efforts to develop weapons, including chemical and biological agents, to deal with the unrest. SADF Chief of Staff, General Constand Viljoen, as well as Generals Liebenberg and Meiring, were seeking an offensive CBW substance that would weaken and incapacitate rioters and was less irritating than tear gas. They consulted Basson and Project Coast. Also, the SADF sought a chemical that would color the skin for about two weeks and allow the identification of frontrunners in the violence.[30]

By 1985, several Project Coast program directors were planning for a massive escalation of the chemical and biological agents production program and working on plans that would have resulted in a weapons program. According to RRL scientist Mike Odendaal, he had received instructions to start a factory where biological agents would be produced in mass form, and 200,000 rand ($100,000 in 1985 U.S. dollars) had already been spent on the plans.[31] A new wing had been added to Roodeplaat Research laboratories for a production-scale laboratory, with fermenters that could produce 300 liters or more of anthrax and other biological agents and a P-4 level laboratory. For the first few years, Project Coast used P-2 to P-3 facilities, and RRL only used two 10-gallon fermenters for growth medium. In 1985, when the new wing for RRL was built, a P-4 facility was added. Basson and his superiors in the SADF (Generals Liebenberg, Nieuwoudt, and Viljoen, as well as Magnus Malan) approved the upgrade.

According to RRL scientist Schalk van Rensburg, when Basson wanted the safety level raised to level 4, two British scientists, on an unauthorized visit from Porton Down, U.K. (which had been privatized) helped and advised.[32] According to Tom Mangold, MI-6 opened a file on Basson after he attended the Second World Conference of Toxicologists in Ghent, Belgium, where he reportedly met with scientists, including some from Porton Down.[33] Consequently, both American and British intelligence agencies knew of Basson's activities during this time but did little against him. However, there is no evidence, besides Basson's claims, that Basson ever visited Porton Down.[34]

In the end, the directors of Project Coast decided not to fund the larger fermenters. According to Odendaal, SADF decided that biological agents would be used in low intensity regional skirmishes and assassinations, but not on a more massive scale.[35] Therefore, in comparison to the USSR, which had scores of big fermenters, the South African program was quite small in size and scale. However, according to many American and South African experts, in terms of the range of biological agents possessed and the science involved, the CBW program was the "second most sophisticated program," next to the Soviet program, and more sophisticated than the Iraqi program that was uncovered in 1995. In our interviews, no comparisons were made with the U.S. program that existed until 1969.

A senior former army officer confirmed that "any thinking person in the SADF" knew that South Africa had developed chemical weapons, at least by the mid-1980s." He confirmed that South Africa was manufacturing chemical weapons from the mid-1980s until the "whole scenario changed" in the early 1990s.[36] Earlier, the army had spent most of its time testing decontamination gasses. Also, at this time, several public statements about developing methods to counter chemical attacks appeared.

Weaponization began in cooperation with ARMSCOR, the state-owned arms producer, which developed unmanned aerial vehicles (UAVs) and missiles that would have the capability to carry chemical and biological agents. All of this was top secret, and the Americans and British only discovered weaponization in 1994. They did not insist that weaponization be included in the chemical and biological memorandum because they had no hard evidence upon which to make such a demand.[37] The South African Ministry of Defense still denies that weaponization took place.

While reports that the former South African government tested battlefield weapons capable of carrying biological agents and chemicals cannot be confirmed, there is evidence that such weapons were developed. Basson, much like his counterparts in other countries (e.g., Iraq), had difficulties developing effective delivery systems for using biological agents in mass casualty weapons. While Project Coast researchers undertook conceptual studies in the aerosolization of biological agents, the evidence available to date indicates that sophisticated aerosolization delivery systems were not developed. However, conceptual studies of such systems were well underway at the time Project Coast was shut down. Much more progress appears to have been achieved developing sophisticated artillery warheads and tactical missiles that were capable of delivering NBC warheads. What types of missiles and warheads were built, possibly tested and sold abroad remain among the most important questions related to South Africa's NBC programs still to be answered.

International Links Established during Project Coast

From 1981 onwards, Basson and Project Coast scientists intensified their international contacts, particularly at conferences on CBW. South African delegations made visits to the U.S., Britain, Taiwan, Israel, and Germany. Basson attended a conference on biological warfare (BW) in San Antonio in 1981. From 1981 to 1986, the Reagan administration followed a policy of "constructive engagement." Reagan administration officials sent signals to the Botha regime that the U.S. was willing to turn a blind eye to American industries and scientists as the South Africans built up their defense industries. Under-Secretary of State William Clark went one step further and welcomed South African defense officials and experts to Washington and facilitated their interaction with U.S. counterparts. The attitude of Clark and others enabled South Africa to gain access to U.S. scientists. At the same time, Basson's trip to San Antonio reportedly attracted the attention of American intelligence, and he was barred entry to the U.S. for scientific purposes.[38]

In 1984, the U.S. Centers for Disease Control (CDC) sent eight shipments of the Ebola, Marburg, and Rift Valley viruses to South Africa. The CDC was concerned with outbreaks of Ebola and other viruses and sought South Africa's assistance in preventing their spread. While CDC motives were benign, suddenly, South Africa possessed viruses that could be used with devastating effect in surrounding countries.

Details of the extent and importance of South African cooperation with Israel in CBW research have not been disclosed. The two countries started working together on covert research related to nuclear weapons after World War II. These links had developed into a mature working relationship by the 1970s. Bilateral cooperation between the two states proved especially fruitful in developing nuclear weapons and testing a number of increasingly sophisticated missiles. Israel and South Africa also cooperated closely in the production of the G-5 artillery gun to fight a conventional war.[39] This line of research that cost millions of rand also explored the feasibility of using NBC warheads for the G-5, and later the G-6 gun. The Israelis also helped South Africa with armored cars and tanks and the Cheetah (a Mirage offshoot). Given the breadth and depth of cooperation, it is quite possible that Israel and South Africa cooperated on CBW efforts. It is significant that Basson went to Israel several times during the 1980s.[40]

New questions surfaced about the apartheid government's international connections and interest in biological warfare and birth control methods in early 2000, after Dr. Larry Ford committed suicide in Irvine, California. Local authorities and the FBI launched a weapons of mass destruction investigation into the Ford case and began investigating claims Ford made to his associates and friends that he served as a consultant to the SADF and had close ties with the CIA. According to Dr. Scharf, the former head of Military Hospital One in Pretoria, Ford visited in the mid-1980s as a guest of the South African Surgeon General. Dr. Scharf remembered a visit by Ford to his hospital as the guest of Knobel in 1984 or 1985. Knobel insisted that Ford be given VIP treatment (at the hospital's expense). Scharf was offended by Ford's request for human placenta that he wanted to use in his research on viruses. Scharf refused to cooperate and claimed that he threw Ford out of his office, after warning him that such activities would be very controversial, if they became public, due to the fact that all Africans viewed babies as sacred.[41]

According to microbiologist Mike Odendaal, researcher at RRL, Ford also visited South Africa again in 1987 to instruct scientists working with a SADF front company on how to turn teabags, doilies, and pornographic magazines into "weapons" that could be used against the ANC by using species of clostridium bacteria. Odendaal reported that the scientists found much of Ford's advice confusing and some went so far as to call him a fraud.

Police investigating this case have been unable to corroborate many of Ford's claims made before his death. For example, Ford claimed that he parachuted into southern Africa during the apartheid era to take blood samples from dead guerrilla fighters in order to help the U.S. government determine the biological warfare agents against which the Soviets were vaccinating their allies.[42] Another long-time associate of Ford claimed that only about one per cent of the story of Ford's activities in Africa has been disclosed.[43]

The results of a closed grand jury investigation of the Ford case have not been made public, but the discovery of biological agents and toxins in Ford's possession renewed questions about whether Basson called upon former associates to conceal biological agents, poisons and drugs overseas. Testimony at the Basson's trial to date has failed to explain where tons of drugs and smaller quantities of deadly toxins whose production Basson oversaw before his retirement from the military in 1993 went and why so many drugs were produced in the first place. One of the prosecutors in the Basson case has acknowledged that the prosecution still does not have a very clear idea about either the purpose of the drugs or their final destination.[44]

At the time of Basson's arrest, investigators found several trunks in his possession that contained documents and items related to Project Coast.[45] The investigators also found in the trunks and among Basson's personal effects a great deal of personal correspondence between Basson and individuals in Switzerland, the United Kingdom, and other countries. One letter was from an individual in the U.K., who lived near Heathrow Airport. This letter described what Basson should do if he needed to leave South Africa quickly. The letter said he should contact "them" when he arrived at Heathrow and that "we will collect you." Other letters, from individuals in other countries, described similar emergency exit plans.

The documents are interesting, given statements made by Juergen Jacomet, a former Swiss military intelligence agent, who worked with

Basson on money-laundering for Project Coast in Europe. He spoke of a right-wing conspiracy and alluded to the existence of an information organization of individuals, including Americans.[46] The death of Dr. Ford and revelations of his South African involvement, and his failed effort to establish the Lake View Terrace Institute raised again the possibility of a right-wing international network, united by a vision of a South Africa once again ruled by whites.

No evidence to date has been found to substantiate concerns expressed by some about possible linkages between Project Coast programs and the intentional use of HIV or microbicide contraceptives.[47] However, the recent revelations since Ford's death have been consistent with reports that the former South African government was already concerned about the future impact of the AIDS epidemic by the mid-1980s. In the 1980s, as the South African government became more aware of the magnitude of the impending AIDS epidemic, the SADF started testing thousands of SADF soldiers for HIV. The secret right-wing *Afrikaner* organization, the Broederbond, also recently acknowledged that they had completed population projections during the mid-1980s. They suggested that whites would be in majority in the future due to the devastating effects that AIDS was projected to have on the black population of South Africa.[48]

Throughout the 1980s, Basson continued his foreign visits and interaction with experts from the U.S., the U.K. and other countries. Most contacts appear to have been legal ones between Project Coast scientists and other scientists and consultants in Europe. Most of the substances and knowledge relevant to biological weapons were not controlled in the 1970s and 1980s as there was not the same level of concern with the possible use of biological agents and chemical substances that emerged during the 1990s.[49] However, Basson and Knobel subsequently claimed that Basson visited Iraq and Iran, the Philippines, North Korea, and Croatia, and met with members of Colombian drug cartels, making contacts and collecting information. What was obtained or exchanged during these visits has not yet emerged.

Project Coast ground to a halt in 1988, due to corruption by Basson and others. According to interviews with Project Coast scientists, between 1982 and 1987, Project Coast was advancing as a sophisticated program.[50] Project Coast had acquired anthrax, cholera, botulinum, and other biological agents, was planning to add a wing to RRL to produce massive amounts of anthrax, and was proceeding with genetic engineering research to produce germs that would harm blacks and not whites. However, as the communist threat receded in 1987-88, and as it seemed possible that the apartheid regime's days were numbered, Basson and others allegedly took large amounts of money that was intended for Project Coast programs and diverted it to their own accounts. Elsewhere in government, top officials were taking funds on a large scale. As the biological warfare program stopped, Basson and others began to plan how to roll Project Coast back in such a way that would be advantageous to them. By 1988, President P.W. Botha, Magnus Malan and Wim de Villiers of ARMSCOR had initiated the privatization and liberalization of the defense industry. They envisaged a transfer of power to Mandela and the ANC and saw the need to keep the defense industry out of their hands. The privatization process opened the door to the type of corruption exhibited by Basson and his colleagues.

In 1988, Basson was supposed to have bought a sophisticated peptide synthesizer for $2.2 million from clandestine sources. Project Coast researchers were attempting to make significant advances in the field of peptides to alter brain function, which was a key to creating a biological weapon that would affect blacks and not whites. However, at the trial of Basson, Dr. Lucia Steenkamp, a Project Coast scientist, refuted claims that Basson had bought the peptide synthesizer, and the prosecution alleged that Basson defrauded SADF by pretending he needed the synthesizer but actually used the money for overseas business deals.[51]

Rollback of Project Coast, 1988-1994

In 1988, conditions for the rollback of the CBW program, Project Coast, improved dramatically, as the pace of change accelerated in South Africa and southern Africa. President P.W. Botha and the South African Defense Force (SADF) realized that the Soviet Union was crumbling and knew they were going to win against the Cubans in Angola.

Suddenly, P.W. Botha changed his position and accepted a change in strategy. The goal became minimal destruction, using cross border raids, and not defeat of the regime's adversaries. As Botha realized there was a greatly reduced external threat, he agreed to enter into negotiations, which had started at a lower level in 1986, to reach a compromise with Nelson Mandela and the ANC. In 1988, the U.S., Cuba, Angola and South Africa negotiated the withdrawal of Cuban troops in exchange for the independence of Namibia, and by the end of the year, a deal was reached. The Soviet and Cuban threat that had helped give rise to Project Coast rapidly began to recede. However, the ANC/MK continued their guerrilla campaign, including the bombing of civilian targets.[52]

At the beginning of 1989, President Botha suffered a stroke and was replaced on an interim basis by F.W. de Klerk, an "outsider" to the state security system (including Project Coast). In April 1989, South African troops were confined to barracks in Namibia and were withdrawn by the end of the year. In September 1989, de Klerk was elected and inaugurated as State President and shunted Botha aside. De Klerk began his own five-year plan of ending apartheid. Part of his task included trying to establish civilian control over the security apparatus and reining in the "securocrats" and secret projects (like Project Coast). Talks with Mandela reached their climax, and top ANC prisoners, such as Walter Sisulu, were released. Finally, in February 1990, de Klerk lifted the ban on the ANC, Pan Africanist Congress of Azania (PAC), and South African Communist Party, and released Nelson Mandela.

De Klerk's decision to release Nelson Mandela and lift the ban on the ANC initiated a four-year period of negotiation and contention. During this period of negotiations, instability and violence, many in the regime believed that they needed insurance against the ANC/MK and the "black onslaught." With this in mind, the CBW program was kept intact by Basson and his associates as insurance and was used in assassination attempts. Also, experiments with chemical warfare apparently continued, with an alleged attack on Mozambican troops as late as January 1992. At the same time, Basson, Philip Mijburgh and others were dismantling Project Coast, privatizing its companies, and allegedly accumulating large sums of money.

Basson began to establish contacts with foreign governments, such as Libya, which might be interested in purchasing CBW secrets. Soon, Basson became the target of investigation from the National Intelligence Service (NIS), SADF counterintelligence, and the Office of Serious Economic Offenses, as well as the CIA and MI-6. The investigations culminated in the Steyn Report of December 1992.

After de Klerk lifted the ban on the ANC and freed Mandela, he addressed the SADF and SAP. De Klerk stressed that the ANC was now a party and not the enemy. Needless to say, many in the security forces did not like the message. On 26 March 1990, President F.W. de Klerk was briefed by Surgeon General Knobel about the defensive side of the CBW program, such as gas masks and protective suits. Knobel informed de Klerk about work with lethal chemical agents, and in response, de Klerk ordered Knobel to stop work on the lethal agents. However, de Klerk was not provided with all of the details about Project Coast, especially about the offensive aspects of the CBW program and its use in assassination activities. The same was true with other SADF projects and "third force" activities.[53] Only with the Steyn Report at the beginning of 1993, did de Klerk become aware of the sophistication and offensive nature of Project Coast.

At the end of 1989, the U.S., backed by Britain and Israel, issued a strongly worded warning to South Africa on rolling back the nuclear weapons program.[54] With the prospect of the ANC taking power, the U.S., the U.K. and Israel did not want to see the program's assets or secrets being sold to adversaries in the Middle East or elsewhere. De Klerk was persuaded by the ultimatum, especially as he saw no future need for nuclear weapons. In addition, South African officials were being forced by the U.S. to take a stand on the Non-Proliferation Treaty (NPT), in time for the June 1990 NPT review conference. According to Prof. Andre Buys,[55] in late 1989, de Klerk decided to end the nuclear program.

In contrast to the nuclear weapons program, no pressure was exerted in 1989 or 1990 over the CBW program, even though the CIA released a report in 1989, which placed South Africa on a list of countries that had developed and stockpiled chemical weapons. However, the main focus of concern for the United States and her allies was nuclear proliferation. For a brief time, between 1987 and August 1990, when South Africa sold the G-6 155mm gun and chemical warfare agents, including NGT (CR) gas (New Generation Tear Gas), to Iraq, the United States became concerned about the proliferation of a conventional weapon that had the capability to throw "exotic" shells.[56] However, there was little or no interest among U.S. policy and intelligence communities about possible proliferation threats associated with South Africa's biological warfare program.

The information the CIA and MI-6 possessed was widely circulated and available within the Bush administration and Major government. This lack of interest changed in 1993, as the U.S. learned more about South Africa's CBW and missile programs. Wouter Basson's trips, particularly to Libya, and access to an informant, who provided the U.S. and allies with key details of Project Coast, increased the interest and concern of the United States, Great Britain and other allies. The new information led the U.S. and Britain to issue a *demarche* in April 1994. Israeli officials probably knew more about the program but did not want the U.S. and Britain to know that they were involved with it.

In 1991, U.S. embassy officials, including the defense attaché, discovered at an arms show that South Africa was running a CBW program, including gas masks and protective suits.[57] The Americans asked the South Africans about the CBW gear but elicited little response. Later, an American delegation was invited to visit Protechnik to view facilities producing CBW protective gear. By September 1991, the U.S. government (and not just the CIA) became aware of Basson and Project Coast and began to look for signs of proliferation, especially to ANC allies, such as Libya.

In 1989 and the early 1990s, violence escalated inside South Africa, in spite of the unbanning of the ANC and the release of Mandela. The ANC/MK reserved the right to resume their urban guerrilla warfare campaign, and violence between ANC and Inkatha supporters escalated in KwaZulu-Natal. In this atmosphere of violence, "third force" agents intensified their activities. The most notorious covert operations unit was the Civilian Cooperation Bureau (CCB).

In April 1989, the CCB attempted to assassinate the Reverend Frank Chikane with poison during a trip to Namibia. Another attempt was made during a trip to the U.S., where one doctor finally diagnosed his malady as organophosphate poisoning. According to the testimony of RRL scientist, Schalk Van Rensburg, to the TRC, the men who tried to kill Chikane with Parathion had poor intelligence. He stated, "They were counting on little (*sic*) forensic capability in Namibia. And too little was smeared over his underwear to kill him when he went to the U.S."[58] Chikane's attempted assassination and several other CCB incidents illustrate the difficulties involved in using biological agents as methods of assassination.[59]

CCB operative Petrus Jacobus Botes (who claimed to have also directed operations by the CCB in Mozambique and Swaziland) asserted that he was ordered, in May 1989, to contaminate the water supply at Dobra, a refugee camp located in Namibia, with cholera and yellow fever organisms. A South African army doctor provided them to him. In late August 1989, he led an attempt to contaminate the water supply. However, the attempt failed to have any effect because of the high chlorine content in the treated water at the camp.[60]

In May 1990, a South African newspaper, *Vrye Weekblad*, reported that the CCB had employed biological agents against SWAPO members. Reportedly, the CCB had nearly 300 people working for it, and reportedly consumed about 0.28 per cent of the entire South African defense budget. Reportedly, the group had authority to operate inside South Africa and in neighboring countries and was disbanded at the end of 1990.[61]

In 1990, violence in KwaZulu-Natal and other parts of South Africa escalated, with assistance provided to Inkatha militants from the CCB and other "third force" agents. In response to rising evidence of "third force" activities, the Harms Commission was established in 1990 and was charged by President de Klerk with investigating "third force" agencies, including the CCB and *Vlakplaas*.

The January 1993 Steyn Report was the most ambitious attempt to uncover the secret projects of the SADF, including Project Coast, with the aim of helping to restore civilian control over the military. On 18 November 1992, de Klerk appointed Lt. Gen. Steyn to investigate SADF secret projects, including Basson and Project Coast and "third force" activities around the country. As a result, de Klerk learned of the activities of Basson, Project Coast, CCB and other covert units.[62]

The CIA and MI6 were concerned and were in touch with the NIS. While the different organizations often had to rely upon information obtained from the same source, it was probable that the information that they received was valid. The NIS had been conducting its own intelligence operation since 1989, investigating the SADF and SAP secret projects. Targets for investigation included Project Coast and Basson, as well as Jan Lourens and Brian John Davie of Protechnik, who were involved in the CBW experiments.

The Steyn team quickly investigated projects that needed to be stopped. However, financial misdealings were not examined.

Investigations went smoothly, until the first report was completed and issued on 20 December 1992 and landed on de Klerk's desk at the beginning of January 1993. President de Klerk decided that firm and decisive action was needed, even though there was no conclusive evidence. In mid-January 1993, de Klerk called Liebenberg in again and announced that he had changed his mind and that he wanted to act assertively. He would fire the generals responsible for the CCB and other secret projects. De Klerk asked Liebenberg to ensure that the SADF policed itself. Subsequently, de Klerk launched another, more random investigation. Instead of acting against Liebenberg and van der Merwe, de Klerk let Liebenberg off the hook, and Liebenberg was not obliged to report back. De Klerk did not even confront the SAP's van der Merwe about the activities of the CCB unit of the SAP and its notorious leader, Eugene de Kock. As a result of the second investigation, 27 generals retired early. Col. Dr. Basson was required to leave the SADF at the end of March 1993 and was given a "soft retirement" and reserve status.[63]

The Steyn Report found that Project Coast was offensive in nature and that Basson, RRL, Delta-G, Medchem, and SADF were all operating completely outside the purview of the civilian government. The SADF was compelled to create an offensive CBW program in order to test defensive measures, and the lack of civilian control meant that the program was used as only a few top SADF leaders saw fit. According to this report, starting in 1985, the ANC and MK escalated their campaign of violence to include civilian targets, and the SADF and SAP retaliated by using methods, such as CBW. These persisted, despite later efforts made to assert civilian control. Gen. Liebenberg and Gen. Meiring, in particular, knew about SADF secret programs, including Project Coast, and took an assertive hand in running them. Gen. Liebenberg signed for Project Coast activities and so did Surgeon General Knobel.

Upon receiving Steyn's report, de Klerk finally ordered the destruction of all lethal and incapacitating CBW agents, as well as an end to such research and operations. He also forced the retirement of Basson at the end of March 1993. In January 1993, the Minister of Defense, Kobie Coetzee, acting on de Klerk's order, authorized all CBW research and development stopped. Project Coast documents containing formulas and experiments were to be transferred to CD-ROMs.

According to Dr. Kobus (Jack) Bothma, in testimony at the Basson trial, an office secretary scanned in the documents from Project Coast onto CD-ROMs. Philip Mijburgh transferred the CD-ROMs to the Ministry of Defense, where they were placed in the vaults, and President de Klerk was given a key to the contents, so that only the State President could open it, along with the Surgeon General, and head of the NIS, Niel Barnard.

Although it seemed that Project Coast had been rolled back, Mijburgh issued destruction documents that were inconclusive. While the South African government believed that it had rolled back Project Coast, four years later, in January 1997, police investigators found that Basson had taken copies of Project Coast documents home and hidden them in trunks.

Whether all CBW agents were destroyed at the beginning or end of 1993 remains a matter of opinion. Also, large quantities of drugs were unaccounted for and were either in possession of Basson or were secreted elsewhere. According to General (ret.) Meiring, all CBW agents were dumped out to sea at the end of 1993. The Forensic Branch of the SAP, headed by SAP General Lothar Neethling, placed all agents destroyed on a schedule. The agents were dumped 200 nautical miles south of Cape Argulhas. While lethal CBW agents were destroyed, the irritants, including NGT (CR) gas, were kept.[64]

According to Dr. Knobel's testimony to the TRC, SADF Counterintelligence destroyed all CBW agents in January 1993. Methaqualone purchased in Croatia was allegedly destroyed then, after the order was received that work on all incapacitants should cease.

On 7 January 1993, Dr. Knobel advised his superiors that South Africa "should conceal" NGT (CR) gas from the inspectors of the Chemical Weapons Convention (CWC). On 14 January 1993, South Africa formally acceded to the CWC. However, work on the dispersion of NGT (CR) gas continued.[65] By March 1993, de Klerk publicly announced that South Africa had dismantled its six nuclear weapons in 1991. By the end of 1993, the South African missile program was rolled back.

On 31 March 1993, Basson was retired by President de Klerk from the SAMS and became a reservist. Basson had also been ordered to destroy Project Coast documentation. However, Basson did not follow, to the letter, the orders of his superiors and kept Project Coast research documentation alive. Transnet, the state-owned transportation and infrastructure corporation that built and maintained railroads, tunnels, airports, and hospitals, immediately employed him. Basson then went to Libya on contract to give advice on military counter-measures to CBW attacks.

In the second half of 1993, peace negotiations between the de Klerk government and Nelson Mandela and the ANC gained momentum. In August 1993, the Office of Serious Economic Offenses (OSEO) informed MI-6 and the CIA of the misdeeds of Basson and Project Coast.

The Americans and British became even more concerned when, in October 1993, Basson made his first trip to Libya on behalf of Transnet. This was the first of Basson's five visits to Libya, with his last visit in October 1995, and it is possible that he sold Project Coast secrets.

In addition, South Africa submitted a Confidence Building Measure (CBM) for 1993, as stipulated by the BWC, which provided details on the rollback of the biological side of Project Coast. In November 1993, the Americans and British objected to the South African CBM and began the process of interacting with South African officials in an effort to see that Project Coast would be rolled back to their satisfaction. According to U.S. Ambassador Princeton Lyman, the South African CBM was not forthcoming on many aspects of the CBW program, including offensive uses, weaponization, and proliferation.[66]

According to Peter Goosen, proliferation expert in the Ministry of Foreign Affairs, the South Africans lacked the technical expertise to submit an acceptable CBM and sought British and American assistance. In the meantime, de Klerk and his colleagues attempted to reassure the U.S. and the U.K. that the CBW program had been rolled back.[67]

In January 1994, negotiations between the de Klerk government and Nelson Mandela and the ANC finally reached settlement, and elections were scheduled for April 27. As the momentous hand-over of power approached, the U.S. and U.K. became increasingly concerned about Basson and others proliferating chemical and biological warfare secrets to other states and/or groups of concern.

On 11 April 1994, Ambassador Lyman and the British High Commissioner, Anthony Reeve, delivered a *demarche* to President de Klerk.[68] The U.S. and Britain demanded that their experts be briefed, that all CBW systems and records, including the CD-ROMs, be destroyed, that abuses of the program be investigated and reported, and that Mandela be informed. According to David Steward, de Klerk's chief of staff, the American and British ambassadors regarded Basson as a "dangerous agent."[69]

Within the American team, there were differences. Ambassador Lyman was primarily concerned with reducing the proliferation threat, and State Department and CIA officials joined him in this approach. However, officials from the National Security Council (NSC) were outraged by evidence of the use of CBW and wanted to see that those responsible were punished. Department of Defense officials were late in joining the U.S. team and felt marginalized. Consequently, they sided with the NSC. Ultimately, Ambassador Lyman was able to prevail and focus on proliferation concerns, even though seeking convictions for past CBW use was part of the *demarche*.[70]

According to Dr. Knobel, then South African Surgeon General, President de Klerk and the South Africans cooperated with the Americans and British.[71] However, Knobel and other South African officials believed that the Americans and British were acting on the basis of questionable and uncorroborated evidence, some of which came from press reports. On 21 April 1994, South Africa responded to the *demarche* and asserted that Project Coast records were a "national asset" and that the CD-ROMs would not be destroyed. According to Knobel, he and Basson were given responsibility for briefing the U.S. and British experts and Mandela.

After the *demarche* and the inauguration of President Mandela in May 1994, American and British delegations arrived for the first of several visits to South Africa. Knobel, Basson and others extensively briefed the delegations over a three-day period and took them on a tour of Roodeplaat Research Laboratories, which had been converted to commercial production. The SADF compiled a large file on Project Coast and gave it to the Americans and British.

South Africa reassured the British and Americans that the three keys to gain access to Project Coast secrets on CD-ROM were in the hands of the President, Surgeon General, and National Intelligence Agency head. The South Africans transferred information, which they had obtained from the Russian and Iraqi programs (including flesh-eating bacteria). Knobel claimed that Basson was offered a job and money by the U.S. and Britain but declined. Three teams (from the U.N., U.S. and U.K.) investigated the January 1992 alleged CBW incident in Mozambique. In 1994 and 1995, American and British teams made more visits to South Africa to facilitate the rollback of the South African CBW program.

Basson and his trips to Libya were the main source of contention between the U.S., Britain and South Africa. In spite of the *demarche*, Basson continued to visit Libya in 1994 and 1995, until he had completed five trips. The U.S. and U.K. kept up the pressure on South Africa to control Basson and suggested that the South African National Defense Force (SANDF), which had replaced the SADF, rehire him. Opinion on the damage done by Basson varies.

According to Mangold and Adams,[72] there is no doubt that Basson was originally invited to Libya to help them with chemical warfare facilities at Rabta. General (ret.) Meiring believed that Basson did not pass secret information on the CBW program to the Libyans or to other foreign governments. However, Meiring suggested that he gave them other information and defensive CBW techniques. There was still secrecy about how the knowledge was passed. Meiring stressed that Basson was always under instructions, and claimed there was nothing that went unnoticed by the SADF.

According to Gen. (ret.) Meiring, much of the information for Project Coast was obtained from the nationals of the U.S., U.K., and Germany. Highly technical advanced knowledge passed from U.S., U.K., and German scientists to the South Africans. The South African government did not want to cause the American and British governments embarrassment by revealing that fact. Ambassador Donald Mahley, U.S. State Department proliferation expert, and his British counterpart had led teams that examined Project Coast documents in 1994.

The range of pathogens that were developed led to the American claim that South Africa had the "second most sophisticated program next to the Soviets." While there was no evidence that South African scientists themselves had genetically modified pathogens to create new ones, there was evidence that Project Coast had obtained the pathogens from elsewhere. In addition, from 1989-93, the South African military still had the capability to launch or deliver a nuclear or CBW payload.

On 18 August 1994, Knobel briefed President Mandela, Defense Minister Modise and his deputy, Ronnie Kasrils. The SANDF also provided a large file on Project Coast. Before April 1994 and the elections, Mandela was only getting sketchy details from de Klerk about what was developed, according to senior ANC officials.

Within the ANC, there was a debate, from 1990-94, about whether to keep the nuclear program. However, the conclusion to roll back the CBW program was unanimous. According to Dr. Ian Phillips, ANC defense expert, the ANC wanted to know where the information about the CBW program had disappeared. The ANC believes that white South African scientists and former operatives who are now living in the Middle East as well as the U.S. and Britain sold many of Project Coast's secrets to foreign sources.

In November 1994, the Office for Serious Economic Offenses (OSEO), a special unit attached to the Attorney General's department, completed an official report on the activities and financial irregularities of a network of companies that supplied the SADF with pharmaceuticals and anti-chemical warfare equipment (i.e., Project Coast). The report sent to Justice Minster Dullah Omar was marked "top secret" and the minister was reported to be studying it.[73] One researcher in the Attorney General's office reported studying Project Coast in early 1993.

A report in *The Sunday Tribune* in December 1994 described the network of companies working with SADF on CBW. The report named the key directors of this network under investigation as Dr. Wouter Basson, Dr. Wynand Swanepoel, and Dr. Phillip Mijburgh (a nephew of Magnus Malan), and noted that all three had served in SADF's medical service (SAMS).

The Weekly Mail and Guardian reported, from correspondence between Basson and Mijburgh, that they were researching the legal aspects of CBW. The same newspaper also reported that SADF military officials used the Council for Scientific and Industrial Research (CSIR) facilities to obtain and develop different strains of germs, some of which were highly toxic to humans.[74]

In 1995, Basson's trips to Libya continued. In February 1995, an article appeared in *The Times* of London on possible South African CBW links to Libya. Evidently, someone in MI-6 tipped off the *Times*. In March 1995, the CIA and DIA informed President Clinton of Basson's activities, who authorized the sending of a delegation to South Africa, which met with Mandela. It is not certain if the delegation met with Basson or if he was in Libya.

Once again, the Americans urged the Mandela government to bring Basson under control by rehiring him. On 15 April 1995, South Africa submitted a much-revised Confidence Building Measure (CBM). This was nearly two years after the U.S. and U.K. challenged the 1993 CBM (no CBM was submitted to the U.N. in 1994). This time U.S. and U.K. objections were addressed satisfactorily. Even so, the Americans and British continued to share concerns about the potential spread of the secrets on the CD-ROMs by Basson and others to states and/or groups of concern.

In early 1995, Generals Meiring and Knobel sat down and discussed Basson, after receiving information from NIA, CIA, and MI-6. Basson had been asked by government and SANDF officials to curb his behavior, but there was no way to do so, except to rehire him. Meiring and Knobel went to Deputy Minister of Defense Ronnie Kasrils and urged that Basson be rehired.[75] Kasrils went to Modise and Steyn and recommended the same. In May 1995, Defense Minister Modise and Secretary of Defense Pierre Steyn rehired Basson as a regular SANDF surgeon (he had been on reserve status).

Evidently, great concern existed within the South African government, the SANDF, and among foreign governments about the possibility that Basson was selling Project Coast secrets. However, even after being rehired by the SANDF, Basson still made another and final trip to Libya in October 1995.[76]

In January 1997, Basson was arrested during a sting operation on charges of fraud and the possession of illegal substances based on his alleged effort to sell 1,000 Ecstasy tablets. A subsequent search of Basson's friend and business associate, Sam Bosch's home, uncovered 5 or 6 trunks and a couple of suitcases that contained secret documents related to Project Coast that were thought to have been destroyed when the CBW program was dismantled.

The senior Truth and Reconciliation Commission researcher, Dr. Villa-Vicencia, rushed to Pretoria, after Basson was arrested, in order to represent the TRC. He was joined by Mike Kennedy, the representative of the National Intelligence Agency (NIA), and representatives from the Office of Serious Economic Offenses (OSEO), and the Gauteng Attorney General's Special Investigation Team. Together they went through the contents of these trunks. After some initial squabbling, an agreement was reached that the NIA would take control and responsibility for keeping these documents secure. Before the documents were turned over to the NIA, the contents of the trunks were inventoried. These documents contained the core of information, which formed the basis of the TRC's investigative work over the next 18 months. The TRC called in Professor Peter Folb, University of Cape Town, to serve as their scientific and technical adviser.

In March 1998, Chandre Gould, another TRC investigator who had access to the documents, and the TRC's Commissioner, Wendy Orr, looked at some of the technical documents that had been found in Basson's trunks. Gould wanted an explanation of some of the pharmaceutical and medical terminology. Orr was horrified by what she did understand, even though there was much that she did not understand in the contents. One of the first documents Dr. Orr examined was the infamous *verkope lys* (shopping or sales list).[77]

The senior TRC investigator, Villa-Vicencia, concluded that the trunks contained a "mixed bag" that included memorabilia, as well as sensitive technical information, which might prove embarrassing to foreign governments, as well as information readily available in open source literature (e.g., formulas for methaqualone and how to build a bomb). He felt that collectively, these documents confirmed the idea that South Africa's biological weapons program had developed some very sophisticated processes and procedures.[78]

At a hastily called meeting of representatives of various agencies at the end of May 1998, two main objections were raised to TRC hearings on Project Coast. One objection to the TRC hearings was that information disclosed during these hearings could lead to the proliferation of weapons of mass destruction that would cause South Africa to violate its international obligations. A second concern was that revelations of the involvement of various foreign governments in the CBW program could jeopardize international relations. South African government officials told the participants that Britain and the U.S. had voiced the strongest objections to the hearings.[79] Dr. Peter Folb, the TRC's scientific adviser, disagreed with the official assessment during this meeting, "because much of the science involved in Project Coast was pedestrian."[80]

The compromise that was reached was to have a small group of representatives from the meeting go through every document in the TRC's possession and decide together which could be placed in the public domain at the hearing. Commissioner Orr, Dr. Folb, and TRC investigators Gould and Jerome Chaskalson represented the TRC. Knobel, his lawyers, NIA officials, and other SANDF members, represented the government. Documents were placed into one of three categories: (1) no restrictions (i.e., ones to be referred to in the hearing and released to the media); (2) ones to be referred to but not released; and, (3) those that would not be mentioned at all.

The President's office did not accept the TRC's decision to hold the public hearings and issued an application to have section 33C invoked, which would require that the hearing be held behind closed doors. Thabo Mbeki's legal adviser and Abdul Minty, Chairperson of the Council for the Non-Proliferation of Weapons of Mass Destruction, formally presented the request for a closed hearing.[81] After extensive discussions, the TRC went ahead with open hearings with the understanding that a government representative would monitor the proceedings to ensure that no proliferation or diplomatically embarrassing information was released. This agreement meant that the hearings were bogged down with legal motions and delays from the first day.

Legal wrangling delayed Basson's appearance before the TRC until the last day of the hearings. However, scientists in charge of Project Coast projects did appear and started to reveal many more details about the covert programs in their testimony in an effort to obtain TRC amnesty and immunity in future legal proceedings. The scientists began to talk to authorities about what CBW weapons and knowledge were developed, how the knowledge and weapons were used, and even some details about what was sold after the 1994 elections.[82] Other individuals, such as Dr. Johan Koekemoer, former research manager of Delta-G, were arrested for being in possession of the designer drug Ecstasy and agreed to testify against Basson. The public also heard about the extensive misappropriation of public funds.

Disclosures from the TRC had international ramifications. In response to testimony at the TRC hearings in June 1998, the British Military Intelligence (MI5) and police reopened files on six people who had died in Britain during the 1980s and 1990s of apparent strokes or heart attacks. The re-opened investigations were initiated to explore which of these deaths might have been murders related to South Africa's secret germ warfare program. These investigations required unprecedented amounts of cooperation between South African and British intelligence services.

The deceased had all worked in Britain against the apartheid regime, or had knowledge of Pretoria's secret operation in the 1980s to acquire and develop chemical and biological weapons, at the time of their death in Great Britain.[83]

Despite the limited knowledge obtained from Basson at the TRC, these hearings played a critical role in opening up secret government activities. The TRC hearings on Project Coast opened "a window on the house of horrors" to public scrutiny and let the public know much more about what went on during the apartheid era. These disclosures, in turn, helped to stimulate a national dialogue that was designed to allow the nation to start to heal.[84] The disclosures also established an important precedent and ensured that South Africa's most important post-1994 trial involving national security issues would be open rather than closed to the public.

The Basson trial has been one of the longest and most complicated trials in South African legal history. Basson was initially charged with multiple counts of fraud, murder, conspiracy to murder and possession of drugs (Ecstasy, Mandrax and cocaine). However, the trial was quickly halted by objections presented by his lawyers. In hindsight, the most important objection raised by the defense related to conspiracy to murder charges against Basson for the poisoning of 200 SWAPO prisoners of war in a Namibian detention camp and his alleged involvement in the murder of five other SWAPO members in Namibia.

The Basson trial suggests that effective measures designed to limit the proliferation of CBW or illegal drugs in the future will require much greater inter-agency cooperation within nation-states and new forms of international cooperation among agencies in several countries. The South African case suggests the need for greater coordination between defense and counterproliferation agencies and agencies whose primary mission are crime solving and prevention.

The Basson trial is also useful for illustrating the complex ways that CBW project managers may be able to exploit transnational financial flows and international corporate instruments to quickly move, launder, and house large sums of money for either political or personal motives.

The Basson trial may also serve as a useful reminder of what may become a more general trend: the initiation or continuation of covert CBW programs primarily as a means to cover illegal personal gains from the sale of weapons (including CBW) and drugs.

Conclusion

In April 2002, the Basson trial came to an end after more than 300 days of actual trial and after almost 200 state witnesses gave evidence and after some 30 000 pages of transcripts had been produced. With many of Basson's former SADF superiors, including Magnus Malan and Dr. Knobel present in the courtroom, Judge Hartzenberg acquitted Basson of all charges. A charge of being in possession of thousands of ecstasy tablets was dismissed when the judge accepted Basson's version of events above that of a drug dealer witness.

The judge accepted Basson's testimony that he had ordered that all Project Coast documents destroyed in 1993. The judge accepted Basson's evidence that he had not packed the trunks and could not be found guilty of possession of cocaine, ecstasy and mandrax, as he was not aware of what was in the trunks. Finally, he rejected the evidence of the forensic auditor that Basson was the beneficial owner of SADF front companies, which stood at the center of the fraud charges. Protests against the acquittal came from Archbishop Desmond Tutu, the Chair of the Truth and Reconciliation, and from many other prominent South Africans, who were appalled that Judge Hartzenburg had sided with "Dr. Death." Immediately, the government sought to appeal the case and then retry Basson.

In January 2003, the Swiss added a request that Basson and former police chief of forensics Lothar Neethling be interrogated in the presence of Swiss officials about arms and nuclear goods trafficking. The Swiss government also wanted other records relating to Project Coast. In the wake of the trial, Namibian officials openly considered applying to extradite Basson to stand trial for the death of more than 200 SWAPO prisoners of war. However, Basson remains covered by a blanket amnesty extended to all SADF personnel who had committed crimes in Namibia while exercising their duties.

On June 3, 2003, the Supreme Court of Appeal in Bloemfontein denied the state's appeal for a retrial of the Basson case. The appeal judges found that Judge Hartzenberg's refusal to remove himself did not relate to an error of law on his part, but that it was a factual finding. Basson had finally escaped punishment for his alleged misdeeds.

In March 2003, South Africa sent a delegation of WMD experts to Iraq supposedly to assist in the disarmament process. The experts included Col. Ben Steyn, adviser to South Africa's surgeon general and an expert on nuclear and chemical weapons and scientist Philip Coleman of Protechnik (the CBW defense firm). Not invited to go to Iraq were Project Coast Wouter Basson, Daan Goosens, or other top Project Coast scientists.

In April 2003, revelations emerged about the attempted sale to American officials of biological pathogens and Project Coast documents by retired General Tai Minaar on behalf of Daan Goosens in May 2002. The story raised new concerns that Project Coast had not been rolled back and that the scientists remain a source of possible proliferation.

During the period when it developed chemical, biological, and nuclear weapons, South Africa was an isolated state that felt threatened by a more powerful state actor, the Soviet Union, which was helping hostile regimes and movements in neighboring states. One response of the apartheid regime to changing threat perceptions in the region was to develop Project Coast.

The decision-making process was secretive and controlled by the military and enabled a nuclear weapons program and a very sophisticated CBW program to be developed with little outside scrutiny. Military and police units used chemical and biological agents for counter-insurgency warfare, assassination, and execution of war prisoners.

As the regime felt increasingly threatened by opposition at home, top political leaders approved plans for research and development of exotic means to neutralize opponents, large-scale offensive uses of the program, and weaponization. However, the plans were not operationalized. The end of the external threat led to a decision to unilaterally dismantle the CBW program prior to a shift to majority rule.

Lack of civilian control over military programs made the rollback difficult, rife with corruption and may have permitted the transfer of findings and materials to other states.

The U.S., U.K. and other countries pressured the South African government to ensure that the CBW program was dismantled and the former project manager, Dr. Wouter Basson, constrained. Since Basson secretly retained copies of Project Coast documents, concerns remain about whether he assisted other states by transferring and selling such information.

The information that has emerged to date about Project Coast suggests that a country possessing chemical and biological weapons is likely to use them against adversaries at home and abroad. The unpredictable, hot and windy environment of southern Africa did not discourage conventional military or counter-insurgency units from experimenting with these weapons.

The South African case also dramatically shows how thin the line is between defensive and offensive weapons. First the Iraqi, and now the South African, cases suggest that it is prudent to assume that if a country is suspected of developing covert nuclear capabilities, it is probably supporting research into the offensive uses of chemical and biological weapons as well. If efforts are being made in the more challenging and expensive nuclear arena, why would a regime not develop the more accessible and less costly chemical and biological weapons?

South African CBW programs also underscore the importance of control by civilians, of transparency, and of accountability. Some aspects of the apartheid regime's management of their CBW programs may be unique. However, this case vividly illustrates what will happen when there is loose accountability of covert NBC research and development by senior military and political leaders. This is especially likely when the government is besieged both at home and on its borders.

The efforts to dismantle the South African CBW program illustrate how difficult effective NBC non-proliferation agreements will be to enforce. For many, the discovery that Wouter Basson secretly kept some of the classified documents is deeply disturbing to those who believe that South Africa developed highly sophisticated CBW capabilities during the Project Coast years.

For others, the science involved in the 10 years of research conducted by Project Coast was considered so pedestrian that they are not worried about the possibility of proliferation. These differing views of the program deserve further research and evaluation by CBW experts.

The likelihood that the South African government still possesses highly sophisticated CBW secrets, which it considers a "national asset," will remain a source of concern for the foreseeable future. As controls on arms sales erode and as high-level corruption increases, the chances that top officials might sell these secrets to states and/or groups of concern increases. The issue for counterproliferation experts is how to prevent such a transfer of deadly information from occurring.

Notes

1. Edward Regis, *The Biology of Doom: The History of America's Secret Germ Warfare Project* (New York: Henry Holt, 1999). Albert J. Mauroni, *America's Struggle with Chemical-Biological Warfare* (Westport, Conn.: Praeger, 2000). Erhard Geissler, et. al., eds., *Biological and Toxin Weapons: Research, Development and Use from the Middle Ages to 1945* (New York: Oxford University Press, 1999). Ken Alibek, with Stephen Handelman (Contributor) *Biohazard.* (New York: Random House, 1999). Tom Mangold and Jeff Goldberg, *Plague Wars: A True Story of Biological Warfare* (New York: St. Martin's Press, 1999). John Prados, "All Weapons Great and Small," *Washington Post, Book World*, 16 January 2000, 7.

2. Interview with Dr. Vernon Joynt of Mechem (explosives warfare program) and the Council for Scientific and Industrial Research (CSIR), Pretoria, South Africa, 14 June 2000.

3. Interview with General (retired) Jannie Geldenhuys, Pretoria, South Africa, 13 June 2000.

4. H.E. Purkitt, "The Politics of Denuclearization: The Case of South Africa". Presentation at the Defense Nuclear Agency's Fourth Annual International Conference on Controlling Arms, Philadelphia, Penn., 21 June 1995. (Earlier draft presented at Institute for National Studies (INSS), U.S. Air Force Academy, Colorado, 9 November 1994.

5. Interview with Gen. (ret.) Georg Meiring, Pretoria, 3 July 2000.

6. Interview with former Defense Minister Magnus Malan, Pretoria, 23 June 2000.

7. Annette Seegers, *The Military in the Making of Modern South Africa.* (New York: St. Martin's Press, 1996).

8. Interview with Magnus Malan, 23 June 2000.

9. Interview with Dr. Vernon Joynt, Pretoria, 14 June 2000. Dr. Joynt claims that Surgeon General Nieuwoudt sent Major Wouter Basson to him in 1978 and offered him the directorship of a chemical weapons program. While Joynt refused, many scientists and specialists accepted research projects by Nieuwoudt and Basson, and many did not tell their superiors.

10. Interview with Magnus Malan, 23 June 2000.

11. See Lt. Gen. (Dr.) D.P. (Niels) Knobel's testimony to the Truth and Reconciliation Commission (TRC), July 1998.

12. Chris Oppermann, "How the taxpayer footed the bill for Project Coast," *Weekly Mail and Guardian* archive, 27 June 1997.

13. According to Helmut Heitmann, defense expert, in a 26 June 2000 interview, the evidence was not conclusive.

Heitmann was among the first journalists to raise questions about South African allegations that the Cubans had used chemical weapons in Angola and highlighted the difficulty of verifying the source of alleged CBW attacks (Heitmann, 1985, 1990; see also Steenkamp, 1989).

14. Interview with Magnus Malan, 23 June 2000. Despite concerns by senior military leaders about the possibility that Cubans might use CBW in Angola, little time was spent on defensive CBW training during the 1970s. From the mid-1970s through the late 1970s only a few hours during one day of training was devoted to CBW of SADF infantry personnel. Most of these sessions focused on the use of CS gas. Many more hours of training were devoted to how to counter urban violence. Interview with Mark Malan, former SADF officer and senior researcher at the Institute for Strategic Studies-South Africa, 23 June 2000.

15. According to Chandre Gould, formerly of the TRC, interviewed 29 June 2000 in Johannesburg, South Africa.

16. Mangold, *Plague Wars,* 236. They estimate four to five million pounds.

17. Interview with Dr. Ian Phillips, 13 June 2000.

18. Interview with Rocky Williams, ISS-South Africa, 5 July 2000.

19. Interview with Gen. (ret.) Meiring, 3 July 2000.

20. Mangold, *Plague Wars,* 243.

21. Mangold, *Plague Wars,* 241.

22. Mangold, *Plague Wars,* 243.

23. Interview conducted in 1997 by Helen Purkitt.

24. Magnus Malan indicated as much in a 23 June 2000 interview.

25. According to Dr. Rocklyn Williams of ISS, Pretoria, interviewed 15 July 2000, he debriefed a SADF sergeant in 1983 who talked about the development of a "black bomb."

26. Mangold, *Plague Wars,* 244.

27. Mangold, *Plague Wars*, 244. In an interview for the television documentary, Dr.

Daan Goosen again acknowledged that the target of Project Coast's work on drugs that would induce infertility was the black population. One line of research was to develop a vaccine, one for males and one for females that could be given surreptitiously or under another pretext. This research was based on open source contraceptive research. Another line of research was work on a [unnamed] product that could have been given without the knowledge of the person receiving it either orally or in some sort of injection. He went on to state, "the most serious problem as told to us [was] the birth rate of the black population, and that it would outgrow the resources of the country and it was very important that this be brought under control. There was no doubt about that. This was given to us by Basson, by the surgeon general…it was very clear that this was the most important project we had to work on." *Frontline transcripts from Plague Wars: A report on biological weapons threats and how the Soviet Union secretly amassed an arsenal of bio-weapons.* Transcript from television show http://www.pbs.org/wgbh/pages/frontline/shows/plague/sa/. (Accessed 15 June 2000)

28. Interviews with a South African journalist, 20 July 2000.

29. According to Chandre Gould, formerly of the TRC, in a presentation, 29 June 2000.

30. Interviews with retired generals Thirion and Geldenhuys, Pretoria, 13 June 2000.

31. Testimony by Dr. Mike Odendaal in the Basson Trial, 24 May 2000. See "HIV Blood Sample Frozen for Chemical Warfare, Basson Trial Hears," *South African Press Association (SAPA),* 24 May 2000.

32. Mangold, *Plague Wars,* 243.

33. Mangold, *Plague Wars,* 242.

34. Dr. Basson told Mangold (*Plague Wars,* 442, note 443) in 1998 that the reason why a detailed investigation by Britain's MI-6, the Security Service, failed to substantiate the allegations that he visited Porton Down is because he used false names and passports for his frequent visits. Another possibility is that Basson met with former Porton Down employees. Several former employees of Porton Down report that they were asked to pose as employees after reporting contacts with Wouter Basson to British authorities. See Michael Evans, "South Africa may have ordered British deaths," *The Times (London),* (14 July 1998), 7 for further details.

35. Testimony by Dr. Odendaal, 24 May 2000. See "HIV..," *SAPA,* 24 May 2000.

36. Interview with former South African military officer, who will remain anonymous, July 2000.

37. Ambassador Princeton Lyman, e-mail to Stephen Burgess, 18 September 2000. Ambassador Princeton Lyman backtracked somewhat from earlier statements made in a

31 August 2000 interview about claims that weaponization took place. Donald Mahley of the U.S. State Department, who was part of the delegation to South Africa after the *demarche* of 11 April 1994, also downplayed evidence of weaponization in a 30 August 2000 interview.

38. Mangold, *Plague Wars*, 242. Skepticism still surrounds Basson and Knobel's claims about Basson's international activities. According to several interviewees, it is doubtful if Basson ever penetrated Porton Down or U.S. and Soviet facilities.

39. According to Gen. (ret.) Sass, interviewed 12 June 2000 in Pretoria.

40. According to Gen. (ret.) Sass, interviewed 12 June 2000 in Pretoria.

41. Interview with Dr. G. Scharf, former Director of Medical Hospital One (Pretoria), 6 July 2000.

42. Arthur Allen, "Mad Scientist," *Salon.com* (http://salonmag.com/ health/ feature/2000/06/26/biofem), 26 June 2000 (accessed August 9, 2000)

43. See Andrew Bluth and Tony Saavedra "The materials are collected at the home of Jerry Nilsson, who was questioned and released, *The Orange County Register,* April 2, 2000 and Tony Saavedra "Surgeon says he doesn't know why he was subjected to a search," *The Orange County Register*, April 5, 2000

44. Interview with South African prosecutor in the Basson case, July 2000.

45. Interview with former TRC investigator, 20 July 2000. In addition to scientific literature, papers from scientific conferences, and government documents marked top secret, investigators found financial records, canceled checks, bags of foreign coins, memorabilia (e.g., a cartoon of Basson carrying a violin case), and several small bottles of scotch and beer cans, which they did not taste. The contents in these trunks were really a "mixed bag" of personal effects and top secret documents.

46. Mangold, *Plague Wars*, 277-8.

47. Dr. Daan Goosen, former managing direct of RRL, claimed that Project Coast never conducted research on HIV as a weapon. However, he acknowledged that Project Coast scientists were planning to do some work that he termed "legitimate work" for a European pharmaceutical company. Interview Transcript from television show http://www.pbs.org/wgbh/pages/frontline/shows/plague/sa/ (accessed 15 June 2000).

48. Interview with South African reporters who covered the TRC hearings, July 2000. Despite the lack of evidence linking Project Coast research with the intentional use of AIDS, allegations that the policies of the former South African government were motivated by AIDS considerations are likely to be raised in the future, as the HIV

epidemic peaks in South Africa. For example, one researcher at the International AIDS conference held in Durban in July 2000 suggested in a paper that projections of huge losses in the black population through AIDS was the real reason why de Klerk had started transition process.

49. As Daan Goosen noted, "biological weapons was a new field, and it was done all over by all countries, even England at Porton Down and the Americans at Fort Detrick. We know they were doing it, and we had contacts with all that work and the weapons that were developed." *Frontline transcripts from Plague Wars: A report on biological weapons threats and how the Soviet Union secretly amassed an arsenal of bio-weapons.* http://www.pbs.org/wgbh/pages/frontline/shows/plague/sa/. (Accessed 15 June 2000).

50. Interview with Jacques Pauw, Johannesburg, 29 June 2000. Pauw had interviewed the Project Coast scientists, including Andre Immelman, Schalk van Rensburg, Mike Odendaal, Daan Goosen, and Peter Lourens.

51. Interview with Col. (ret.) Johann Smith, 30 June 2000. Negotiations with Mandela and the end of the Angolan war led Basson and others to take advantage of a window of opportunity to get rich. He was able to deceive top generals and salted away millions. Smith was certain that Basson turned to dealing Ecstasy and other drugs, because his money was in Swiss banks, and he still needed to raise cash in South Africa.

52. Interview with Brig. Gen (ret.) Bill Sass, July 1994. See Purkitt, "The politics of denuclearization," for further details of changes made at the end of P.W. Botha's rule.

53. Interview with David Steward, 26 June 2000.

54. According to Dr. Renfrew Christie, interviewed 26 June 2000, the U.S., backed by Israel and the U.K., issued a "hostile nation warning" to South Africa in January 1990 to destroy the nuclear weapons program in order to keep it out of ANC hands. Christie claimed that, in the 1980s, the Israel had been involved in South African NBC programs, and the U.S. and Britain did not object to South Africa developing those programs.

55. Interview with Prof. Buys, 14 June 2000.

56. According to Col. Mike Ferguson, former Defense Attaché to South Africa, interviewed 23 May 2000 in Washington, D.C.

57. According to Col. Mike Ferguson, interviewed 23 May 2000.

58. Testimony of RRL scientist, Schalk Van Rensburg, to the TRC on 9 June 1998.

59. Bumbled assassination attempts using BW devices seem to have been pretty

common. This fits with what BW terrorist experts have found in other cases. See Carus, *Working Paper on Bioterrorism*, 88.

Carus classifies this incident as probable or possible use but with no authoritative confirmation. In some cases, a biological agent was used, but there was no information to indicate whether the perpetrator knowingly caused the infection. The probability of intentional contamination for these cases is difficult to determine. See Carus, 90.

60. Jacques Pauw, *Into the Heart of Darkness: Confessions of Apartheid's Assassins* (Johannesburg: Jonathan Ball, 1997).

61. Pauw, *Into the Heart of Darkness*, 226.

62. Interview with David Steward, 26 June 2000.

63. According to General (ret.) Meiring, interviewed 3 July 2000. Basson's soft retirement meant that he was no longer an active member of the SADF but continued to draw a paycheck as a reserve SADF officer and doctor at a military hospital.

64. According to General (ret.) Meiring, interviewed 3 July 2000.

65. See Knobel's testimony to the Truth and Reconciliation Commission, July 1998.

66. Interviews with Ambassador Princeton Lyman, Washington, D.C., 25 May and 31 August 2000.

67. Interview with Peter Goosen, proliferation expert, Ministry of Foreign Affairs, Pretoria, 15 June 2000

68. According to Dr. Ian Phillips, ANC defense expert, interviewed 13 June 2000, Anglo-American cooperation on South Africa's NBC program was not as smooth as it may have seemed. During the 1989-94 period, the British were upset with the Americans at the latter's efforts to promote their own "solution for South Africa."

69. Interview with David Steward, 26 June 2000.

70. Interview with Ambassador Lyman, 31 August 2000.

71. Interview with Dr. Knobel, 15 June 2000.

72. Mangold, *Plague Wars*, 243.

73. *Weekly Mail and Guardian*, 15 December 1994.

74. Koch and Fleming, *Weekly Mail and Guardian,* 15 December 1994.

75. General (ret.) Meiring, interviewed 3 July 2000.

76. Although Basson's trips to Libya did decline after he was "rehired," the South African government at one point placed Basson under an undeclared "house arrest."

77. The *"verkope lys"* was a list of items, allegedly ordered by Dr. Basson and given to CCB operatives. This list includes anthrax-infected cigarettes; shampoo poisoned with an insecticide, and poisoned chocolates. Wendy Orr, *From Biko to Basson* (Saxonwold, South Africa: Contra Press, 2000): 328-9. See Appendix C for the complete list.

78. Interview with Dr. Villa-Vicencia, former senior investigator for the TRC, 21 July 2000.

79. For additional details of this meeting that included representatives of the old and new military and political guard, see Orr, 331-2. Dr. Orr notes that she arrived at this hastily called meeting and found that she was the only TRC (and the only woman) representative among the 40 participants.

80. Orr, *From Biko to Basson,* 332. She notes that Dr. Folb made himself forever unpopular with many participants at this meeting by making this observation.

81. Chandre Gould confirmed the agreement regarding the status of documents in a telephone interview in July 2000.

82. For example, Dr. Jan Lourens, a bio engineer who worked at Delta G and later headed Protechnek, was one of the scientists who applied for amnesty to the TRC after Basson's arrest. He called the claims "nonsense" that Project Coast was a defensive program.

83. Michael Evans, "South Africa may have ordered British deaths," *The Times* (14 July 1998), 7.

84. Paraphrase of comments made by Dr. Villa-Vicencia, former senior investigator for TRC during an interview in July 2000.

CHAPTER 4

Not with Impunity:
Assessing U.S. Policy for Retaliating to a Chemical or Biological Attack[*]

Harry W. Conley

Senator Jesse Helms: Suppose somebody used chemical weapons or poison gas on people in the United States . . . would they damn well regret it?

Secretary of Defense William Perry: Yes.

Helms: I want to know what the response will be if one of these rogue nations uses poison gas or chemical weaponry against either us or our allies. . . . What is the response of this country going to be?

Perry: Our response would be devastating.

Helms: Devastating—to them?

Perry: To them, yes. . . . And I believe they would know that it would be devastating to them.

Helms: Let the message go out.

> —Testimony of Secretary of Defense William Perry
> before the Senate Foreign Relations Committee
> March 28, 1996

How should the United States determine its response to a chemical or biological attack against American personnel or interests? The current

---

[*] This paper was written with support of the USAF Counterproliferation Center, 2000-2001. Originally published in Chairman of the Joint Chiefs of Staff Strategy Essay Competition, Essays 2001 (Washington, D.C.: National Defense University Press, 2001).

U.S. retaliation policy, known as *calculated ambiguity,* warns potential adversaries that they can expect an "overwhelming and devastating" response if they use chemical or biological weapons (CBW) against the United States or its allies.[1] Implied in this policy is a threat of nuclear retaliation, but the specifics of the U.S. response are left to the imagination. By not identifying a specific response to an attack, this intentionally vague policy is designed to maximize flexibility by giving the United States a virtually unlimited range of response options.[2] While ambiguity gives flexibility to policymakers, it also enhances deterrence by keeping adversaries guessing. But there is a downside to flexibility and ambiguity. Because it is easier to prepare to execute a specific strategy than it is to prepare for a broad range of possibilities, military preparedness suffers—at least at the strategic level—under a policy of ambiguity. It is not surprising that the policy of calculated ambiguity, which is intended to place doubt in the minds of potential adversaries, has engendered uncertainty among those who would implement the policy. This uncertainty could manifest itself in strategic unpreparedness. I argue that the United States needs a clearer reprisal policy, one that strikes a better balance between flexibility and preparedness.

In general, national policy should facilitate strategy development. If a policy fails to provide enough substance for making strategy, the policy should be revised. Adjectives such as *overwhelming* and *devastating* are the only guidelines that the calculated ambiguity policy provides to strategy makers. Because current policy aims to achieve unlimited flexibility through ambiguity, there is simply not enough substance in the policy to support strategy development. Absent a strategy, military means may not be able to support policy ends. In making the case that the current reprisal policy hampers strategic preparedness, I examine existing policy and assess its strengths and weaknesses, then suggest means for clarifying the policy with a view toward better balancing flexibility and preparedness. Having proposed a policy that better supports strategy development, I present an analytic framework consisting of four critical variables that must be considered in formulating strategies for responding to a chemical or biological attack.

Current Reprisal Policy

President William Clinton's National Security Strategy (NSS) called weapons of mass destruction (WMD) "the greatest potential threat to global stability and security."[3] The NSS further stated, "Proliferation of advanced weapons and technologies threatens to provide rogue states, terrorists, and international crime organizations with the means to inflict terrible damage on the United States, our allies, and U.S. citizens and troops abroad."[4] At his confirmation hearing in 1997, Secretary of Defense William Cohen asserted, "I believe the proliferation of weapons of mass destruction presents the greatest threat that the world has ever known."[5] Barry Schneider, director of the U.S. Air Force Counterproliferation Center, claims, "There are perhaps one hundred states that have the technical capability to manufacture and deploy biological weapons."[6] That Americans will be subject to a chemical or biological weapon attack is not a matter of *if*, but *when*.

In 1969, President Richard Nixon stopped all biological weapons programs in America. More recently, the United States has begun to destroy its chemical weapons stockpile in accordance with the Chemical Weapons Convention.[7] The United States no longer has the option of responding in kind to a chemical or biological attack. This situation has thrown U.S. retaliation policy into a conundrum: How best to respond to a WMD attack when the only WMD in the arsenal is nuclear? Albert Mauroni, author of *America's Struggle with Chemical-Biological Warfare*, writes, "Our national policy of responding to enemy use of CB [chemical and biological] weapons has shifted over the years from one extreme to the other; from retaliation using similar CB weapons to massive conventional retaliation to (most recently) nuclear retaliation."[8]

Prior to the Gulf War, President George Bush and other officials let it be known that nuclear weapons might be used against Iraq, if Iraq were to use its weapons of mass destruction against coalition forces.[9] However, in private, Bush reportedly ruled out the use of nuclear weapons.[10] During *Desert Shield*, Secretary of State James Baker coined the term *calculated ambiguity* to describe this policy of secretly planning not to use nuclear weapons yet publicly threatening just the opposite.[11] Defense Secretary William Perry's testimony at hearings in 1996 on the Chemical Weapons Convention made it clear that ambiguity was still the policy for the

Clinton administration. When asked what the U.S. response to a chemical attack would be, Perry replied, "We would not specify in advance what our response to a chemical attack is, except to say that it would be devastating."[12] When asked if the response could include nuclear weapons, Perry responded, "The whole range [of weapons] would be considered."[13] Perry's successor, William Cohen, reiterated the policy in 1998: "We think the ambiguity involved in the issue of nuclear weapons contributes to our own security, keeping any potential adversary who might use either chemical or biological [weapons] unsure of what our response would be."[14] It appears that the current Bush administration will advocate the same policy of ambiguity as did its predecessors. For example, National Security Advisor Condoleezza Rice threatens "national obliteration" to those who would use such weapons.[15] Robert Joseph, the Bush administration's senior advisor on counterproliferation issues, argues nuclear weapons should be an "essential component of the U.S. deterrent posture against [proliferation of mass destruction weapons]."[16]

Nuclear weapons have always been a lightning rod for controversy, so it should come as no surprise that an intense debate has been raging over the possible use of nuclear weapons in a U.S. reprisal against a CBW attack. At issue is the decades-long clash between so-called deterrence hawks, who advocate a prime role for nuclear weapons in the calculus of deterrence, and the counterproliferation doves, who maintain that there are safer ways to deter the use of chemical and biological attacks and that the United States should reject first use of nuclear weapons. Deterrence theory, long relegated to the proverbial back burner, is witnessing a resurgence, driven in no small part by this reprisal policy, which, when taken at face value, allows the United States to use nuclear weapons in response to something other than a nuclear attack. According to deterrence hawks, the potential threat to American interests from these other attacks is so large that only by threatening absolute devastation with nuclear weapons can the United States deter such attacks.[17] The deterrence doves, on the other hand, place primacy on countering nuclear proliferation. The dove position is that the goal of nuclear nonproliferation will be irreparably damaged if America continues to maintain a policy that allows nuclear first use. The United States should renounce nuclear retaliation, they argue, and instead threaten a massive conventional response.[18]

Evaluating Current Policy

Is the current policy of calculated ambiguity viable? In assessing the current policy, one must answer two questions: What are the general criteria for evaluating a reprisal policy, and to what degree does the current U.S. policy satisfy these criteria?

To answer the first question, I submit that retaliatory policy should be measured against two key criteria. First, does the policy meet its stated objective? Second, does the policy support the development of strategy? The objective of stated U.S. reprisal policy is clear: to deter the use of chemical and biological weapons against U.S. interests. Colin Gray defines *deterrence* as "a condition wherein a deteree—the object of deterrent menaces—chooses not to behave in ways in which he would otherwise have chosen to behave, because he believes that the consequences would be intolerable."[19] Thus, there is no purpose in having a publicly stated reprisal policy if the United States does not believe that this policy will cause the deteree to avoid undesirable behavior. Moreover, it is important that a reprisal policy deter not only state actors but nonstate actors as well. To be effective against states and nonstate actors, the "deterrent menaces" of the policy must be applicable against each. Finally, the target audiences of the policy must perceive the threat as *credible*.

There are two essential objectives of deterrence in a reprisal policy. Perhaps the most important objective is deterrence of CBW first use. Deterring first use sometimes fails, which leads to the second objective: preventing recurrences or escalation of CBW attacks. Preventing recurrences can be accomplished with threats or direct military action. A primary mechanism for deterring or preventing escalation is punishment, the threat and execution of which is intended to serve as a deterrent against further CBW attacks on the part of the adversary or other parties. For example, the swift trial and conviction of Timothy McVeigh could deter other terrorists who may be considering actions against the United States. Thus, in evaluating a reprisal policy, it is important to determine policy applicability to state and nonstate actors, its credibility, and the degree to which the stated policy addresses the two objectives of deterrence.

The second criterion in evaluating reprisal policy is the degree to which the policy supports strategy development. If a policy requires military action that cannot be well executed, the policy is flawed. Military forces may not be able to accomplish a proposed action because the forces do not have the necessary means, such as equipment. Conversely, if there is no viable strategy, military forces may not be able to carry out an action even if they have the proper equipment. In this case, the forces are strategically unprepared.[20] Policy must enable the development of strategy. Gray defines *strategy* as "the bridge that relates military power to political purpose."[21] *Military strategy*, according to Drew and Snow, is "the art and science of coordinating the development, deployment, and employment of military forces to achieve national security objectives."[22] Drawing from these definitions, if a policy (political purpose) is not clearly defined, I conclude that the development of strategy is problematic. Thus, a viable policy must embody clear national security objectives for the development of strategy.

The 1998 cruise missile strikes against terrorist facilities in Afghanistan and Sudan provide an illustration of both the thinking of the Clinton administration leadership relative to reprisal policy and how this U.S. action was intended as punishment and prevention of further attacks. In his address to the Nation announcing the strikes, Clinton stated that a key reason for the U.S. response was "the imminent threat [the facilities] presented to our national security."[23] These strikes served several purposes: they sent a strong signal of U.S. willingness to retaliate, they served as a form of punishment against terrorist behavior, and they decreased the likelihood that those facilities could be used again.

Weaknesses

Does the current policy of calculated ambiguity meet the stated objective of deterrence, and does it support the development of strategy? When measured against these two key criteria, existing policy has some significant shortcomings. One of the weaknesses of the policy is its credibility. Would an American President really use nuclear weapons in retaliation for a CBW attack? It would seem that the threshold of damage would have to be high for a President to consider using nuclear weapons, yet the stated policy does not address thresholds of damage. The main reason for the policy's lack of credibility is that it fails to address proportionality. Adjectives such as *overwhelming* and *devastating* in policy bring to mind a massive response. Yet one of the widely held tenets of the international law of armed conflict—the rule of proportionality—holds that armed action "must be measured and not excessive in the sense of being out of proportion to the original wrong nor disproportionate in achieving its redress."[24]

Suppose an adversary killed several dozen American soldiers with a biological attack. Taken at face value, the current policy would seem to stipulate a response out of proportion to the original attack. A disproportionate response would surely trigger an international furor over U.S. actions. Moreover, it is not clear that threatening massive retaliation is the best deterrent against CBW use. Avigdor Haselkorn writes in *The Continuing Storm*, "Frequently, the bigger and more indiscriminate the threat, the less believable it is in the eyes of the target audience."[25] Unfortunately, current policy wording may commit the United States to a massive response when the situation does not actually call for this.[26] In their statements, policymakers seem to imply that all potential CBW events are equal, with each demanding the same massive response. In reality, of course, future CBW events will vary widely, and U.S. policy should be worded carefully to allow for a tailored response, appropriate to the situation.

Another shortcoming of the current policy is its implicit focus on state actors, when in fact the threat of CBW from nonstate entities may be greater than the threat from states. It does not seem likely that Rice's phrase "national obliteration" would have much deterrent effect on terrorist groups. The current policy begs two questions: Does the threat of a nuclear response deter terrorists? Would the United States ever launch a nuclear weapon into a sovereign state in response to a terrorist attack? The answer to both questions is, "very unlikely." While terrorists are a highly likely source of CBW attacks, the current policy all but ignores these nonstate threats.

Strengths

The calculated ambiguity policy does have one strong feature. The more uncertain an adversary is about U.S. response, the less likely it is to use chemical or biological weapons. As Paul Bernstein and Lewis Dunn write, "deliberate ambiguity creates significant uncertainty for an adversary regarding the nature of our response to CBW use."[27] Indeed, ambiguity deters, as long as the adversary perceives U.S. willingness and ability to respond forcefully. Since the ambiguity in the current policy incorporates the possibility of nuclear retaliation, one must ask: are today's chemical- and biological-capable adversaries deterred by the U.S. threat to retaliate with nuclear weapons? Even Scott Sagan, an articulate advocate of abandoning the role of nuclear weapons in U.S. reprisal policy, concedes that nuclear weapons contribute "the extra margin of deterrence" against CBW use.[28] The inherent deterrent value of nuclear weapons is a strength of the current policy, but policymakers must clarify the conditions under which nuclear weapons might be considered.

Failure to Support Strategy Development

I have argued that the current U.S. reprisal policy has weaknesses that should be redressed, the most important of which is a lack of clarity. The policy is so ambiguous that it hampers the development of strategies that are necessary to implement the policy. There is ample evidence that the policy fails to support strategy development.

The first piece of evidence demonstrating that the current policy fails to support strategy development is the waffling of the Bush administration during the Gulf War. During that conflict, the United States faced a foe that was known to have used chemical weapons in the recent past and was suspected of possessing biological weapons.[29] Bush and his top advisors struggled to answer the question, "What should the United States do if Iraq uses these weapons?"[30] In *Crusade*, Rick Atkinson describes the alternatives that were considered. These included a recommendation by General Norman Schwarzkopf to threaten nuclear weapons; air strikes against the presidential palace; a proposal to strike dams on the Tigris and Euphrates above Baghdad; a Brent Scowcroft suggestion to attack the oilfields; and a hint by Richard Cheney that Israel would retaliate with nuclear weapons if attacked with CBW.[31] There was no consensus on how to respond.[32] In the end, writes Haselkorn, "The ambiguity of the U.S. position on the proper response to Iraq's use of weapons of mass destruction was as much a result of the conflicting stands within the Bush administration as it was part of a calculated policy."[33] The widely varying views taken by these influential individuals should be of great concern. Had retaliation been called for, uncertainty and lack of consensus among

U.S. political and military leaders would have created difficulties in planning and executing a response.

The second piece of evidence that suggests the current policy is not pragmatic is the persistent stumbling over the issue by the Clinton administration. In *An Elusive Consensus*, Janne Nolan concludes that confusion over U.S. reprisal policy persisted throughout the Clinton administration.[34] The most visible issue the administration grappled with was the African Nuclear Weapons Free Zone (ANWFZ) Treaty, in which the United States promised not to use nuclear weapons in Africa. To assuage Pentagon concerns, the administration issued a declaration reserving the U.S. right to use nuclear weapons against states that employ weapons of mass destruction against U.S. interests. In another incident, a senior Pentagon official publicly argued for development of a new, earth-penetrating nuclear weapon that could be targeted against a Libyan chemical weapons plant. Pentagon spokesman Kenneth Bacon had to later issue a clarification, to "correct the impression . . . that the U.S. had accepted a policy of nuclear preemption against Libya," which would be in violation of the ANWFZ Treaty.[35] This waffling and stumbling by the last two administrations raise the question of whether it is possible to develop sound military strategy when policy is unclear. The answer appears to be no.

The third piece of evidence that the flawed reprisal policy has hampered strategy development is the disconnection between statements of grand strategy (including the National Security Strategy) and the National Military Strategy (NMS) of the Chairman of the Joint Chiefs of Staff. Recent grand strategy documents have trumpeted the national security threat posed by chemical and biological weapons, whereas NMS barely gives a nod to the CBW threat. A perusal of these two documents highlights the disparity in focus between the grand strategy and the military strategy. President Clinton's 1999 National Security Strategy makes numerous references to a counter-WMD strategy, including the previously cited statement that WMD presents "the greatest potential threat to global stability and security,"[36] as well as the following: "Because terrorist organizations may not be deterred by traditional means, we must ensure a robust capability to accurately attribute the source of attacks against the United States or its citizens, and to respond effectively and decisively to protect our national interests."[37] The NSS also specifically addresses the issue of reprisal: "The United States will act to deter or prevent such [WMD] attacks and, if attacks occur despite those efforts, will be prepared to defend against them, limit the damage they cause, and respond effectively against the perpetrators."[38] The predominant focus of the NMS, on the other hand, is the Nation's two-major theater war (MTW) strategy, with relatively minor emphasis on weapons of mass destruction. The National Military Strategy concedes that the use of WMD by an adversary is "increasingly likely" and states that the Armed Forces must be able to detect, destroy, deter, and protect forces from the effects of weapons of mass destruction, and restore affected areas.[39] But the NMS barely addresses the challenges of WMD use by nonstate actors, and it does not discuss retaliation.

The evidence is clear: because of an ambiguous policy of CBW reprisal, there is no strategy to link military capabilities with political objectives. Given the increasing likelihood that a CBW will be used against the United States, it is time to begin redressing the broken link. The timeframe immediately following the first large-scale use of chemical or biological weapons against Americans is certain to be filled with extreme emotions. During a chemical or biological crisis, leaders will be inclined to make emotional judgments. As Terry Hawkins, Director of Nonproliferation and International Security at Los Alamos National Laboratories, warned, "If you don't have the preplanning, it will be almost impossible to deal with in the panic of the moment."[40] Two things need to change to rectify this situation. First, the policy must be clarified. Second, the strategy bridge linking ends and means must be developed.

Clarifying the Policy: Balancing Flexibility and Preparedness

Two steps must be taken to clarify U.S. reprisal policy: make regime survival and accountability the hallmark of the policy, and determine under what conditions nuclear weapons would be used.

Rather than making vague threats such as "national obliteration," the primary feature of U.S. reprisal policy should be a guarantee to bring to justice those responsible for a chemical or biological attack. Responsible persons would include those leaders who directed the action, as well as their lieutenants who executed it. Making regime survival and accountability the hallmark of the reprisal policy has many benefits. First, it applies equally well to state and nonstate actors, a distinct advantage over the current policy. Second, a promised retribution against the responsible parties does not have to be implemented immediately. Recent U.S. experiences with terrorism, including the joint Yemeni-Federal Bureau of Investigation inquiry into the U.S.S. *Cole* bombing (which netted six suspects and prompted others to flee to Afghanistan), the embassy bombings in Africa, and the downing of Pan Am Flight 103, demonstrate the effectiveness of American and international justice systems when patience and diligence are applied to challenging scenarios. Third, focusing the reprisal actions on those responsible for CBW attack averts the potential criticism of a disproportionate U.S. response, which would be likely under the current policy. There is certainly solid precedent for threatening regime destruction. At his meeting with Iraqi Foreign Minister Tariq Aziz 2 weeks before *Desert Storm*, James Baker told Aziz, "If there is any use of weapons [of mass destruction], our objective won't just be the liberation of Kuwait, but the elimination of the current Iraqi regime, and anyone responsible for using those weapons would be held accountable."[41] Finally, direct threats against the decision-makers responsible for the attacks—instead of promising "national obliteration"—would enhance policy credibility as a deterrent.[42]

The second major change to current U.S. reprisal policy should be to clarify when nuclear weapons would be used. In existing policy, when to use nuclear weapons is left as an open issue. Some argue this ambiguity enhances deterrence. The mushroom cloud is indeed one of the enduring images of the 20th century, and only the most ardent of the nonproliferators would argue that the threat of nuclear weapons has no deterrent effect. Nuclear weapons may simply be too good a deterrent to take off the table. Yet, because current policy provides no guidance on the conditions under which nuclear weapons would be considered, planning and strategy of both conventional and nuclear responses have been severely hampered. When and if to use nuclear weapons in a reprisal is a controversial issue. Bernstein and Dunn capture the issue well:

> There is no way to resolve fully these competing considerations related to what punishment to threaten. It would be dangerous to rule out the possibility of a nuclear response to CBW use,

particularly in the face of egregious and highly damaging attacks. But it would be equally imprudent to rely exclusively on nuclear threats for deterrence of CBW use.[43]

Nuclear weapons should be considered *only* in the most horrifying and damaging attacks. Policy should reflect the reality that nuclear weapons will be used only in the most extreme circumstances. This will enable planners and strategists to get on with the business of planning and developing strategies for conventional responses, which will be the most likely kind of response directed by the President.

Robert Joseph asserts that "for deterrence to work, the adversary must be convinced of our will and capability to respond decisively. On this score, ambiguity and uncertainty play very much against us."[44] My suggestions—to emphasize regime survival/accountability and clarify the role of nuclear weapons—would result in a less ambiguous policy. Given the current situation, in which U.S. planning and strategy have been paralyzed due to an unclear policy, it is time to make these clarifying changes to policy. The benefit—a clear policy that supports strategy development—outweighs the drawbacks.

Analytic Framework: Four Critical Variables

How should the United States determine its response to a CBW attack? Guided by political objectives inherent in a clearly articulated reprisal policy, the crisis response analysis can proceed by examining four key variables: context (wartime or peacetime), adversary class, number and type of casualties, and identification of perpetrators. These four variables form the genesis of an analytic framework that can enable policymakers and planners to begin developing reprisal strategies.

Context

The U.S. response to a "bolt-out-of-the-blue" CBW attack is likely to be far different than if the Armed Forces were attacked during a conflict or period of hostilities. During hostilities, the mindset of American leaders and the public is at a higher state of alert. If casualties in a conflict have already occurred from conventional means prior to a CBW attack, the leadership and the public may be somewhat hardened and may not react as strongly as they would in a peacetime scenario. Moreover, during hostilities, U.S. forces are likely to use CBW defense equipment, such as masks and detection equipment, which could serve to minimize the adverse impacts of a CBW attack. In fact, depending on the nature and scope of the attack, U.S. forces could "take it in stride," with little if any change in operational plans. In this case, a specific reprisal action may not be necessary.

The international legal standards for retaliation during peacetime are much higher. Richard Erickson makes the point that reprisal has a "very low level of acceptability" in international law. He claims, "The general view is that articles 2(3) and 2(4) of the U.N. Charter have outlawed peacetime reprisals . . . . When states have relied upon it, the U.N. Security Council has condemned their action soundly."[45] Thus, reprisals in peacetime will have to pass a stricter set of criteria.

Adversary Class

The second variable to consider in reprisal calculations is adversary class. Is the perpetrator a state or nonstate actor? While international law gives clear guidance as to how states may legally respond to attacks from other states, the law is murky when dealing with nonstate actors; hence, any proposed U.S. retaliatory action must take this difference into account. For example, despite the evidence and strong justification for its actions against the Afghanistan and Sudan terrorist facilities, the United States was subject to much condemnation from the international community, not to mention internal criticism. U.S. reprisal attacks against nonstate actors are likely to require much more evidence and justification compared to similar actions against state actors. Many kinds of military actions can be taken against a state actor, whereas the kinds of actions that can be taken against nonstate actors may be limited. The nature of the reprisal, therefore, will be heavily influenced by the type of actor involved.

Number and Type of Casualties

The number of American casualties suffered due to a WMD attack may well be the most important variable in determining the nature of the U.S. reprisal. A key question here is how many Americans would have to be killed to prompt a massive response by the United States. The bombing of marines in Lebanon, the Oklahoma City bombing, and the downing of Pan Am Flight 103 each resulted in a casualty count of roughly the same magnitude (150–300 deaths). While these events caused anger and a desire for retaliation among the American public, there was no serious call for massive or nuclear retaliation. The body count from a single biological attack could easily be one or two orders of magnitude higher than these events. Using the rule of proportionality as a guide, it is debatable whether the United States would use massive force in responding to an event that resulted in only a few thousand deaths. However, what if the casualty count was around 300,000? Such an unimaginable result from a single CBW incident is not beyond the realm of possibility: "According to the U.S. Congress Office of Technology Assessment, 100 kg of anthrax spores delivered by an efficient aerosol generator on a large urban target would be between two and six times as lethal as a one megaton thermo-nuclear bomb."[46] Would the deaths of 300,000 Americans be enough to trigger a nuclear response? In this case, proportionality does not rule out the use of nuclear weapons.

Besides just the total number of casualties, the type of casualties—predominantly military versus civilian—will also impact the nature and scope of the U.S. reprisal action. Military combat entails known risks, and the emotions resulting from a significant number of military casualties are not likely to be as forceful as if the attack were against civilians.

World War II provides perhaps the best examples for the kind of event or circumstances that would have to take place to trigger a nuclear response. A CBW event producing a shock and death toll roughly equivalent to the attack on Pearl Harbor might be sufficient to prompt a nuclear retaliation. President Truman's decision to drop the bombs on Hiroshima and Nagasaki—based on a calculation that up to one million casualties might be incurred in an invasion of the Japanese homeland[47]—is an example of the kind of thought process that would have to be conducted prior to a nuclear response to a CBW event. Victor Utgoff suggests:

> If nuclear retaliation is seen at the time to offer the best prospects
> for suppressing further CB attacks and speeding the defeat of the
> aggressor, and if the original attacks had caused severe damage

that had outraged American or allied publics, nuclear retaliation would be more than just a possibility, whatever promises had been made.[48]

Even the "overwhelming and devastating" conventional response threatened by Secretary Perry[49] would seem unlikely unless there were large number of Americans or allies killed. In any event, it is imperative that policymakers and planners consider that the number and type of casualties, as well as the attendant public opinion resulting from those casualties, will play a significant role in determining the nature of U.S. reprisal actions.

Identification of the Perpetrator

Before taking action against the parties responsible for a CBW attack, the United States is compelled to demonstrate that it has strong enough evidence linking the perpetrators to the act itself. How strong does the evidence have to be? Erickson writes, "The threshold for what constitutes sufficient evidence varies. Factors that must be considered are the threat, the response contemplated, and the audience to be persuaded."[50] Stronger evidence may result in the ability of the United States to conduct a stronger response. As a final consideration on the issue of evidence, policymakers must consider the possibility that there could be a large-scale attack with heavy U.S. or allied casualties, yet with insufficient evidence to allow for a reprisal.

In the final analysis, the U.S. response must be determined by a thorough cost/benefit calculation. Decision-makers must ask what the potential results of a reprisal, both internationally and domestically, would be. Are there any unanticipated consequences? Are there any vulnerabilities in the strategy? These are the kinds of tough questions that must be answered prior to determining a reprisal action. Current policy, with its reliance on an "overwhelming response," is not useful in many potential situations. It has been, in the words of Bernstein and Dunn, "a false justification for inaction—for avoiding tough resource allocation decisions needed to improve our ability to defend against hostile CBW acts."[51]

Implications and Conclusion

The suggested policy clarifications and the strategic framework proposed above could serve to bound and focus policy debates and, if implemented, would enable strategists to begin to link military capabilities better with political objectives. Adapting these policy changes has implications for at least two elements of U.S. military power: intelligence and special operations. If regime survival becomes the hallmark of U.S. reprisal policy, then the U.S. intelligence community must be challenged to improve intelligence collection against organizations suspected to be involved with chemical and biological weapons. Successfully collecting this needed intelligence requires new ways of thinking about intelligence, improved cooperation among domestic and allied intelligence agencies, and increased budgets to reflect the national priority and concern for weapons of mass destruction.

Being ready to retaliate following a CBW attack against the United States also implies an increased emphasis on special operations forces (SOF). In such situations, "SOF, because of their unique skills, regional expertise, cultural sensitivity and operational experience, may be the force of choice for meeting the strategic requirements of the National Command Authorities."[52] Finally, the United States must continue its investment in chemical and biological defense. If CBW defense equipment can mitigate the effects of a CBW attack, the adversary may see no advantage in using weapons of mass destruction.

Ultimately, the aim of CBW retaliation policy is deterrence. Although an element of ambiguity certainly can serve to enhance deterrence by keeping adversaries guessing about the response to an attack, it seems more likely that the United States is stuck with the current approach because there has not been much of the critical thinking needed to devise a more robust policy. In other words, the current policy of calculated ambiguity—with its over-reliance on the nuclear "big stick"—is a cop-out. America is paying full price for this half-policy, the result of which is that the Armed Forces may be strategically unprepared to respond when the time comes.

Former National Security Advisor Sandy Berger, in the days following the cruise missile strikes against Sudan and Afghanistan, said that U.S. strikes "have made it clear that those who attack or target the

United States cannot do so with impunity."[53] To back up this statement with a credible deterrent threat requires the United States to have a robust, well-considered retaliation policy. Without a viable reprisal policy, America is fated to fall victim to the panic of the moment.

Notes

1. Prepared statement of William J. Perry, Hearing before the Committee on Foreign Relations, U.S. Senate, 104th Congress, 2d session, March 28, 1996, quoted in Scott D. Sagan, "The Commitment Trap," *International Security* 24, no. 4 (Spring 2000), 85.

2. Because the *calculated ambiguity* policy seeks to maximize the options available to policymakers, it could also be called *absolute flexibility*.

3. William J. Clinton, *A National Security Strategy for a New Century* (Washington, DC: The White House, December 1999), 6.

4. Ibid.

5. Testimony of Secretary William S. Cohen, quoted in *Proliferation: Threat and Response, 1997*, Office of the Secretary of Defense, January 15, 2001, http://www.defenselink.mil/pubs/prolif97/index.html.

6. Barry R. Schneider, *Future War and Counterproliferation: U.S. Military Responses to NBC Proliferation Threats* (Westport, CT: Praeger, 1999), 199.

7. Albert J. Mauroni, *Chemical-Biological Defense* (Westport, CT: Praeger, 1999), 171. The Chemical Weapons Convention, effective 1997, "outlines a verifiable ban on all production, storage, and use of chemical weapons."

8. Albert J. Mauroni, *America's Struggle with Chemical-Biological Warfare* (Westport, CT: Praeger, 2000), 4.

9. Stephen I. Schwartz, "Miscalculated Ambiguity: U.S. Policy on the Use and Threat of Use of Nuclear Weapons," January 15, 2001, http://www.nyu.edu/globalbeat/nuclear/schwartz0298.html.

10. Ibid.

11. Ibid.

12. Senate Foreign Relations Committee, 104th Congress, 2d session, testimony of Secretary of Defense William J. Perry, March 28, 1996.

13. Ibid.

14. Secretary of Defense William S. Cohen, quoted in Sagan, 85.

15. Condoleezza Rice, "Promoting the National Interest," *Foreign Affairs* 79, no. 1 (January/February 2000), 61.

16. Robert G. Joseph and Barry M. Blechman, "Deterring Chemical and Biological Weapons," *Transforming Nuclear Deterrence*, Institute for National Strategic Studies, http://www.ndu.edu/ndu/inss/books/tnd/tnd2.html.

17. Three recent publications that provide excellent discussions of the two sides of this heated debate are Victor A. Utgoff, "Nuclear Weapons and the Deterrence of Biological and Chemical Warfare" (The Henry L. Stimson Center, Occasional Paper No. 36, October 1997), Sagan, "The Commitment Trap," and "Responding to the Biological Weapons Challenge: Developing an Integrated Strategy" (Alexandria, VA: Chemical and Biological Arms Control Institute, 2000).

18. Ibid.

19. Colin S. Gray, "Deterrence in the 21st Century," *Comparative Strategy*, 19, no. 3 (July/September 2000), 256.

20. The 1980 failed Iranian hostage rescue attempt is a good example of this second case. U.S. military forces had clear political objectives (rescue the hostages), and they had the equipment; they lacked, however, a viable strategy, joint doctrine, training, and interoperability. In other words, the United States was not "strategically prepared" for the *Desert One* operation.

21. Colin S. Gray, *Modern Strategy* (New York: Oxford University Press, 1999), 17.

22. Dennis M. Drew and Donald M. Snow, *Making Strategy* (Maxwell Air Force Base, AL: Air University Press, 1988), 18.

23. William J. Clinton, "The Fight Against Terrorism," President's address to the Nation, August 20, 1998, *Vital Speeches of the Day* 64, no. 23 (September 15, 1998), 706–707.

24. Richard J. Erickson, *Legitimate Use of Military Force Against State-Sponsored International Terrorism* (Maxwell Air Force Base, AL: Air University Press, 1989), 180.

25. Avigdor Haselkorn, *The Continuing Storm: Iraq, Poisonous Weapons and Deterrence* (New Haven, CT: Yale University Press, 1999), 49.

26. Sagan advocates removing nuclear weapons from the U.S. reprisal calculus because American leadership may feel committed to responding to a CBW attack with nuclear weapons based on strong policy declarations and promises to allies. Sagan calls this conundrum the *commitment trap*.

27. Paul I. Bernstein and Lewis A. Dunn, "Adapting Deterrence to the WMD Threat," in *Countering the Proliferation and Use of Weapons of Mass Destruction*, Peter L. Hays, Vincent J. Jodoin, and Alan R. Van Tassel, eds. (New York: McGraw-Hill, 1998), 159.

28. Sagan, 114.

29. Mauroni, *Chemical-Biological Defense*, 26–27.

30. Ibid., 28.

31. Rick Atkinson, *Crusade: The Untold Story of the Persian Gulf War* (Boston: Houghton Mifflin, 1993), 86–87.

32. McGeorge Bundy reported that some of these differing opinions became public: "The President's associates . . . sometimes disagreed with each other. The most notable of these disagreements was that between some Pentagon officials and John Sununu, the White House Chief of Staff, who at one point found it prudent to give assurance that there was no likelihood of resort to tactical nuclear weapons. Nameless Pentagon sources then rebuked him for the military error of telling the enemy what we were not going to do. Bundy, "Nuclear Weapons and the Gulf," *Foreign Affairs* 70, no. 4 (Fall 1991), 86.

33. Haselkorn, 60.

34. Janne E. Nolan, *An Elusive Consensus* (Washington, DC: The Brookings Institution Press, 1999), 81.

35. Ibid.

36. Clinton, *A National Security Strategy for a New Century*, 6.

37. Ibid., 15.

38. Ibid., 20.

39. John M. Shalikashvili, *Shape, Respond, Prepare Now: A National Military Strategy for a New Era* (Washington, DC: Chairman of the Joint Chiefs of Staff, 1997), http://www.dtic.mil/jcs/core/nms.html.

40. Terry L. Hawkins, "The Role and Limits of Science and Technology," Presentation to Air War College NBC Seminar, Los Alamos National Laboratory, Los Alamos, NM, September 12, 2000.

41. James A. Baker III, *The Politics of Diplomacy* (New York: G.P. Putnam's Sons, 1995), 359.

42. Making regime accountability the linchpin of U.S. reprisal policy would imply some modest changes to today's military force structure. According to Bernstein and Dunn, there is a significant challenge for the United States in "operationalizing and projecting a credible threat [of regime elimination]." (159). To meet this challenge—of making credible the threat of regime elimination—the United States should place more emphasis on human intelligence and special operations.

43. Ibid.

44. Joseph and Blechman.

45. Erickson, 180.

46. Congressional report cited in Randall J. Larsen and Robert P. Kadlec, *Biological Warfare: A Post Cold War Threat to America's Strategic Mobility Forces* (Pittsburgh, PA: Matthew B. Ridgway Center for International Security Studies, University of Pittsburgh, 1995), 7.

47. Richard B. Frank, *Downfall* (New York: Random House, 1999), 338. Frank discusses the current debate over the number of casualties that Truman expected and the methodology for determining those estimates. Whether he believed 25,000 or 250,000 U.S. servicemen would be killed in an invasion of the Japanese homeland, Truman made the decision. His calculus in World War II is not dissimilar to what might face a future U.S. President if extremely large numbers of Americans are killed by a chemical or biological attack.

48. Victor A. Utgoff, *Nuclear Weapons and the Deterrence of Biological and Chemical Warfare*, Occasional Paper No. 36 (Washington, DC: The Stimson Center, 1997), 3, http://www.stimson.org/pubs/zeronuke/utgoff.pdf.

49. Perry, quoted in Sagan, 85.

50. Erickson, 105.

51. Bernstein and Dunn, 152.

52. *United States Special Operations Forces Posture Statement* (Washington, DC: U.S. Special Operations Command, 1998), 38.

87

53. Dian MacDonald, "Berger: Those Who Attack U.S. 'Cannot Do So With Impunity'," USIS Washington File, August 23, 1998, http://www.fas.org.man/dod-101/ops/docs/98082303_tpo.html.

CHAPTER 5

Pointing the Finger: Unclassified Methods to Identify Covert Biological Warfare Programs

Dorothy L. DuBois

Introduction

> *"The current expectation that U.S. [United States] Intelligence will be able to thwart future BCW [biological and chemical weapons] attacks is exceedingly high. Our fear is not that someday, somewhere, an attack will succeed and the IC [Intelligence Community] will be accused of failure. Our fear is that people will die – a lot of people."* [1]
>
> -   John C. Gannon

Biological weapons have been called "the poor man's nuclear bomb" due to their comparatively cheap production costs. While Richard Preston's *The Cobra Event* gave one U.S. president nightmares, Russian defector Ken Alibek told the world that at its height, the Soviet biological warfare (BW) program employed more than 60,000 people.[2] And in the frequently quoted warning of Robert Blitzer, in 1997 head of the FBI's Domestic Terrorism/Counterterrorism Planning Section, "it's not a matter of *if* it's going to happen, it's *when*."[3] Other experts maintain that the threat of a successful mass casualty attack using a biological agent has been over exaggerated in the media, that the number of states possessing an offensive BW program has remained relatively steady over the last fifteen years and, with the rollback of the South African and Russian/Soviet programs, has even decreased. Some also suggest that states suspected of having an offensive BW program and also sponsors of terrorism would be reluctant to cede control over a mass casualty weapon to terrorist organizations.[4]

89

How can the intelligence community (IC) assist policymakers to assess the potential case against states and terrorist groups that perpetrate BW while still protecting sources and methods of gathering intelligence? The intelligence community can work closely with the scientific community to identify existing BW programs and possibly use rational models predictive of a state or group's likelihood of developing an offensive BW program. This chapter will show how *models* for predicting development of a BW program and unclassified *indicators* can be used to "point the finger" by applying them to four case studies of actual or alleged programs. It will conclude with a discussion of the current state of cooperation between the intelligence and scientific communities and offer several suggestions for their enhanced cooperation.

What factors must be present for a state or terrorist group to develop or acquire biological or other mass casualty weapons? Three unclassified *models* will be examined to elucidate these factors – an "assimilation model" that examines a state or group's proclivity for a BW program based on its material base and threat perceptions, a model developed by the Russian Foreign Intelligence Service (FIS), and a model described by the United States (U.S.) Office of Technical Assessment (OTA).

What are the *indicators* that a state or terrorist group has a covert, offensive biological warfare program? This chapter will consider 26 indicators that mark an outbreak of disease as a suspicious BW agent and will discuss them in relation to natural outbreaks of infectious disease.

The chapter will then examine four case studies, two incidents of suspicious outbreaks of disease indicative of a covert BW program and two incidents of alleged state use of biological weapons. The *models* for acquisition or development of a covert BW program will be applied to the cases, and the cases will be evaluated for common factors from the *models* that may be applied to future, similar instances. Being able to make a credible and logical assessment of future adversaries' likelihood of developing a BW program or the existence of a BW program is vital to the protection of U.S. national security.

The final portion of the chapter will consider the state of cooperation between the intelligence and scientific communities with regard to identification of BW threats, particularly since the terrorist attacks of 11 September 2001, and will propose ways in which this cooperation might be enhanced. The intelligence and scientific communities have improved their important cooperation but many improvements may still be made.

Models for Acquisition or Development of an Offensive BW Program

In this section, three models or sets of indicators of the development or acquisition of a biological warfare capability will be considered. Models can be used by intelligence and other analysts to focus their analysis and to compare various state and non-state actors. For instance, the usefulness of a particular model can be evaluated by using it to study an admitted past possessor of BW capability, such as the former Soviet Union (FSU) or South Africa. Once a model is validated as useful it can be applied to other cases of suspected proliferants to evaluate the likelihood of possessing a covert BW program. Models can also be even more effective when combined with analysis of suspicious outbreaks of infectious disease. Models are thus another open-source tool available to postulate possession of a BW capability.

The first model is an "assimilation model" based on a goal-instrument relationship developed by Jean Pascal Zanders of SIPRI (Stockholm International Peace Research Institute). It is applicable to state and non-state actors and is useful for assessing a group's predisposition to develop a BW program in the absence of a great deal of information in the form of official or public pronouncements. The second model is based on a 1993 report by the Russian Foreign Intelligence Service. Given that the former Soviet Union developed the largest BW program in history, it is useful to consider their perspective on the subject. The third model, developed by the U.S. Office of Technology Assessment, is a set of observable indicators of research and development signatures, weaponization and testing signatures, production signatures, and stockpile and delivery signatures.

Assimilation Model

The "assimilation model" examines the relationship between an actor's goals and the instruments available to it or of interest to it to achieve those goals. As defined by Zanders, "Assimilation is the process by which political and military imperatives, as constrained by a political entity's material base, become reconciled with each other so that a new weapon, weapon system, or arms category becomes an integral part of the political entity's mainstream military doctrine."[5] The model considers a dual decision-making track existing in a state of creative tension – a political track consisting of security and budgetary decisions, and a military track using threat information and political inputs to determine military doctrine and strategy. The model has *thresholds* that must be crossed for adoption of a weapon or weapon system along with applicable military *considerations*. The *thresholds* are classified as intrinsic or extrinsic, and military *considerations* relate to the attributes of a weapon and the operational "balance between potency and logistical considerations."[6]

Intrinsic Thresholds

Intrinsic thresholds are related to an entity's material base. This consists of the entity's physical base: "geographic location, territorial size, population, presence of natural resources, access to resources abroad, etc. – as well as the level of education, of scientific, technological, and industrial development, of economic strength, and so on."[7] Intrinsic thresholds will be higher for non-state actors than for states, as they will be higher for developing countries than for developed countries.[8] For example, non-state actors will not have the territory, population, national resources, or economic strength of states. Similarly, the physical base of a developing country will be less than that of a developed country. That said, with the continuing global expansion of the biotechnology industry, the increased number of biotechnologists being trained in developed countries, and the industry's attendant characteristic of being information rather than capital-intensive,[9] these intrinsic thresholds relating to the potential capabilities of actors may be lowered, particularly to the extent that extrinsic thresholds such as budgetary restrictions apply.[10]

Extrinsic Factors

Extrinsic factors relate to an entity's domestic or international environment. One important factor relating to BW acquisition or development is the tension between political or social constraints regarding weapons of mass destruction or casualty and threat perceptions.

Another is the nature of the group's structure. Norms against weapons of mass casualty were strengthened even as the weapons themselves were developed – witness the 1925 Geneva Protocol and the 1972 Biological and Toxin Weapons Convention (BWC). Norms, both domestic and international, against biological weapons must be overcome to develop a WMD program and the perception of a high level of internal or external threat may help accomplish this.[11] If a credible threat is perceived, BW may be sought as a means of assassination for political opponents, as a strategic weapon and deterrent to other WMD possessor states in the region, or as a counterinsurgency weapon.[12] Historically, states with possession of a WMD capability did not develop norms against these weapons until the state's monopoly had disappeared or was balanced asymmetrically. Despite proliferation of WMD, this sense of power may still exist for a state within a confined region, leading to the non-development of norms against WMD. The group's structure is also of importance to the acquisition or development of WMD. A vertically integrated and ideologically consistent group will be more capable to develop a high volume program in secrecy than a group organized in small cells. While an organization with a small cell structure might offer the security of decentralization, it would lack the material base of a larger entity required for a high volume BW program.

Military Considerations

Military considerations also play a large role in the adoption of BW by a state or non-state actor. Both state and non-state actors will look to balance weapon effectiveness with logistical considerations in achievement of their goals.[13] States typically have considered the following factors when selecting a BW agent for use as a weapon: reliability, virulence, incubation period, contagiousness, no widespread immunity, low or no susceptibility to common medical treatments, suitability for production in necessary quantities, ease of transport, stability, ability to survive environmental stresses, and availability of protective measures for friendly troops.[14] Military uses such as "denying terrain, degrading combat effectiveness by forcing the enemy to don protective clothing, degrading the operability of facilities and equipment together with imposing the need for elaborate decontamination procedures, causing terror and psychological exhaustion, flushing out enemy troops from strongholds, incapacitation, and crop destruction,"[15] in addition to casualty production, are all factors states will consider when seeking or adopting a BW capability and integrating its use into their military doctrine. Non-state actors may use a similar effectiveness-logistical consideration calculus when seeking a BW weapon. Terrorists, in particular, may consider BW agents and substances that, while not useful for large-scale military applications outlined above, may meet their own needs.[16]

In summary, the assimilation model provides a means of considering intrinsic and extrinsic thresholds and military applications in evaluating an actor's potential for acquiring or developing a BW capability. This model would be useful for establishing a theoretical likelihood for an actor to acquire biological weapons. Examples of the use of this model will be discussed in the analysis of the case studies.

Russia's Foreign Intelligence Service Model

The Russian FIS report entitled "A New Challenge after the Cold War: Proliferation of Weapons of Mass Destruction," described indicators of a WMD program in four areas: political, economic, scientific-technical, and military-technical. It stated that indicators in all four areas must be analyzed to determine a country's involvement in or capability for a WMD program. The model was developed to consider all WMD programs and may be applied to BW programs as well as CW (chemical warfare) and nuclear weapons programs. Indicators that may be observed are highlighted below.

Political Indicators

The model starts with the assumptions that a political decision to embark on a WMD program has been made and that it has been kept secret. It may be noted that these political indicators are very applicable to the past WMD programs of the FSU and South Africa. Political indicators of covert BW programs are:

- Not becoming a party to treaties or instruments renouncing WMD. Not participating in international fora or negotiations on such treaties or instruments.

- Refusal or obstruction of international monitoring of facilities.

- Creation of an administrative structure with extraordinary powers directly subordinate to the highest political leadership or army command.

- Creation of foreign economic agencies or intelligence service units with large financial resources to buy materials, equipment, and technology abroad. Creation of ostensibly private companies for the same purpose.

- Active promotion of WMD by groups closest to the highest levels of power.

- Psychological manipulation of the public to accept WMD as a part of military doctrine.

- No governmental reaction to accusations of a state's proliferation.

- Overt or covert support to proliferating countries.

Economic Indicators

The Russian FIS model considers the strongest BW indicator to be the share of the government's budget devoted to the military, and it notes that this information is often absent, concealed, or contradictory in nature. General indicators include the development of defense and civilian industry sectors and types of imports. Specific direct and indirect indicators are:

- A large military budget.

- Presence of nuclear, biological, or chemical programs.

- Presence of required specific production capabilities.

- Importation of "WMD components, raw materials for their production, specialized equipment, and 'dual-use' technologies."

- Scientific or technological advancement beyond apparent civilian need of specific production capabilities.

- Unexpectedly high budgetary allocations for ostensibly civilian sectors such as biotechnology.

Scientific-Technical Indicators

This set of indicators focuses on technical capabilities, human resources, and means of expanding scientific potential.

- Presence of raw materials.

- Importation of non-indigenous raw materials or components.

- Presence of required technologies.

- Presence of required production capacity.

- Required scientific or technical specialists are present and a system for training others exists.

- Ability or programs to attract needed specialists from abroad is present.

- Scientific centers are created.

- Scientific and production firms with required specialties are present.

- A supercomputer or powerful computer network for running simulations is present.

Military-Technical Indicators

Military-technical indicators revolve around a doctrine that incorporates the use of WMD and the presumption that WMD will be used against itself. Direct and indirect indicators include:

- Technical units in the military relating to the use of WMD.

- Reinforced or hardened facilities for the government and military.

- Training of personnel to deploy WMD in warfare and to operate in a WMD environment.

- Storage facilities with high security measures.

- Possession of appropriate delivery systems.

- Intensified intelligence activities against specific enemy targets.

- A highly developed program for civil defense.

The Russian FIS model presents an organized way to look at indicators for a possible covert WMD program. Taken together, these indicators, many of them openly observable, form a useful checklist for evaluating a country's likelihood with regard to proliferation of weapons of mass destruction.[17]

U.S. Office of Technology Assessment (OTA) Model

As is acknowledged by many authors and experts in the field, detection of a covert BW program is very difficult to do, and even under the best of circumstances is likely to produce only circumstantial evidence and not the "smoking gun" so sought after in international fora. Several factors contribute to this, and perhaps most important among them is the dual-use nature of equipment and feedstock materials. Also, as technology develops, production can take place in much smaller and less visible locations than in the past. The dual-use nature of equipment makes it possible to convert legitimate facilities to BW agent production in a very short time, thus possibly obviating the need for dedicated facilities. The speed with which BW agents may be grown and the potency of small quantities mean that large stockpiles may not be necessary. And finally, as will be discussed in more depth below, when BW agents that are endemic to the affected area are used, they can be very difficult to distinguish from natural outbreaks of disease. That said, this model, taken from the Office of Technology Assessment's (OTA) *Technologies Underlying Weapons of Mass Destruction*, focuses on signatures as indicators. Observable indicators for each signature – research and development, weaponization and testing, production, and stockpile and delivery – are outlined below.

Research and Development Signatures

The OTA model evaluates many of the same indicators found in the Russian FIS model, but it is careful to place them within the overall context of a country's behavior and the transparency of its defense program. Indicators could include biological research facilities under military control, production of vaccines in excess of domestic needs, and the purchase of dual-use materials and equipment. Analysis of a state's open source scientific and technical information can allow the monitoring of research trends, identification of institutions and individuals associated with biotechnical research, and the identification of sudden halts in certain types of research that might be indicative of military censorship. The assessment acknowledges that monitoring publications can only provide a very broad measure of a country's activities, as many of the articles from countries of interest are not published or available in English. Also, because much of the basic science is already understood and available, very little preliminary research would be necessary.

Weaponization and Testing Signatures

Any weaponization development would have no obvious civilian application and would be an indicator in and of itself. Indicators observable via overhead imagery could include field tests of aerosols, tests of weapons' effectiveness against large animals, and the burial of animals used at weapons testing sites. Observation of indicators in this category is made difficult because much testing could be done inside production facilities. The sensitivity of many BW agents to sunlight would necessitate testing at night, and legitimate activities such as crop dusting or the use of conventional smoke bombs could be used as a clandestine way of testing BW delivery. Weaponization and testing signatures may be more susceptible to detection through on-site inspections.

Production Signatures

Advances in production technology, particularly in developed countries, have made detection of production signatures more difficult. Small, continuous-flow fermenters capable of producing large quantities of agent quickly have replaced the large, batch fermenters and refrigerated storage vaults of the past, thus greatly reducing the size of production facilities. Smaller facilities may be buried underground or hidden within larger, legitimate, commercial plants. That said, several indicators could be detected via overhead imagery. Tight security and secrecy around an ostensibly civilian facility, including "double or triple fencing, watch towers, and air-defense missile batteries," could be an indicator, although it would be possible to conceal these measures from overhead satellites. The existence of very extensive microbiological production plants that were much more sophisticated than known civilian facilities could be an indicator. Another could be the existence of facilities unassociated with vaccine production with large numbers of test animals, especially "primates, horses, rats, mice, rabbits, sheep, goats, or chickens (for producing eggs)."[18] Finally, observable changes in ostensibly civilian production facilities could be an indicator. Production signatures are more observable via on-site inspections than overhead imaging. On-site inspections can determine plant layout and physical containment measures, plus they can also reveal the types of equipment and materials in use.

Stockpile and Delivery System Signatures

A few indicators could be observable via overhead imagery, but more could be detected only through on-site inspections. Observable indicators could include refrigerated bunkers or igloos for storage of large amounts of BW agents, storage depots for BW munitions near suspected production facilities, and heavy trucks for the transportation of munitions or for decontamination use.

In summary, for this model, the signatures discussed are indicators that could be observed via open sources and overhead imagery. There are other indicators that could be observed via on-site inspection, but until an inspection protocol is put into place for inspections to be carried out under the BWC, non-coercive or coercive on-site inspections are likely to remain a rarity. Also, human intelligence is noted as a valuable source of information.[19] These indicators and sources of information are not considered as they are beyond the scope of this study.

Summary of Models

Models present an organized process for examining the open source information available regarding a state's predisposition or actions taken towards developing a BW capability. The assimilation model approaches the problem from resource base and a normative political-military decision-making process. The Russian FIS model is based on experience, and points to indicators that would be particularly valid for a highly centralized state with an industrial base and significant monetary resources available to devote to the problem. Finally, the US-based model is indicative of the approach taken by a country with a robust microbiological technical base, a relatively transparent defense structure, and an open society. Models provide a starting point for considering the issue and can be used in conjunction with examinations of possible use of BW or accidental releases to better draw conclusions about an entity's BW capabilities.

Unnatural versus Natural Outbreaks of Disease: Indicators

While most experts agree that detection of a covert biological weapons program is difficult at best, many also agree that the careful and thorough examination of outbreaks of disease can yield significant clues.[20] Even though there are significant ways in which unnatural outbreaks of disease differ from natural outbreaks, distinguishing between the two remains difficult. It is in this arena, perhaps more than any other, that the close cooperation between the public health community and the intelligence community could be most beneficial.

This section will discuss the general parameters for investigation of outbreaks of disease and sources of information on outbreaks. It will then consider some characteristics of natural outbreaks of disease and characteristics of unnatural or suspicious outbreaks.

Investigation of Outbreaks of Disease

The initial steps taken in an analysis of a disease outbreak are the same whether the outbreak is suspicious or initially thought to be a natural outbreak. Two principal types of information are collected: personal interviews, particularly of those involved, and biological samples. The first step in an investigation is definition of the disease, including a case definition. The case definition is broad enough to include all likely cases and is refined as the investigation proceeds. As the definition becomes more precise, previously analyzed cases are reanalyzed and discarded if they do not fall within the revised parameters.

The next steps are to locate the earliest cases of exposure and determine the victims' physical location and the time when symptoms began to manifest. Determination of locations and case histories may lead to environmental sampling and possible identification of the causative agent. Finally, laboratory analysis and attempts to isolate and cultivate the putative agent will occur. At the end of this process, the identity of the disease should result.[21]

An outbreak of disease could result from one of several causes. Natural outbreaks are by far the most common versus the accidental release of a BW agent being developed as part of a covert BW program, the field testing of an agent, the small scale use of an agent against a target, a larger scale attack, a criminal attack, or a terrorist attack.[22]

The free flow of information regarding outbreaks of disease is facilitated by databases such as ProMED Mail, which makes it possible for medical, veterinary, and agricultural professionals to exchange and monitor disease outbreak information real time. This also makes it more difficult for states or non-state actors to conceal information on outbreaks of disease. Information in this forum is free of governmental influence.[23] Other media for the dissemination of disease outbreak information include the *Weekly Epidemiological Record* published by the World Health Organization, the *Morbidity Mortality Weekly Report* published by the Centers for Disease Control, the *Communicable Disease Intelligence* from Australia, and the *Monthly EPI Comment* from South Africa.[24]

Indicators of Natural Outbreaks of Disease

This section will outline some of the characteristics of natural outbreaks of disease. Some of the characteristics of unnatural or suspicious outbreaks of disease outlined in the following section may also apply to natural outbreaks. This possibility of overlap between the two categories is indicative of the difficulty of distinguishing between the two.

Natural outbreaks are usually characterized by a gradual increase in cases until the majority of the population has been exposed to the disease, after which there is a gradual decline in the number of cases. [25] In a natural outbreak, cases may continue to occur throughout the outbreak and will be widely spread in location. [26] There will be a gradual increase in the incidence of disease as it is spread from person to person in the case of a communicable disease. [27] Natural outbreaks may also originate from a point source with many victims making contact with the agent at the same time. This could be common with exposure to food-borne pathogens. In this case the outbreak would exhibit a compressed epidemic curve (a temporal plotting of the incidences of the disease) which may peak in days or hours. A second peak could occur after the first if the agent is contagious and is passed on. [28]

Indicators of Unnatural or Suspicious Outbreaks of Disease

While most experts on the subject agree that a definitive model for distinguishing between natural and unnatural outbreaks of disease does not exist, many authors list several common indices to differentiate the two. Since determination that an outbreak of disease is of unnatural origin is one of the more effective ways of detecting the existence of a covert BW program or a BW attack, a thorough listing of possible indicators drawn from multiple sources is presented below. As will be seen, several of the indicators are common to natural outbreaks of disease as well.

- Origination from a point source with many victims coming into contact with the agent at the same time.

- Origination from a line source with many victims coming into contact with the agent at the same time.

- A compressed epidemic curve which may peak in days or hours. If the disease is contagious and passed from person to person, there may be a second peak after the first.

- A large epidemic, especially if it occurs in a discrete population.

- More severe disease than is normally expected for the pathogen.

- Unusual routes for exposure for the pathogen, such as inhalational anthrax instead of dermatological anthrax.

- A disease that is unusual for the affected area or for the season in which it appears.

- An endemic disease found outside its established range.

- A disease that is impossible to transmit naturally without the presence of its usual vector, when that vector is not present.

- Multiple epidemics of different diseases.

- Different diseases in the same patient.

- A disease that attacks animals as well as humans.

- Unusual strains of disease or antibiotic resistant strains different from expected disease strains. If an agent is isolated in a laboratory culture for some time before its use, it may stand out against the background strains of the disease, as they continue to evolve in nature.

- A strain of disease last seen some years before the outbreak.

- Higher attack rates in different areas. For instance, if an agent were released indoors, those inside the location would have higher exposure rates and, therefore, higher attack rates. Likewise, if an agent were released outdoors, lower exposure rates would be expected for those who were inside at the time of release.

- Intelligence information that a group has access to an agent.

- Claims by a group that it has perpetrated an attack.

- Direct evidence of an attack such as equipment or munitions.

- Pulmonary disease in the absence of a natural high-concentration aerosol.

- High military and civilian casualties when both are collocated.

- High morbidity and mortality.

- High morbidity and mortality in relation to the number of individuals potentially exposed.

- Lower disease rates for those with filtered air supplies or closed ventilation systems.

- Failure of a group or state to cooperate with an investigation of an outbreak or refusal of offers of assistance.

- The sudden demand for large quantities of a specific vaccine greatly in excess of previously known requirements.

- A specific disease in a population with high immunity to that disease as a result of vaccination. This could suggest a modified agent.

- An outbreak of disease in a target population for which a suspected or potential adversary is known to have been vaccinated.[29]

While there are many overlapping indicators for classification of natural and unnatural outbreaks of disease, a thorough and patient investigation over time will usually reach a valid determination in the end. This section outlined some of the standard steps to be taken in an investigation of an outbreak. Disease investigation is, however, much more complicated than simply taking the steps outlined here, as it involves computer databases for analysis and requires specially trained health professionals. As described in this section, there are several sources, both governmental and non-governmental, of information on outbreaks. Finally, a likely determination of whether an outbreak is natural or unnatural can be made by a skilled epidemiologist in many cases by performing an epidemiologic investigation and applying a set of indicators to the outbreak.

Presentation of Case Studies

Four disease outbreaks are presented below. The first two outbreaks are a limited smallpox epidemic in Aralsk, Kazakhstan, USSR in 1971 and the anthrax outbreak in Sverdlovsk, Russia, USSR, 1979. Both outbreaks are alleged to have been caused by release of BW agents – as a result of field-testing in the Aralsk case and accidentally in the Sverdlovsk case.

The second two outbreaks of disease are the 1978-1980 outbreak of anthrax in Zimbabwe and two outbreaks of cholera in Burma in 1993 and 1994. Both outbreaks are alleged to have been the result of BW attacks by the governments of the two states against sectors of the people, and both were alleged to have occurred during counterinsurgency campaigns.

Aralsk, Kazakhstan, USSR – 1971

A limited smallpox epidemic occurred in Aralsk, Kazakhstan, from July through October 1971. There were 10 infections, and 3 resulted in death. The index case for this epidemic likely was exposed to smallpox on 30 July 1971. She was an ichthyologist aboard the research ship *Lev Berg*. The *Lev Berg* left Aralsk on 15 July, traveled east and south of Vozrozhdeniye Island, and then made a port call on 29 July at Uyaly. The ship made another port call at Komsomolsk-on-Ustyurt on 31 July and at Muynak on 4 August. It returned to Aralsk on 11 August.[30]

The index case had been vaccinated against smallpox and probably for this reason contracted a relatively mild form of the disease. She began to manifest symptoms on 11 August.[31] The index case transmitted the virus to her younger brother, who was also vaccinated, who also contracted a less severe form of the disease and fully recovered. He began to show symptoms on 27 August. The boy returned to school before medical authorities had diagnosed smallpox but was later quarantined after the diagnosis had been made. Six adults and 2 children from 4 households contracted smallpox over the period from 10 September through 2 October. The adults ranged in age from 24 to 60, with a median age of 34.5, and the two children were 4 years old and 9 months old. Both children and one adult were unvaccinated, and all of them died from a rare, highly lethal, hemorrhagic form of the disease. The remaining adults were vaccinated and contracted either a discrete or a varioloid form of the illness and survived.[32]

The public health response began on 22 September when a diagnosis of smallpox was clinically confirmed. The two known cases at that time were transferred to an isolation unit, their contacts were identified, and their residences disinfected. On 23 September, a 150-bed isolation unit for contacts of the patients was established, and house-to-house interviews were started. A vaccination program began with vaccination centers being set up at the train station and airport. Quarantine of the city was established, and individuals without vaccination certificates were prohibited from traveling out of Aralsk. A virologist arrived from Moscow on 23 September, and the city was placed under quarantine on 24 September. On 25 September, the smallpox diagnosis was confirmed via laboratory tests. Additional medical personnel arrived from Moscow, Alma-Ata, Aktyubinsk, and Leningrad; a medical headquarters with a director for the outbreak was established. On 26 September, the military took over enforcement of the quarantine from the civil authorities. Autopsies were performed on the victims by civil authorities during the period 24 September through 7 October.[33]

During the outbreak 274 people were isolated, and 270 visits were made to homes and schools, with 20,000 to 25,000 people clinically examined daily. Hospital personnel worked in anti-plague protective gear and were quarantined, and the smallpox hospital and isolation units were guarded by police on a 24-hour basis. Nine hundred sixty-four buildings and 10,400 kg of household goods were disinfected. A total of 36,276 residents of Aralsk were vaccinated, resulting in a 100 per cent vaccination rate for the population by 5 October. The quarantine of Aralsk was lifted on 11 October. Post-outbreak measures included continued epidemiological surveillance, disinfection of the hospital and isolation units, and additional house-to-house calls.[34]

The official report posited that the index case most likely had contracted the disease during the port calls at either Uyaly or Komsomolsk-on-Ustyurt. It offered Afghanistan as a second, but less likely, hypothetical source via transmission through Tajikistan or Uzbekistan, due to extensive economic and shipping links between those republics and Aralsk. Under this second hypothesis, the index case would have contracted the disease in Aralsk, not during port calls. The official report on the outbreak remained secret until early 2002.[35]

The ichthyologist stated during an interview in May 2002 that she did not leave the ship at any point during the voyage. Since none of the male crew members, who were allowed to go ashore during port calls, became ill with smallpox, it is unlikely that she contracted the illness from one of them. Smallpox was considered eradicated from the USSR in 1936, and the last reported, imported case was in 1961. Yet the smallpox outbreak was not reported to the World Health Organization (WHO).[36]

Vozrozhdeniye Island was a primary open air, field-testing site for the Soviet BW program from 1936 to at least 1990, with a 17-year hiatus from 1937 through 1954.[37] A military facility housed several hundred people, who lived and worked on the island beginning in 1954. Personnel received regular immunizations and hardship benefits. The northern part of the island included a residential area and an airport, and the southern portion of the island housed the BW testing complex. Agents tested included anthrax, botulinum toxin, brucellosis, plague, Q fever, smallpox, tularemia, typhus, and Venezuelan equine encephalitis. Special strains developed for high virulence or survivability were tested on the island. Vozrozhdeniye Island was declared as a testing site for outdoor aerosol tests in the Russian BWC declaration of July 1992. The site was officially closed on 18 January 1992, and this was confirmed by a United States Department of Defense (DOD) inspection in August 1995.[38]

The *Lev Berg* was probably south of Vozrozhdeniye Island on 30 July, and the prevailing winds in the area blew from north to south over the island during that time of the year. The primary testing season for BW agents was April through August, and the index case spent most of her time working on the deck of the ship casting fishing nets. In a 2001 interview, Dr. Pyotr Burgasov stated that 400 grams of a smallpox weapon was exploded on the island, and the *Lev Berg* came within 15 km of the island, within the contamination radius of the smallpox. He confirmed that the index case contracted smallpox as a result of the test. Burgasov stated that he informed KGB chief Yuri Andropov of the event, and Andropov directed that it not be reported further.[39]

In conclusion, an epidemiological analysis of the outbreak assesses that the index case contracted smallpox as a result of exposure to an open-air smallpox test conducted on Vozrozhdeniye Island while her ship sailed near it on or about 30 July, and that this was the origin of the smallpox outbreak in Aralsk.[40] Former first deputy director of Biopreparat Ken Alibek stated that the description of the case was factual, and stated that it was "talked about" when he worked at Biopreparat.[41]

Sverdlovsk, Russia, USSR - 1979

On 2 April 1979, between the hours of 1330 and 1600[42], an accidental release of anthrax spores occurred at the military compound known as Compound 19 in Sverdlovsk. Two Soviet sources have stated that a problem with the plant's filtration system caused the release.[43] An aerosolized plume was released, possibly from a rooftop ventilator at height of approximately three to four meters.[44] It traveled in a southeasterly direction about 15km per hour over the Chkalovskiy section of the city and into the surrounding countryside.[45] The pattern of animal deaths indicated a plume of 50km in length.[46]

Livestock, including sheep and cows, in six villages lying along the extended axis of the plume south of the city were infected at the same time as humans. The livestock deaths began on 5 April.[47] While livestock and human deaths occurred almost concurrently, anthrax was recognized as the cause of the animal deaths first due to veterinarians' greater familiarity with the symptoms of anthrax in animals. Roadblocks were established 12km south of Sverdlovsk to check for suspected contaminated meat. Carcasses of infected animals were burned. Public health measures similar to those taken in response to human cases (see below) were taken for confirmed animal cases and included the vaccination of humans associated with the animals.[48]

In response to the crisis, an emergency meeting of local officials took place on 9 April, at which it was decided to conduct a house-to-house survey in the Chaklovskiy *rayon*. At the beginning of the outbreak, before anthrax had been identified as the cause, hospital quarantine measures were taken, and victims were isolated and restricted to only two area hospitals. Morgues and burials were also isolated. The Ministry of Health was contacted on or about 9 April, and authority for dealing with the crisis was ceded to the central government. The central government dispatched experts from Moscow to take charge of the situation, undertook a vigorous public health campaign, and posited tainted meat as the cause of the outbreak. On 12 April, Dr. Vladimir Nikiforov, an infectious disease expert, was sent with several assistants from Moscow to supervise the medical treatment of the victims. Deputy Minister of Health, Dr. Pyotr Burgasov, was dispatched from Moscow on or about 13 April as the senior official in charge of handling the outbreak. Dr. Nikolay Babich headed the local public health efforts.[49] Intelligence community documents report that Defense Minister Ustinov and Health Minister Petrovski visited Sverdlovsk in early May.[50] Reportedly, work on virulent anthrax ended by 15 April.[51]

On 18 April, leaflets describing anthrax symptoms and warning against consumption of meat bought in unofficial markets were distributed in the southern part of Sverdlovsk. Leaflets were distributed on 19 April describing four methods of anthrax transmission: cutaneous, inhalational, gastrointestinal, and via insect bites. It also described two forms of the disease: cutaneous and systemic. The leaflets described symptoms and public health measures to be taken in case of infection.[52] During the epidemic, buildings were washed with a chlorine solution and roads were paved, which Burgasov attributed to preparations for the upcoming May Day celebrations rather than to public health measures. In the Chalovskiy *rayon*, where the majority of the victims worked, the interior and exterior of the ceramics factory buildings were washed.[53] According to eyewitnesses, hundreds of stray dogs in the affected area were killed.[54]

The public health response to individual fatalities followed a set pattern. An autopsy of the victim was conducted, and the victim was encased in a coffin treated with lime. Interment then proceeded in a specific part of the Vostochniy cemetery. Police prevented family members from entering the cemetery for the burials, and burial charges and cemetery plots were funded by the government. Antibiotics were given to victims' surviving family members. The victims' houses were disinfected, and their bed linens and suspect clothing removed. The outsides of the houses were washed in a chlorine solution.[55] Residents of the affected area received a series of three inoculations, reportedly with vaccine from Georgia, while residents at Compound 19 were inoculated with vaccine reputed to have been produced there.[56] A reported 80 per cent of 59,000 persons in the area were vaccinated at least once. Two vaccination campaigns occurred, one beginning in mid-April and a second beginning on or about 11 May.[57]

The earliest human victims began to display symptoms on 4 April, with the first deaths occurring 7-8 April, and an official diagnosis of anthrax was made on 10-11 April. Laboratory tests confirmed the diagnosis on 12 April and the last death occurred 16 May. The total number of deaths is not known with absolute certainty, but it is likely 64 to 68. Based on primate experiments showing that anthrax spores can remain dormant in the lungs for up to 100 days after exposure, it seems reasonable that all of the deaths in the 2 April – 16 May period resulted from one release. Biologist Matthew Messelson estimates that the release was a minimum of 2-4 mg to a maximum of 300-600 mg,[58] while the U.S. intelligence community's early estimate was 22 pounds.[59]

Victims were primarily older men. Seventy-five percent were male, and half were older than 45. All of the women except one were 32 or older. No one under the age of 24 was a victim.[60] Guillemin reports that "only one person per household was affected."[61] Causes of death were not always listed as anthrax; other causes included pneumonia and sepsis. The deaths were three times the average yearly number of anthrax deaths in the USSR.[62] A 1998 report of polymerase chain reaction analysis of tissue samples determined that up to four strains of anthrax were present in victims, which was judged to be indicative of an unnatural cause for the outbreak.[63] If it had been a natural outbreak, only one strain of anthrax would have been expected. A Russian military officer who worked at Compound 19 in 1979 confirmed in 1993 that the facility had many strains of anthrax.[64]

Local governmental records on victims were absent, confiscated by Dr. Burgasov, and there were allegations that autopsy and other case records were confiscated by the KGB. The KGB also reportedly confiscated records from the ceramics factory. All birth, marriage, and death records were unavailable.[65] While records documenting human cases disappeared, veterinary records did not.[66] Soviet officials attributed the lack of available documentation to the negligence of local officials.[67]At the time of the event and for years afterwards, rumors abounded amongst the local population that the cause was a biowarfare plant, Compound 19, in Sverdlovsk.[68]

When initially confronted with the event by U.S. State Department officials during the first Biological Weapons Convention (BWC) review in 1980, Soviet officials denied that there had been an anthrax outbreak. This initial denial was subsequently changed to an acknowledgement with an attribution to tainted meat products resulting from improper meat processing procedures. The USSR on 21 March 1980 admitted that there had been cases of intestinal anthrax but denied that the anthrax outbreak had any bearing on a possible violation of the BWC.[69] Soviet authorities maintained that tainted meat was sold to workers at the ceramics factory.

Many of the victims' surviving family members reported that they had not eaten any meat bought from private sources immediately before the outbreak. [70] Despite the official explanation for the outbreak, a formerly secret Soviet document dated 5 June 1979 states that anthrax was "isolated from samples of soil, air, washings from a woolen wall hanging, the outside part of a door," indicating airborne anthrax. [71] The Soviet government resisted the 1983 and 1988 attempts of American teams to investigate the incident, and the Russian government obstructed the later investigation by an American team in 1992. [72] Russian President Boris Yeltsin acknowledged in an interview in 1992 that the outbreak was caused by the military BW development and production facility in Sverdlovsk. In July 1992, a Russian BWC declaration admitted that research and development of biological weapons occurred after Soviet accession to the BWC; however, it denied that BW agents were produced or stored in Sverdlovsk. [73] The Russian delegation to the BWC Ad Hoc Group negotiations still promulgated the tainted meat explanation as recently as March 1997. [74]

Additional governmental actions and communications about the incident took place. As has been well reported, in 1986 a team of American experts received a presentation in Moscow on the attribution to tainted meat, followed by a reciprocal visit in 1988 of a team of Soviet scientists to institutions in Washington, D.C., Baltimore, and Cambridge. The tainted meat explanation was judged plausible by some U.S. scientists even though unsupported by epidemiological or clinical evidence. [75] Burgasov asserted that infected meat had been sold by mistake, specifically at the ceramics factory, where up to a third of the victims had worked. Burgasov further claimed that male heads of households performed more physically strenuous labor and therefore ate more meat than other family members. He explained that this was why more men than women were victims and why almost no children were casualties. [76] Burgasov claimed that there were no deaths of workers at Compound 19, but this was later refuted. [77] During 1992 and 1993 investigations, there were instances in which governmental participants contradicted one another on the facts of the incident and their beliefs about its likely cause. [78] Compound 19 commander in 1992, General A.T. Kharechko, is quoted in Guillemin's *Anthrax* as having said "The rumors ... that an explosion took place on the territory of our institution and that anthrax pathogen was discharged into the external environment do not have any real basis, primarily because we have never had any explosion of that sort."[79] It can be noted that this is actually a true denial of an explosion, not a denial of an anthrax release or of a biological weapons program.

Zimbabwe, 1978-1980

The world's largest recorded outbreak of anthrax among humans occurred in Zimbabwe, with 10,738 cases reported by the government from January 1979 through December 1980. There were 182 human deaths, mostly from cutaneous anthrax.[80] The outbreak manifested in three provinces covers the period November, 1978 through October, 1980, during which 9,711 cases were recorded.[81] A human epidemic followed a severe epizootic in cattle, in which, for example in the Lupane district of Matabeleland, at least 5% of the cattle population died and in which some owners lost up to 50% of their herds.[82]

The first reported human case was on 24 November 1978 in the Nkai district of the Matabeleland province. It was a case of cutaneous anthrax, and the victim reported that he had skinned and butchered infected cattle. The outbreak remained localized in the Nkai district from November 1978 through June 1979, until it spread to the contiguous Que Que district. In October 1979 it spread westward into the contiguous Lupane district, and in November 1979, the outbreak spread to the non-contiguous districts of Insiza, Umzingwane, and Bubi to the south and east. Anthrax continued to spread among humans and cattle, and by October 1980, all districts of Matabeleland except the Binga district had been affected. A total of 2,065 human cases were reported in the Matabeleland province for the period January 1979 through October 1980, with 36 deaths, representing a mortality rate of 1.74%.

Anthrax spread to the Que Que district of the Midlands province in June 1979, spreading to additional districts in November and December 1979, and January and March 1980. Ninety-eight percent of the cases and 99% of the deaths in the Midlands were localized in the Que Que district, where it affected two communal farming areas while leaving the commercial farming areas almost completely untouched. A large shoe factory in the province, processing over 130,000 hides yearly, had no recorded cases, and urban areas also had no reported cases. There were a total of 6,609 cases and 101 deaths for the period June 1979 through October 1980, representing a mortality rate of 1.53%.

Anthrax entered the Mashonaland province in the Sanyati communal farming area on 29 September 1979, with cases appearing in new districts month by month through January 1980. The first case was cutaneous anthrax, and the victim reported that he had cut up and eaten an infected cow. There were some cases recorded from commercial farming areas, but most cases originated in the communal farming areas. There were 1,037 cases in Mashonaland during the period September 1979 through October 1980 and 14 deaths, resulting in a mortality rate of 1.35%.[83]

All forms of anthrax – cutaneous, medistinal and gastrointestinal – occurred, along with the two major complications, septicemia and meningitis. Uncomplicated cutaneous anthrax accounted for approximately 95% of all cases, and the mortality rate was 1.55%.[84] The prevalence of the cutaneous form was consistent with most scientific literature, which cites the prevalence as 95% for cutaneous, 5% for inhalational, and 0-5% for gastrointestinal. The aggregate mortality rate was slightly higher than what would be expected for cutaneous anthrax alone, which is less than 1% in treated cases.[85] This could be because the aggregate mortality rate of 1.55% includes non-cutaneous cases. Of the cutaneous cases, 74% of the lesions were on the head, neck, face, and upper limbs, 13% were on the lower limbs, and 13% were on the trunk.[86]

Various authors writing about the outbreak describe efforts to control the outbreak among livestock as being largely unsuccessful due to the disruption caused by the ongoing armed conflict between the state and guerrillas. A veterinary team sent to begin a vaccination campaign in the Matabeleland was ambushed, but despite this disruption they managed to vaccinate some 8,000 cattle in areas including commercial farms.[87] The breakdown of civil administration also appears to have contributed to the extent of the oubreak, and attempts to persuade the rural people to have their cattle vaccinated were mostly unsuccessful. Efforts to control the outbreak in remote areas were eventually abandoned.[88] Numerous authors attributed the outbreak to the breakdown of veterinary services in the tribal areas.[89] Dr. Meryl Nass, however, stated that "routine anthrax vaccination of livestock was not practiced to a large extent in Zimbabwe before 1979, according to local veterinary experts." She maintained that this meant that the breakdown of veterinary services was not a contributing factor to the early development of the outbreak.[90]

In sheer number of cases the 1979-1980 anthrax outbreak was a catastrophic departure from Zimbabwe's experience with anthrax both after but especially before the outbreak. There were no reported cases of human or bovine anthrax during the period October 1976 to September 1977,[91] and only two human cases had been reported in 1978.[92] For the period from 1926 through 1977, 311 cases of human anthrax and 20 deaths were reported, a mortality rate of 6.43%. The highest recorded number of cases was in 1967 with 86, which also saw the most deaths at 6.[93] For the period 1981 through 1985 the number of anthrax cases continued to be much higher than the historical rate before the 1979-1980 outbreak. This period saw a total of 4,124 cases reported. Two hundred ninety-five cases was the lowest total reported during the period and was the total number of cases reported in both 1983 and 1984.[94] For the period 1988 through 1995 the number of reported cases dropped dramatically to a total of 169 cases, with the largest numbers being 89 and 30 in 1991 and 1992, respectively.[95] Recent outbreaks have included the following:

- September 2000 in the Mt. Darwin district – 70 animal deaths, seven human cases, and no human fatalities.

- November 2000 in the Makoni district – 25 animal deaths, 15 human cases, and 2 human fatalities.

- November 2000 in the Mhondoro communal farming area – 44 animal deaths, possibly 630 human cases, and 9 human fatalities.[96]

- October 2001 near the town of Kwekwe – 5 animal deaths, 15 human cases, and 1 human fatality.[97]

- November 2002 in Bindura – unknown animal cases, 20 human cases, and 2 human fatalities.[98]

In the outbreaks reported for 2000-2002, the government was described as having quickly deployed veterinary services to conduct vaccination campaigns in the affected areas. Various accounts blamed either the movement of cattle related to squatting on commercial farms and the poor state of disease control. Conversely, various members of the government have attributed recent outbreaks to deliberate sabotage by white farmers.[99]

The 1979-1980 outbreak began and was localized for six months in the district of its original focus. It then spread outward largely to contiguous districts through communal farming areas, while mostly bypassing the commercial farming areas. It spread in areas where vaccination of cattle was still possible, although vaccination was not likely to be absolutely complete or effective. Some authors did not attribute the outbreak to a single point source and concluded that cattle acquired the disease locally, presumably from spores already present in the soil.[100]

Initial studies of the outbreak attributed the spread among cattle to direct contamination of pastures and posited that vultures feeding on dead carcasses could account for some of the spread across areas with no previously known bovine cases. Watering holes were also implicated in the "hopping" nature of the spread, both because vultures wash themselves after feeding and because cattle in the terminal stages of the disease could discharge anthrax bacilli from the nose, mouth, and intestinal tract into water. Cattle in communal farming areas mingled at watering holes, while water was usually piped directly to restricted paddock areas in commercial farms. The implication was that in communal farming areas the disease could be spread via contaminated water, and the water in commercial farms would not be contaminated. Evidence for these theories was not judged to be conclusive by the studies. Authors noted that human lesions of the lips, tongue, and mouth were rare, leading to the conclusion that eating infected meat was probably not an important cause. This was supported when most patients stated that they had not handled infected meat.[101] Cutaneous lesions resulting from the handling of hides during slaughter were thought to be a primary cause until the advent of later theories about the role of biting and non-biting flies.[102]

Although the evidence was not conclusive, several authors cited the possible role of biting and non-biting flies in spreading the disease. It was noted that the peak months of the spread of the disease and the highest numbers of human cases coincided with the rainy season and the highest prevalence of horse flies (*Tabanidae*). A study of the location of lesions in children revealed that the majority were located on the head, neck, or face – areas that were more exposed when they were carried about on a parent's back. Likewise, nearly 85% for all cases had cutaneous lesions on exposed areas. It was postulated that in addition to biting, flies could be attracted to existing cuts and abrasions. The flies could contaminate the cuts with spores adhering to their legs/bodies or by vomiting spores/bacilli into the cuts.[103]

Author Meryl Nass, MD took a dim view of the various insect vector explanations. In her 1992 article "Anthrax Epizootic in Zimbabwe 1978-1980: Due to Deliberate Spread?" she noted that many authors dispute insect transmission of anthrax in cattle. Dr. Nass pointed out that several investigators encountered great difficulty when attempting to infect cattle by parenteral injection because of a relatively large volume of blood needed to be transferred to achieve an infection. She cited successful attempts to use stable flies to infect mice and guinea pigs with anthrax, but she maintained that these results could not be extrapolated to cattle and humans due to the differences in susceptibility to infection and the required dose sizes. Dr. Nass also ruled out horse flies as vectors for the same reasons, judging that even the horse fly's increased infective capacity over stable flies would not be sufficient to infect cattle or humans.

Dr. Nass noted the explosive nature of the outbreak when compared with the number of anthrax cases in Zimbabwe both before and after 1978 - 1980. She noted that most anthrax outbreaks are localized, while this outbreak spread to encompass 17% of the land area of the country. Many cases occurred in areas where there were no previous recorded anthrax cases, and cases were confined almost exclusively to communal farming areas. There were 4 outbreaks with only 11 cattle deaths in the commercial farming areas and no anthrax deaths among white Zimbabweans, which seemed suspicious in the context of the ongoing civil war in Zimbabwe. Finally, Dr. Nass noted that the outbreak coincided with the final months of the civil war in Zimbabwe, which saw an escalation of tactics by the Rhodesian military. Dr. Nass judged that cattle were likely the primary object of attack due to their economic importance. The economic importance of cattle was highlighted by several other authors.[104]

Since the outbreak there have been several claims that it was a deliberate counterinsurgency attack by Rhodesian forces. In March 1997, Dr. Tim Stamps, then Minister of Health for Zimbabwe, stated his belief that the anthrax outbreak was the result to a BW attack by Rhodesian security forces.[105] An alleged former Rhodesian intelligence officer confirmed the attack in a confidential communication to David Martin in 1993.[106] A search of open source literature did not reveal documentary or conclusive proof of these allegations.

While theories on insect vector transmission are judged by many authors to be inconclusive, the reality of 10,738 human cases of anthrax from January 1979 through December 1980 remains. This period also coincided with an escalation and the conclusion of the civil war in Zimbabwe, during which there are credible reports of the use of other BW agents by government forces against the insurgents.[107]

Burma, 1993-1994

During the night of 12 August 1993, aircraft, presumed to be Burmese Air Force (BAF), dropped an unknown number of devices consisting of a radiosonde in a white box with a 2 meter parachute and one or two balloons attached in the Karen districts of Thaton and Mudraw. The balloons were said by the villagers to have contained a "foul-smelling 'black-yellow-green' liquid." Villagers found the devices, but Burmese officials did not attempt to recover them. After a period ranging from three days to two weeks, villagers in the drop area and some areas downriver began to be ill with a disease resembling cholera or shigella. The disease was highly contagious and most lethal for adults over 15 years of age, resulting in over 300 deaths. This area had previously reported a few deaths per month from dysentery; in September 1993, 185 deaths due to dysentery were reported.

Several Karen villages in the area were quarantined by the Burmese military. Villagers said that the troops stopped entering the villages after the epidemic began, and that the soldiers remained healthy. Villagers believed that the soldiers had been vaccinated against the disease. In a location where there were soldiers encamped in a village, the soldiers required the villagers to engage in basic sanitation measures and to stay out of their encampment. The epidemic had abated by December 1993.

A similar incident was reported in January 1994 in the Karen Dta Greh township. Similar devices were reported to have been dropped at night, and a disease resembling cholera spread in the area of the drops, causing more deaths among adults than children. In both cases, it was reported that the disease was curable with basic medicines which were unavailable to the villagers. An additional similar incident was reported in 1985 before the 1993-94 incidents, when at least one balloon with an attached packet of "powder" was dropped by a BAF aircraft, followed by a cholera epidemic with 10-20 fatalities. Another incident was reported in which a device identical to those dropped in August 1993 was recovered near another location, Manerplaw, although it was not known when the device was dropped.[108]

Members of the organization Christian Solidarity International (CSI) investigated the incidents in late 1994 and concurred with an assessment by the Karen Human Rights Group (KHRG) that the radiosondes were originally manufactured to be used with weather balloons, not to be dropped with parachutes from low-flying aircraft. The KHRG also stated that the low-powered, very high frequency transmissions could only be received along a straight line of sight, which they speculated would only be receivable by the aircraft, if at all. Finally, the KHRG noted that Germany acknowledged in 1991 that 15 Burmese Army officers had received biological warfare defense training from the German Army. Both the KHRG and the CSI group believed that the white boxes contained bacteria which were released over the Karen villages.[109]

Tests were conducted on the boxes at the Porton Down Defense Research Establishment, which were inconclusive. Although the devices were described as "consistent with the covert use of germ warfare," an actual BW attack was not confirmed. Other examinations were made by Thai and Canadian scientists, who concluded that the boxes were innocuous pressure-measuring devices.

An alternative explanation for the outbreaks of disease was that they were caused by a particularly virulent, new strain of cholera, *vibrio cholerae* 0139. The strain was almost unknown before 1992, when it caused a major epidemic in India, spread to Bangladesh, and then to Thailand in early 1993. Due to its virulence and resistance to many anti-cholera drugs, *v. cholerae* 0139 has become the main cause of diarrheal disease in South Asia. This explanation has been accepted by Canadian officials, and it is difficult to make a conclusive assessment of the likelihood that these were BW attacks based on the available open source information.[110]

Analysis of Case Studies

The analysis of the case studies will focus on the three models for analyzing acquisition or development of a covert BW program and the 26 indicators of unnatural or suspicious outbreaks of disease presented in this chapter. A final summary of the cases and the applicability of the models and indicators will conclude the analysis.

Assimilation Model

As the Aralsk and Sverdlovsk cases occurred in the same country, under the same form of government, and in relatively close temporal proximity, they are analyzed together. The "assimilation" model would predict a high likelihood of the Soviet Union developing a BW program (Table 1). The USSR had a material base that was very capable of supporting the development of such a program, and its high threat perception would have led to norms against BW being overcome. The Russian government has admitted that the Soviet regime did develop chemical and nuclear weapons in addition to biological weapons as strategic weapons.[111] The BW program was developed in secrecy within the Soviet security structure, a vertically integrated and ideologically consistent entity. The Soviets very clearly balanced logistical considerations in weapons and delivery system design, choosing and enhancing agents for maximum efficacy, and designing ballistic missiles to effectively deliver them. The Soviet cases exhibited six of the seven factors considered in the model.

The "assimilation" model would predict a high likelihood of Rhodesia developing a BW program. Rhodesia had a material base that was capable of supporting the development of a limited program and its high threat perception from the civil war would have led to norms against BW being overcome. Anthrax was endemic in Zimbabwe and thus would have been available for development as a biological weapon. The program was developed in secrecy within the security structure, an ideologically consistent entity. In addition to the possible use of anthrax, other alleged weapons included toxins, poisons, bacteriological cultures, and cholera. Agents such as poisons were used tactically for assassinations of insurgency leaders. Alleged agents such as cholera, which was alleged to have been used to contaminate rivers,[112] and anthrax would have been used as strategic weapons. By choosing agents endemic to the area such as cholera and anthrax, the Rhodesians were able to conceal their source. These agents were also used to target specific insurgent areas and groups. In this way the Rhodesians balanced weapon effectiveness with the ability to conceal their source and considerations of the weapons' utility in counterinsurgency tactics when selecting agents for employment. The Zimbabwe case exhibited all of the factors considered in the model.

The "assimilation" model would predict a low likelihood of Burma developing a BW program. Burma's material base would have had a limited capability of supporting the development of a BW program. Its GDP per capita was $650 compared to Zimbabwe's $2,160.[113] In 1993 Burma ranked 130th out of 173 countries according to the UN's Human Development Index ranking. Zanders' "assimilation" model places strong emphasis on the necessity for a physical base to support the development of a BW program, and it seems unlikely that Burma possessed enough of a material base to support anything other than a very rudimentary program. Burma's government had largely prevailed over insurgent groups, and the Karen group had been substantially weakened. Thus the government would not be likely to perceive the villagers as a high threat level.[114] Thus norms, if there were any, against BW would be less likely to be overcome. The Burma case exhibited one of the seven factors considered in the model. The following table summarizes the case studies when analyzed using the "assimilation" model.

Table 1. Assimilation Model Analysis of Cases

Indicators	Aralsk & Sverdlovsk	Zimbabwe	Burma
Material base	Yes	Yes	No
Credible threat	Yes	Yes	No
Insurgency	No	Yes	Yes
Vertically integrated structure	Yes	Yes	Not evaluated
Ideological consistency	Yes	Yes	Not evaluated
Program developed in secrecy	Yes	Yes	Unknown
Military considerations a factor	Yes	Yes	Unknown
Overall Likelihood	**High**	**High**	**Low**

Russian FIS Model

The Soviet Union outbreaks exhibited most of the indicators listed in the Russian FIS model. The indicators are evaluated based on accounts of the Soviet BW program in Ken Alibek's *Biohazard* and Tom Mangold and Jeff Goldberg's *Plague Wars*. The Soviet cases were consistent with 25 out of 30 indicators.

While less information is available on the Rhodesian BW program than for the FSU program, numerous elements of the Russian FIS model are applicable. The indicators are evaluated based on accounts of the Rhodesian BW program in Tom Mangold and Jeff Goldberg's *Plague Wars*, and *The Rollback of South Africa's Chemical and Biological Warfare Program* by Dr. Stephen Burgess and Dr. Helen Purkitt.[115] The Zimbabwe case exhibited 13 of the 30 indicators.

Less open source information was available on an alleged Burmese BW capability than for any of the other cases studied; nevertheless a few elements of the Russian FIS model are applicable. The indicators are evaluated based on Andrew Selth's account.[116] The Burma case exhibited 6 of the 30 indicators.

The evaluation below reflects the state of indicators in the various countries at the time of the incidents, as described in the sources used for the assessments.

Table 2. Russian FIS Model Analysis of Cases

Indicators	Aralsk & Sverdlovsk	Zimbabwe	Burma
Political			
Not a party to treaties or instruments renouncing WMD; not participating in fora or negotiations on such.	No	Yes	No
Refusal or obstruction of international monitoring of facilities.	Yes	Unknown	Unknown
Creation of an admin structure w/ extraordinary powers subordinate to highest pol leadership or army command.	Yes	Yes	Unknown

Creation of foreign econ agencies, intel units or ostensibly private cos. with large financial resources.	Yes	Yes	Unknown
Active promotion of WMD close to highest levels.	Yes	Yes	Unknown
Psychological manipulation of public to accept WMD.	Yes	Unknown	Unknown
No reaction to accusations of a state's proliferation.	No	Unknown	No
Overt or covert support to proliferating countries.	Yes	Yes	Unknown

Economic

Large military budget.	Yes	Unknown	Unknown
Presence of nuclear, biological, or chemical programs	Yes	Yes	Yes
Required specific production capabilities	Yes	Unknown	Yes
Importation of WMD components, etc.	Yes	Unknown	Unknown
Advancement beyond civilian needs for prod capabilities	Yes	Unknown	Unknown
High budget allocations for ostensibly civilian sectors such as biotechnology.	Yes	Unknown	Unknown

Scientific-Technical Indicators

Presence of raw materials.	Yes	Yes	Unknown
Importation of non-indig raw materials or components.	Yes	Unknown	Yes
Presence of required technologies.	Yes	Yes	Yes
Presence of required production capacity.	Yes	Yes	Yes
Required scientific/tech specialists present and system for training others exists.	Yes	Yes	Unknown
Ability or programs to attract needed specialists from abroad.	No	Unknown	Unknown
Scientific centers are created.	Yes	Unknown	Unknown
Presence of scientific and production firms w/ required specialties.	Yes	Unknown	Unknown
Supercomputer or powerful computer network for running simulations is present.	Unknown	Unknown	Unknown

Military-Technical Indicators

Tech units in military relating to WMD.	Yes	Unknown	Unknown
Reinforced/hardened facilities for government & military.	Yes	Unknown	Unknown
Training to deploy WMD in warfare and to operate in a WMD environment.	Yes	Yes	Yes
Storage facilities with high security measures	Yes	Unknown	Unknown
Possession of appropriate delivery systems.	Yes	Yes	Unknown
Intensified intelligence activities against specific enemy targets.	Unknown	Yes	Unknown
Highly developed program for civil defense.	Yes	Unknown	Unknown
Overall Likelihood	**High**	**Medium**	**Low**

U.S. Office of Technology (OTA) Model

The Soviet outbreaks exhibited all 14 of the signatures of a BW program as described in the U.S. OTA model. This reflects the model's usefulness in evaluating a very large scale program in a developed country.

The limited material available combined with the scale of the Rhodesian and Burmese programs made this model less useful in these cases than it was for the Soviet cases. The Rhodesian program exhibited none of those signatures per se, however it did have two similar signatures. Under research and development signatures, while not stated in the OTA model, a similar factor is the allegation in *Plague Wars* that "doctors and chemists from the University of Rhodesia were recruited by the CIO and asked to identify and test a range of chemical and biological agents which could be used in the war against the nationalist guerrillas."[117] For weaponization and testing signatures, allegations of experimentation and testing of poisons, toxins, bacteriological cultures, and cholera may be found in *Rollback*.[118]

Finally, the alleged Burmese program exhibited a few of the signatures of a BW program as described in the OTA model. [119] As with the Rhodesian program, the limited material available combined with the small scale of the possible Burmese program made this model less useful. The Burmese case exhibited 2 of the 14 signatures. The indicators are considered for the cases below:

Table 3. OTA Model Analysis of Cases

Indicators	Aralsk & Sverdlovsk	Zimbabwe	Burma
Research and Development Signatures			
Research facilities under military control.	Yes	Unknown	Unknown
Production of vaccines in excess of domestic needs.	Yes	Unknown	Unknown
Purchase of dual-use materials and equipment.	Yes	Unknown	Yes
Sudden halts in research indicative of military censorship or other indicators of military censorship.	Yes	Unknown	Unknown
Weaponization and Testing Signatures			
Field tests of aerosols.	Yes	Unknown	Unknown
Tests of weapons' effectiveness against large animals.	Yes	Unknown	Unknown
Burial of animals used at weapons testing sites.	Yes	Unknown	Unknown
Production Signatures			
Tight security and secrecy around an ostensibly civilian facility.	Yes	Unknown	Yes
Very extensive microbiological production plants much more sophisticated than known civilian facilites.	Yes	Unknown	Unknown
Facilities unassociated with vaccine production with large numbers of test animals.	Yes	Unknown	Unknown
Observable changes in ostensibly civilian production facilities.	Yes	Unknown	Unknown

Stockpile and Delivery System Signatures

Refrigerated bunkers or igloos for storage of large amounts of BW agents.	Yes	Unknown	Unknown
Storage depots for BW munitions near suspected production facilities.	Yes	Unknown	Unknown
Heavy trucks for the transportation of munitions or for decontamination use.	Yes	Unknown	Unknown
Overall Likelihood	**High**	**Low**	**Low**

Indicators of Unnatural or Suspicious Outbreaks of Disease

The Aralsk and Sverdlovsk cases had 13 and 14, respectively, of the 26 indicators and exhibited the highest number of indicators of the 4 cases studied. The events held 11 of the indicators in common. These common indicators were a point source origination, a compressed epidemic curve, severe disease, unusual exposure routes, unusual diseases for the area, unusual strains of the diseases, a higher attack rate depending on location of the victim, pulmonary disease, high morbidity and mortality, the failure of the government to cooperate with an investigation, and sudden demand for vaccines. A credible Russian official who was in a position of authority at the time (Yeltsin), later acknowledged that a BW facility was responsible for the outbreak in Sverdlovsk. Although the Russian government continues to deny that Sverdlovsk was a BW facility, it has admitted that the USSR had a BW program. This admission, coupled with the relatively large amount of information known about the cases, makes these cases good tests of the predictive ability of the indicators for other cases about which less is known.

Less is known about the Zimbabwe case, but the correlation with the indicators was still relatively strong. When the outbreak is compared to the list of generic indicators, it exhibited 10 of the indicators. The exhibited indicators were a point source origination, a large epidemic curve, unusual extent of the disease for the area, a disease that attacks both animals and humans, a higher attack rate depending on location of the victim, claims of attack by the perpetrator, pulmonary disease, the failure of the government to cooperate with an investigation, sudden demand for vaccine, and outbreak of disease for which a potential adversary was vaccinated.

As has been noted, the amount of substantiated, open source information available on a possible Burmese program is substantially less than that available for the former Soviet program or the Rhodesian program. When the outbreak is compared to the list of generic indicators, it exhibited six of the indicators. Exhibited indicators are shown below in italics. The exhibited indicators were a point source origination, a compressed epidemic curve, a large epidemic, severe disease, a higher attack rate depending on location, and high mortality.

Table 4. Indicators of Unnatural or Suspicious Outbreaks of Disease Analysis of Cases

Indicators	Aralsk	Sverdlovsk	Zimbabwe	Burma
Point source origination	Yes	Yes	Yes	Yes
Line source origination	No	No	No	No
Compressed epidemic curve	Yes	Yes	No	Yes
Large epidemic	No	Yes	Yes	Yes
Severe disease	Yes	Yes	No	Yes
Unusual exposure routes	Yes	Yes	Undetermined	Undetermined
Unusual for the area or season	Yes	Yes	Yes	No
Endemic disease outside established range	Yes	No	No	No
Impossible to transmit naturally without vector	No	No	No	No
Multiple epidemics of different diseases	No	No	No	No
Different disease in the same patient	No	No	No	No
Disease that attacks animals and humans	No	Yes	Yes	No

Unusual strains of disease	Yes	Yes	Unknown	Probable
Strain of disease seen some years before outbreak	Unknown	Unknown	Unknown	No
Higher attack rate depending on location	Yes	Yes	Yes	Yes
Intelligence information about agent	Unknown	Unknown	Unknown	Unknown
Claims of attack by perpetrator	No	No	Yes	No
Direct evidence of attack – equipment, munitions	No	No	No	Undetermined
Pulmonary disease	Yes	Yes	Yes	No
High military and civilian casualties when collocated	No	Unknown	No	No
High morbidity and mortality	Yes	Yes	No	Yes
Low disease rates for those with controlled air supplies	Unknown	Unknown	Unknown	Unknown
Failure to cooperate with investigation	Yes	Yes	Yes	No
Sudden demand for vaccine	Yes	Yes	Yes	No
Disease in population with high immunity	Yes	No	No	No
Outbreak of disease for which adversary was vaccinated	N/A	N/A	Yes	Unknown
Overall Likelihood	**High**	**High**	**Medium**	**Low**

Conclusions about the Cases and the Models

The following chart summarizes the assessment of the likelihood that a case was indicative of a covert BW program for each case using each of the models.

Table 5. Summary of Analytic Models and Cases

Case	Assimilation Model	Russian FIS Model	U.S. OTA Model	Indicators of Unnatural or Suspicious Outbreaks
Aralsk	High	High	High	High
Sverdlovsk	High	High	High	High
Zimbabwe	High	Medium	Low	Medium
Burma	Low	Low	Low	Low

The Soviet cases illustrate the utility of the models in indicating the existence of a covert BW program. The Soviet program was officially acknowledged by the Russian government, and despite later denials by the government, a credible Russian official admitted that the Sverdlovsk plant was a BW installation. In the Sverdlovsk case, the disease was localized in a distinctive area indicative of a plume; a rare form of the infection was prevalent; animals as well as humans were affected; and multiple strains of anthrax were isolated in victims.[120] Although the Russian government has not officially acknowledged the Aralsk case, it has admitted that Vozrozhdeniye Island was used for open air testing of BW agents. Thus the case is strong that these incidents were what they appeared to be – accidental releases of BW agents. Given that they strongly correlated with the models and indicators used, this serves to validate the models and indicators.

The Zimbabwe case is more difficult. As has been shown, the amount of substantiated, open source information available on the Rhodesian program is substantially less than that available for the former Soviet program. Given the inadequacy of open source information, the use of the models considered likely would not lead an analyst to conclusively suspect that Rhodesia had a covert BW program. While the "assimilation" model indicated a high likelihood of a covert BW program, the Russian FIS model and the U.S. OTA model, both most applicable to large programs in developed countries, had medium and low correlations, respectively. This outbreak is an example of the difficulty in positively identifying outbreaks of disease as indicators of a BW attack or capability. In this case, additional, reliable human intelligence would enable a more definitive conclusion. As has been described in *Plague Wars* and *The Rollback of South Africa's Chemical and Biological Warfare Program*, Rhodesia did employ poisons, toxins, and bacteriological cultures. The government is alleged to have used cholera and other chemical and biological agents to foul water supplies.[121] All of these measures were undertaken as part of the government's counterinsurgency efforts, which heightened during the period of the 1978-1980 anthrax outbreak. Given the magnitude of the outbreak, its anomalous nature, and its timing, the event is assessed as likely to have been a BW attack. This case highlights the need for close cooperation between the intelligence community and the scientific community.

An analysis of the 1993-1994 outbreaks of cholera in Burma based on models and indicators for the acquisition or development of BW capability points to a low likelihood that the outbreak was a BW attack. As with the Zimbabwe case, the inadequacy of open source information likely would not lead an analyst to suspect that Burma had a covert BW program when using the models as determinants. The suspicion of a covert BW program is only slightly strengthened by comparing the information known about the events to indicators of an unnatural outbreak of disease. In this case as in the Zimbabwe case, additional, reliable human intelligence and additional epidemiological information could lead to a more definitive conclusion.

The preceding case studies and analyses show that when more information is available, a more definitive conclusion may be made about the likelihood of a state's possession of a covert BW program. In the Soviet cases, defectors and declassified reports provided a great deal of critical information, as did analysis of overhead imagery. In both Soviet cases, extensive epidemiological work produced a definitive portrait of the outbreak, which made analysis of it much more conclusive. These cases demonstrate the results that may be achieved from the synergy of epidemiological and intelligence analysis.

In the Rhodesian case, epidemiological information was more extensive than open source intelligence information. Open source intelligence information was largely unsubstantiated, and scientific information regarding the possible spread of the disease was judged by some to be inconclusive. In this case, the models were of some use when combined with an analysis of the indicators of a suspicious outbreak of disease. Still, additional, credible intelligence combined with definitive scientific information on the role of biting flies as vectors could enable a more conclusive determination.

Finally, as was seen with the Burmese case, sketchy information, both intelligence and epidemiological, make it very difficult to reach a judgment on a possible covert BW program. Additional information in both realms is necessary before a conclusion can be reached and could be obtained through a close partnership between the intelligence and scientific communities.

Cooperation between the Intelligence and Scientific Communities

Cooperation between the intelligence community and public health experts is vital to achieving a full understanding of outbreaks of infectious disease as indicators of covert biological weapons programs. Dr. Jonathan Tucker and Col Robert Kadlec commented on this in a Spring 2001 article in *Strategic Review*, noting that problems in making accurate assessments of outbreaks arise due to lack of coordination between the public health and intelligence communities. Dr. Tucker and Col Kadlec suggested various means of enhancing coordination between the two communities. This section will review their comments and will contribute assessments and suggestions made by analysts from the intelligence community (IC).

Dr. Tucker and Col Kadlec cited the response to the West Nile virus outbreak of 1999 as indicative of the coordination problems plaguing the various local, state, and federal agencies involved. They maintained that the outbreak highlighted major coordination problems between the veterinary and public health communities, and likewise between the intelligence and public health communities. The authors noted that timely dissemination of information available as a result of the veterinary investigation of the outbreak would have been of great use to the public health investigators dealing with the outbreak. Dr. Tucker and Col Kadlec found that the intelligence communities "connection of the dots" in this case lead to an unwarranted suspicion of Iraqi involvement. They asserted that full and open coordination with trained epidemiologists would have ruled this out. The authors attributed the lack of such coordination to the greatly differing organizational cultures, logistical and security barriers, and an extant sense of mutual distrust.

Dr. Tucker and Col Kadlec had several recommendations to "bridge the gap" between the public health and intelligence communities. They recommended institutionalization of exchanges of personnel and training between the two communities, with "temporary details" of six months to one year. They also recommended the creation of an "intra-governmental coordinating body of experts from public health and intelligence agencies that would meet periodically to review unusual outbreaks of infectious disease when some suspicion of covert biowarfare or bioterrorism exists."[122]

A discussion with various intelligence community analysts in February 2003 yielded a more rosy picture of the current state of interaction in the post-9/11 world, but a near mirror image of the difficulties and frustrations encountered when working with partners in the public health community. Analysts acknowledged a residual cultural distrust between the two communities, but stated that this fell away as individuals got to know each other on a personal basis. The IC analysts also cited logistical and administrative restrictions necessary to maintain security as barriers to interaction. IC analysts lauded the very significant interaction with partners in the Department of Homeland Security (DHS) and the National Institutes of Health (NIH) since 11 September 2001. They agreed with some of the suggestions made by Dr. Tucker and Col Kadlec for enhanced cooperation between the two communities and put forth several of their own.[123]

IC analysts believed that as interaction between the public health community and the IC increased, their partners in the public health community gained a greater understanding of IC analysts' motives. They noted an evolving understanding of the need for closer cooperation between the two communities among the senior levels of public health agencies. The analysts noted that when they reached below the senior levels of those agencies, they sensed residual misperceptions about the intelligence community among lower ranking officers. They saw mistrust as stemming from a perception that the two communities have different agendas. The analysts saw the fact that the United States does not have an offensive BW program as a positive for the relationship – it allowed scientists and IC analysts to realize that they are on the same side. They noted that when they made visits to laboratories, and scientists did not focus on where they worked, all participants, whether IC or scientific, clearly realized that they were eager to find the same information to get at the truth. The analysts perceived that before the 2001 anthrax attacks the scientific and health community tended to think that the BW threat was overblown. This has now changed, and public health officers look to the IC for more threat information. IC analysts now felt that they and the scientific community were more "on the same sheet of music." This was especially so with officials in Homeland Security. The IC analysts felt that the public health community was becoming more aware of the insidious nature of some interlocutors who want information from them.

The IC analysts also noted obstacles to interaction dictated by the security measures necessary for an intelligence organization. They said that collegial interactions were somewhat restricted, as they were unable to talk readily to individuals openly and freely, due to both security considerations and lingering cultural differences. They noted that very few of their interlocutors have security clearances, and that this restricts the flow of information. They further lamented the impracticality of clearing scientific partners for isolated projects and were unsure that the public health agencies would be willing to make the commitment to engage fully in the classified world. This kind of commitment would involve outlays for secure communications, clearances, and SCIFs (Sensitive Compartmented Information Facilities).

The analysts believed that enhanced interaction on an issue dependent basis was logical and reasonable. Certain issues, such as biodefense, lend themselves to interaction with NIH, Centers for Disease Control, DHS, and Health and Human Services Officials. For other issues, enhanced interaction is not logical, as the IC analysts would tend to rely upon their own sources of information. While interaction with federal officials has increased, the analysts saw more interaction likely in the future with officials at the state level. They believed that while contacts in the academic community were developing at a slower pace, they would be likely to accelerate as universities started to institute academic departments for the study of homeland security or biological warfare. The incentive for increased publication would increase contacts. Finally, the IC analysts noted that they made and maintained contacts outside the IC during interagency working groups that bring together professionals under a policy umbrella. They found it beneficial to maintain contacts in these groups for the future, and they noted that they leveraged cleared contacts at State, DoD, and the NSC as conduits to the scientific community.

The IC analysts concurred with Dr. Tucker and Col Kadlec's suggestion for rotational assignments for scientists from CDC and USAMRIID into the IC. They noted that it would be easier to clear these individuals for such assignments, and they would start with more knowledge of the IC than would individuals without a federal government affiliation. They would welcome rotations by members of the public health community as specialists in certain IC branches for assignments of six months to one year, as these would be good opportunities for exchanges of knowledge and cross-cultural pollenization between the communities. The analysts would also welcome rotational assignments or conferences with experts in cultural and historical issues for various regions of concern. They believed that this type of interaction would be more practical than purely scientific exchanges. The analysts thought that periodic review of unusual outbreaks of infectious diseases should be accomplished virtually due to the fast pace of outbreaks. Finally, the IC analysts also advocated issue-based conferences to be held on an ad hoc basis. They noted that a "neutral" sponsor such as the National Defense University would be welcomed by both communities, and they envisioned attendance at such conferences of experts from the public health, intelligence, academia, and policy communities.

The analysts noted that technical depth in the IC had been enhanced in the last five years; as expectations have increased, so has the need to have analysis backstopped by the scientific credentials of the analysts. The number of PhDs working in the IC has greatly increased over the last ten years, and they described it as being "in good shape," both technically and substantively. That said, they noted that they do not stay current in most subspecialties of basic research. They said that as there are so many scientific fields that contribute to any given subject, it is not possible for the analysts to have knowledge as in-depth as the scientist working in the lab. This level of detail is neither needed nor desired for the majority of the work the analysts do.

The IC analysts summarized by saying that the IC and public health communities are making very good progress on increasing interactions, IC analysts are staying abreast of developments and increasing technical depth when warranted, and communication with other agencies and communities is coming along very well.[124]

Conclusion

> *"BW programs have become more technically sophisticated as a result of rapid growth in the field of biotechnology research and the wide dissemination of this knowledge. Almost anyone with limited skills can create BW agents. The rise of such capabilities also means we now have to be concerned about a myriad of new agents."*[125]
>
> - George Tenet, 11 February 2003

As the threats to our nation increase and become more complex, so too must the integration of all elements of national power grow and become more profound. The difficulty of effectively "pointing the finger" using unclassified information was made apparent when the world watched in early 2003 as Secretary of State Colin Powell made the case for Iraq's continuing possession of weapons of mass destruction. These realities make it imperative that the intelligence community and the public health community work together to protect our nation.

Models of behavior and indicators for disease outbreaks provide a framework for assessing suspicious outbreaks of disease as indicators of covert BW programs. Using these tools to assess events can help to determine if further investigation is warranted and the directions such investigations might take. Using the framework they provide, preliminary and tentative conclusions about incidents may be drawn.

As shown by the amount of publicly available and declassified information on the 1971 smallpox epidemic in Aralsk, the 1979 outbreak of anthrax in Sverdlovsk, and the 1978-1980 anthrax outbreak in Zimbabwe, it is clear that international scrutiny of suspicious outbreaks of diseases will occur. Given the advent of the Internet and websites such as

ProMED, it is likely that international suspicion will be aroused sooner than was the case before the maturation of the Information Age. Open source reporting of observable traits common to suspicious outbreaks can speed initial evaluation of events and spur international demand for investigations or explanations. Evaluation based on open source reporting can be readily shared with interested parties without risking the compromise of intelligence sources or methods. Finally, open source information may be more readily received by international parties, as it would be independently verifiable by them.

The open source arena is one in which the intelligence community and the scientific community can easily collaborate. While both communities describe a culture of distrust, the events of 11 September 2001 have served to bring them closer together in achieving the common goal of defending our nation and people. Interaction between the communities continues to increase, as members of both have shown a strong willingness to reach out to the other. The stakes are high, and a strong partnership between the intelligence community and the public health community will further strengthen our defenses against weapons of mass destruction.

Notes

1. John C. Gannon, "The U.S. Intelligence Community and the Challenge of BCW," in *The New Terror: Facing the Threat of Biological and Chemical Weapons*, ed. Sidney D. Drell et al. (Stanford, CA: Hoover Institution Press, Stanford University, 1999), 132.

2. Ken Alibek, *Biohazard*, (New York, NY: Random House, 1999), 43.

3. Jonathan B. Tucker, "Bioterrorism: Threats and Responses," in *Biological Weapons: Limiting the Threat*, ed. Joshua Lederberg (Cambridge, MA: The MIT Press, 1999), 285.

4. W. Seth Carus, "Biological Warfare Threats in Perspective, " *Critical Reviews in Microbiology* 24, no. 3 (1998): 149-155.

5. Jean Pascal Zanders, "Assessing the Risk of Chemical and Biological Weapons Proliferation to Terrorists," *The Nonproliferation Review* (Fall 1999): 17-34.

6. Ibid.

7. Ibid.

8. Ibid.

9. U.S. Congress, Office of Technology Assessment, *Technologies Underlying Weapons of Mass Destruction, OTA-BP-ISC-115* (Washington, DC: U.S. Government Printing Office, December 199c 3), 84-5.

10. Zanders, "Assessing the Risk," 17-34.

11. Ibid.

12. Jonathan B. Tucker, "Motivations For and Against Proliferation: The Case of the Middle East," in *Biological Warfare: Modern Offense and Defense*, ed. Raymond A. Zilinskas (Boulder, CO: Lynne Rienner Publishers, 2000), 29.

13. Zanders, "Assessing the Risk," 17-34.

14. U.S. Congress, *Technologies*, 77.

15. Zanders, "Assessing the Risk," 17-34.

16. Zanders, "Assessing the Risk," 17-34.

17. Russian Federation, Foreign Intelligence Service, "A New Challenge after the Cold War: Proliferation of Weapons of Mass Destruction," 5 March 1993, in FBIS Report: Proliferation Issues, JPRS-TND-93-007, 1-39.

18. U.S. Congress, *Technologies*, 104.

19. Ibid., 99-107.

20. For example, see David R. Franz, Peter B. Jahrling, Arthur M. Friedlander, David J. McClain, David L. Hoover, W. Russell Byrne, Julie A. Pavlin, George W. Christopher, and Edward M. Eitzen, Jr., "Clinical Recognition and Management of Patients Exposed to Biological Warfare Agents," in *Biological Weapons: Limiting the Threat*, ed. Joshua Lederberg (Cambridge, MA: The MIT Press, 1999), 77-79, Graham S. Pearson, "The Essentials of Biological Threat Assessment," in *Biological Warfare: Modern Offense and Defense*, ed. Raymond A. Zilinskas (Boulder, CO: Lynne Rienner Publishers, 2000), 55-83, and Mark Wheelis, "Investigation of Suspicious Outbreaks of Disease," in *Biological Warfare: Modern Offense and Defense*, ed. Raymond A. Zilinskas (Boulder, CO: Lynne Rienner Publishers, 2000), 105-117

21. Mark Wheelis, "Investigation of Suspicious Outbreaks of Disease," in *Biological Warfare: Modern Offense and Defense*, ed. Raymond A. Zilinskas (Boulder, CO: Lynne Rienner Publishers, 2000), 110-1.

22. Pearson, "The Essentials of Biological Threat Assessment," in *Biological Warfare*, 67.

23. Mark Wheelis, "Investigating Disease Outbreaks under a Protocol to the Biological and Toxin Weapons Convention," *Emerging Infectious Diseases* 6, no. 6 (November-December 2000): 595-600.

24. Ad Hoc Group, "Use of Investigative Epidemiology as a Tool in the Investigation of Unusual Outbreak of Disease and Alleged Use of Biological Weapons," *The Biological and Toxins Weapons Convention (BTWC) Database*, 8 December 1995, n.p., on-line, Internet, 2 February 2003, available from http://www.brad.ac.uk/acad/sbtwc/adhocgrp/wpindex.htm.

25. John G. Bartlett, MD, ed., *Bioterrorism and Public Health: An Internet Resource Guide*, (Montvale, NJ: Thompson Medical Economics, 2002), 91.

26 Pearson, "The Essentials of Biological Threat Assessment," in *Biological Warfare,* 67.

27. Jonathan B. Tucker, "Bioterrorism: Threats and Responses," in *Biological Weapons: Limiting the Threat*, ed. Joshua Lederberg (Cambridge, MA: The MIT Press, 1999), 308.

28. John G. Bartlett, MD, ed., *Bioterrorism and Public Health: An Internet Resource Guide*, (Montvale, NJ: Thompson Medical Economics, 2002), 91.

29. Ibid., 91-2, Pearson, "The Essentials of Biological Threat Assessment," in *Biological Warfare*, 67-8, Wheelis, "Investigations" in *Biological Warfare*, 108-113, Franz, et al, "Clinical Recognition" in *Biological Weapons*, 77-9, Tucker, "Bioterrorism," in *Biological Weapons*, Ad Hoc Group, "Use of Investigative Epidemiology" *The Biological and Toxins Weapons Convention (BTWC) Database* n.p., Ad Hoc Group, "Unusual Outbreaks of Disease and Their Investigation," *The Biological and Toxins Weapons Convention (BTWC) Database*, 26 July 1996, n.p., on-line, Internet, 2 February 2003, available from http://www.brad.ac.uk/acad/sbtwc/adhocgrp/wpindex.htm , Maj Donald L. Noah and LTC Annette L. Sobel, "Biological Warfare Training: Infectious Disease Outbreak Differentiation Criteria, *Military Medicine* 163, no. 4 (April 1998): 198-201, Wheelis, "Investigating Disease Outbreaks," *Emerging Infectious Diseases,* 595-600, and BG Russ Zajtchuk, ed., *Textbook of Military Medicine: Medical Aspects of Chemical and Biological Warfare* (Washington, DC: Office of the Surgeon General Department of the Army, 1997), 449, U.S. Congress, *Technologies*, 107-113.

30. Jonathan B. Tucker and Raymond A. Zilinskas, eds., *The 1971 Smallpox Epidemic in Aralsk, Kazakhstan, and the Soviet Biological Warfare Program*, Occasional Paper No. 9 (Monterey, CA: Center for Nonproliferation Studies, July 2002), 12.

31. Ibid., 17-9. The official report states that the index case began to sicken on 6 August, while she recalled in a May 2002 interview that she began to have symptoms on 11 or 12 August.

32. Ibid., 13-5.

33. Ibid., 23-7, 31-46.

34. Ibid., 31-59, 1.

35. Ibid., 30.

36. Ibid., 17-20.

37. Ibid., 20.

38. Gulbarshyn Bozheyeva, Yerlan Kunakbayev, and Dastan Yeleukenov, *Former Soviet Biological Weapons Facilities in Kazakhstan: Past, Present, and Future*, Occasional Paper No. 1 (Monterey, CA: Center for Nonproliferation Studies, June 1999), 4-7, and Jeanne Guillemin, Anthrax: *The Investigation of a Deadly Outbreak* (Berkley, CA: University of California Press, 1999), 185.

39. Tucker and Zilinskas, eds., 9, 20-1.

40. Ibid., 21. Ronald M. Atlas, Ph.D. and Richard Clover, M.D., "Implications of the 1971 Smallpox Outbreak in Aralsk, Kasakhstan, for U.S. Smallpox Vaccination Policy,"*CNS Occasional Papers: #9 Commentaries*, n.p., on-line, Internet, 9 September 2002, available from http://cns.miis.edu/iiop/cnsdata?Action=1&Concept=0&Mime=1& collection=CNS+Web+S. The authors of this commentary agree with Tucker and Zilinskas' conclusion.

41. Ken Alibek, Lecture Question and Answer Session, SAIC, Tyson's Corner, VA, 12 September 2002.

42. Guillemin, 234. Guillemin places the date and time of the release based on extensive interviews with victims' surviving family members and survivors of the incident. Ken Alibek, in his book *Biohazard*, identifies the date of the accident and the release as being during the night of 30 March. As Guillemin's date and time are based upon epidemiological research conducted with survivors and surviving family members, and as it is consistent with established dates of death and the expected course of anthrax in humans, it is used instead of Alibek's date and time, which are based on information that is second-hand at best.

43. One source is retired counterintelligence officer General Andrey Mironyuk in 1993, quoted in Guillemin, 187. The second is Ken Alibek, *Biohazard*, (New York, NY: Random House, 1999), 73-4.

44. Guillemin, 196, 224. Guillemin cites General Valentin Yevstigneyev as the source for the rooftop ventilator release information. Also in Alibek, 73-4, Alibek cites exhaust pipes as the source of the release, but does not specify a height.

45. Guillemin, 234.

46. Raymond A. Zilinskas, ed., *Biological Warfare: Modern Offense and Defense*, (Boulder, CO: Lynne Rienner Publishers, Inc., 2000), 79.

47. Matthew Messelson, Jeanne Guillemin, Martin Hugh-Jones, Alexander Langmuir, Ilona Popova, Alexis Shelokov, Olga Yampolskaya, "The Sverdlovsk Anthrax Outbreak of 1979," *Science* 266, no. 5188 (19 November 1994): 1202-8.

48. Ibid., 106, 115, 202-5.

49. Guillemin, 234, 105-6, 112-5, 44.

50. Defense Intelligence Agency, *Trends and Developments: Foreign Technology Weapons and Systems* (Washington, D.C.: Defense Intelligence Agency, 1980), 13. <u>Document is now declassified</u>.

51. Guillemin, 224.

52. Guillemin, 14.

53. Ibid., 15, 98-9, 127, 235. The chief epidemiologist at the Sanitary Epidemiological Station (SES) maintained that Burgasov ordered the buildings washed, but Burgasov denied this.

54. Ibid., 142.

55. Ibid., 87, 103, 117, 127, 128-9, 133, 181

56. Anthony Rimmington, "From Military to Industrial Complex? The Conversion of Biological Weapons' Facilities in the Russian Federation," *Contemporary Security Policy* 17, no. 1 (April 1996): 80-112.

57. Guillemin, 134-5.

58. Ibid., 234, 273, 189, 242.

59. *Soviet Biological Warfare Threat*, U.S. Government White Paper (Washington, D.C.: Defense Intelligence Agency, 1986), 4. (Unclassified.)

60. Guillemin, 237. The lack of deaths among young people and children could be explained by differences between the immune systems and reactions to inhalatory infections of the young and children and the reactions of older adults.

61. Ibid., 64.

62. Ibid., 34, 87, 91.

63 Paul J. Jackson, Martin E. Hugh-Jones, Debra M. Adair, Gertrude Green, Karen K. Hill, Cheryl R. Kuske, Lev M. Grinberg, Faina A. Abramova, Paul Keim, "PCR Analysis of Tissue Samples From the 1979 Sverdlovsk Anthrax Victims: The Presence of Multiple *Bacillus antracis* Strains in Different Victims," *PNAS Online* 95, no. 3, 3 February 1998, 1224-1229, on-line, EBSCO Host, 3 October 2002.

64. Guillemin, 195.

65. Ibid, 45, 60, 70, 113, 115-116, 161, 164, 166, 214. A Russian official related that the Soviet Council of Ministers ordered that the KGB records be destroyed on 4 December 1990.

66. Ibid., 199-201.

67. Ibid., 93.

68. Ibid., 83, 103, 129, 135, 143-4, 150, 155.

69. Ibid., 8.

70. Ibid., 85, 88.

71. Ibid., 226.

72. Ibid., 93, 119, 137, 147-148.

73. Ibid., 163, 185, 256.

74. Zilinskas, ed., 78.

75. Guillemin, 10.

76. Ibid., 25-6. Guillemin reports that one six-year-old girl contracted cutaneous anthrax.

77. Ibid., 29, 230.

78. Ibid., 16-22, 44-7. Guillemin relates that Dr. Babich maintained that there were no intestinal lesions or symptoms, while Dr. Nikiforov's report judged the cases to be gastrointestinal anthrax based on the amount of damage to intestinal organs. Photographic slides presented by the two primary pathologists involved in the case, who performed the majority of the autopsies, showed intestinal lesions. These pathologists believed the cause to be inhalational anthrax. The assistant chief sanitary inspector of the Sverdlovsk Oblast Sanitary Epidemiological Station (SES) asserted an animal outbreak before the human cases, while Dr. Babich maintained that animal deaths occurred after the human deaths began. Dr. Vladimir Nikiforov's son stated that his father had been coerced into supporting the tainted meat explanation, and he shared his father's information, which he believed supported inhalational anthrax, with investigators. The two primary pathologists involved in the case, who performed the majority of the autopsies, believed the cause to be inhalational anthrax.

79. Ibid., 107.

80. Meryl Nass, MD, "Anthrax Epizootic in Zimbabwe, 1978-1980: Due to Deliberate Spread?," *The PSR Quarterly* 2, no. 4 (December 1992): 198-209.

81. J.C.A. Davies, "A Major Epidemic of Anthrax in Zimbabwe, Part I," *The Central African Journal of Medicine* 28, no.12 (December 1982): 291-8.

82. W.E. Kobuch, J. Davis, J. Fleischer, M. Isaacson, and P.C.B. Turnbull, "A Clinical and Epidemiological Study of 621 Patients with Anthrax in Western Zimbabwe," *Salisbury Medical Bulletin* 68: 34-8, and J.A. Lawrence, C.M. Foggin, and R. A. I. Norval, "The Effect of War on the Control of Diseases of Livestock in Rhodesia (Zimbabwe)," *Veterinary Record* 107 (1980): 82-5.

83. Davies, "A Major Epidemic, Part I," 291-8.

84. J.C.A. Davies, "A Major Epidemic of Anthrax in Zimbabwe, Part II," *The Central African Journal of Medicine* 29, no.1 (January 1983): 8-12, and Davies, "A Major Epidemic of Anthrax in Zimbabwe, Part I," 291-8.

85. James C. Pile, MD, John D. Malone, MD, Edward M. Eitzen, MD, MPH, Arthur M. Friedlander, MD, "Anthrax as a Potential Biological Warfare Agent," *Archives of Internal Medicine* 158, no. 5, March 9, 1998, n.p., on-line, Internet, 16 February 2003, available from http://archinte.ama-assn.org/issues/v158n5/ffull/ira705l2.html.

86. Davies, "A Major Epidemic, Part II," 8-12.

87. A.O. Pugh, and J.C.A. Davies, "Human Anthrax in Zimbabwe," *Salisbury Medical Bulletin* 68: 32-3.

88. Lawrence, et al, "The Effects of War on the Control of Diseases of Livestock in Rhodesia (Zimbabwe)," 82-5.

89. Ibid., Davies, "A Major Epidemic, Part I," 291-8, Davies, "A Major Epidemic, Part II," 8-12, Pugh and Davies, "Human Anthrax in Zimbabwe," 32-3, and M. Turner, "Anthrax in Humans in Zimbabwe," *The Central African Journal of Medicine* 26, no. 7 (July 1980): 160-1.

90. Nass, "Anthrax Epizootic in Zimbabwe,: 198-209.

91. Davies, "A Major Epidemic, Part II," 8-12.

92. Nass, "Anthrax Epizootic in Zimbabwe," 198-209.

93. Davies, "A Major Epidemic, Part II," 8-12.

94. Nass, "Anthrax Epizootic in Zimbabwe," 198-209.

95. "The Status of Anthrax in Zimbabwe," *World Health Organization Collaborating Center for Remote Sensing and Geographic Information Systems for Public Health*, n.p., on-line, Internet, 18 February 2003, available from http://www.vetmed.lsu.edu/whocc/zimbabwe.htm.

96. John Lawrence, posting to ProMED-mail, 21 Dec 2000, n.p., on-line, Internet, 16 February 2003, available from http://www.fas.org/ahead/disease/anx/2000/dis-anx-001224-afzwe.htm.

97. "15 Get Anthrax in Zim After Eating Sick Cows," *Dispatch Online*, 27 October 2001, n.p., on-line, Internet, 16 February 2003, available from http://www.dispatch.co.za/2001/10/27/foreign/ANTHRAX.HTM, Challiss McDonough, "Zimbabwe/Anthrax," *VOA News Report*, 26 October 2001, n.p., on-line, Internet, 16 February 2003, available from http://www.globalsecurity.org/military/library/news/2001/10/mil-011026-3dc94681.htm, and Roderick Mukumbira, "Zimbabwe: The Anthrax Scare That Never Was," *Africanews* 68 (November 2001), n.p., on-line, Internet, 16 February 2003, available from http://www.peacelink.it/afrinews/68_issue/p2.html.

98. "Anthrax Outbreak at Settlement Leaves Two Dead," *The Herald (Harare)*, 5 November 2002, n.p., on-line, Internet, 16 February 2003, available from http://allafrica.com/stories/200211080083.html.

99. "15 Get Anthrax in Zim," *Dispatch Online*, McDonough, "Zimbabwe/Anthrax," *VOA News Report*, Mukumbira, "Zimbabwe: The Anthrax Scare," *Africanews*, and "Anthrax Outbreak at Settlement," *The Herald (Harare)*.

100. Davies, "A Major Epidemic, Part II," 8-12, and Kobuch, et al, "A Clinical and Epidemiological Study," 34-8.

101. Davies, "A Major Epidemic, Part II," 291-8, and Turner, "Anthrax in Humans in Zimbabwe," 160-1.

102. Pugh and Davies, "Human Anthrax in Zimbabwe," 32-3.

103. Davies, "A Major Epidemic, Part II," 8-12, Kobuch, et al, "A Clinical and Epidemiological Study," 34-8, D.R.A. McKendrick, "Anthrax and Its Transmission to Humans," *The Central African Journal of Medicine* 26, no. 6 (June 1980): 126-9, and Turner, "Anthrax in Humans in Zimbabwe," 160-1.

104. Nass, "Anthrax Epizootic in Zimbabwe," 198-209, Turner, "Anthrax in Humans in Zimbabwe," 160-1, Lawrence, et al, "The Effects of War on the Control of Diseases of Livestock in Rhodesia (Zimbabwe)," 82-5, and Pugh and Davies, "Human Anthrax in Zimbabwe," 32-3.

105. Mangold, *Plague Wars*, 219-21.

106. Ibid., 222, and David Martin, *The Use of Poison and Biological Weapons in the Rhodesian War*, (Harare, Zimbabwe: Southern African Research and Documentation Centre, 1993), 7.

107. See Dr. Stephen Burgess and Dr. Helen Purkitt, *The Rollback of South Africa's Chemical and Biological Warfare Program*, (Maxwell AFB, AL: USAF Counterproliferation Center, April 2001), and Mangold, *Plague Wars*.

108. "Is the SLORC Using Bacteriological Warfare?, Preliminary Report Based on Information Independently Gathered by the Karen Human Rights Group," 15 March 1994, n.p., on-line, Internet, 4 February 2003, available from http://www.ibiblio.org/freeburma/humanrights/khrg/archive/khrg94/04_03_15.html,and "Burma and Biologicals: BW?," *ASA Newsletter* no. 47 (1995): 12.

109. Ibid., Andrew Selth, "Burma and Weapons of Mass Destruction, Working Paper," *SDSC Working Papers* no. 334 (July 1999): 1-24, and Andrew Selth, "Burma and Exotic Weapons," *Strategic Analysis* 19, no. 3 (June 1996): 413-433.

110. Ibid., and Andrew Selth, "Burma and Biological Weapons," *Jane's Intelligence Review* 007, no. 011 (1995): 518.

111. Tom Mangold and Jeff Goldberg, *Plague Wars* (New York, NY: St. Martin's Press, 1999), 83-5.

112. Burgess, *Rollback*, 6-9.

113. United Nations Development Programme, *Human Development Report 1994*, (New York, NY: Oxford University Press, 1994), 129-31.

114. Selth, "Working Paper," 12-3.

115. According to David Martin in *The Use of Poison and Biological Weapons in the Rhodesian War*, as of 1993 Zimbabwe was not a signatory to the BWTC. According to Dr. Burgess and Dr. Purkitt in *Rollback*, 8-9, "SADF Special Fores and SAP officers stationed in Rhodesia had studied ... the use of chemical and biological agents."

116. Selth, "Working Paper," 7-11. Several analyses have concluded that Burma may have had a chemical warfare program, possibly targeted at the country's insurgents. It has also been alleged that Burma may have dual-use facilities built with the assistance of German firms. Burmese military officers received BW defense training in Germany.

117. Mangold, *Plague Wars*, 222.

118. Burgess, *Rollback*, 9.

119. Ibid., 6. Possible dual-use facilities are described as being highly secure locations.

120. Joshua Lederberg, ed., *Biological Weapons: Limiting the Threat* (Cambridge, MA: MIT Press, 2000), 77-9, and Jackson, et al.

121. Burgess, *Rollback*, 6-9.

122. Jonathan B. Tucker and Robert P. Kadlec, "Infectious Disease and National Security," *Strategic Review* 29, no. 2 (Spring 1999), 12-20.

123. Intelligence Community Analysts, Personal Interview, Central Intelligence Agency, Langley, VA, 13 February 2003

124. Ibid.

125. "DCI's Worldwide Threat Briefing, The Worldwide Threat in 2003: Evolving Dangers in a Complex World," *Central Intelligence Agency*, 11 February 2003, n.p., on-line, Internet, 11 February 2003, available from http://www.cia.gov/cia/public_affairs/ speeches/dci_speech_02112003.html.

CHAPTER 6

The Worldwide Biocruise Threat

Michael E. Dickey

Introduction

Emerging from the Cold War as the sole remaining superpower, the United States faces regional stability challenges in several places around the world. The loss of a bi-polar superpower world has led to the emergence or resurgence of numerous regional conflicts, which threaten regional stability and potentially impact global economic stability. In order to meet those challenges the U.S. military has become more expeditionary in nature than ever before. As the world's predominant military power, both in nuclear and conventional terms, state and non-state actors have abundant reasons to avoid meeting the U.S. military in a "head to head" action in order to achieve their goals. The 1990-91 Gulf War effectively highlighted the conventional warfare capabilities of the U.S. military and the foolishness of attempting to prevail against it in open conventional combat. However, the result of that preeminence in U.S. conventional power has been the emergence among potential adversaries of a distinct asymmetric threat. This threat could have major adverse impacts on deployed U.S. military forces as well as on the U.S. homeland unless adequate steps are taken to counter this threat.

Not new to the world's conflict stage, the ongoing proliferation of both biological weapons and cruise missiles is alarming. While it appears that biological weapons have not been employed against an opposing armed force since World War II (North Korean assertions that the United States employed biological weapons during the Korean Conflict were proven in 1998 to be a fabrication,[1] and United States claims that the Soviet Union employed a "yellow rain" biological or chemical agent in Cambodia were never proven), they have been used in

145

numerous small-scale criminal acts. Recent improvements in biotechnology have made them both easier and cheaper to produce than any other weapons of mass destruction (WMD). Although prohibited from manufacture, stockpiling, or use by the Biological Weapons Convention (BWC), numerous nations are known to have biological weapons programs and others are strongly suspected of having them. Further, the relative ease of manufacture and weaponization of biological agents (compared to other WMD) makes them a threat-in-being as opposed to one that may emerge in the future.

Closely coupled to the proliferation of biological WMD is the proliferation of modern delivery systems, which could enable a state or non-state actor to attack the U.S., or deployed U.S. forces, with potentially devastating results. While the proliferation of ballistic missiles has drawn much public attention over the last several years, the ongoing proliferation of cruise missiles, unmanned aerial vehicles (UAV), and remotely piloted vehicles (RPV) presents an even greater threat. These delivery systems have enjoyed several successful engagements in the anti-ship mode, notably by Argentine forces against the British during the Falklands/Malvinas conflict, as well as their more recent land attack variant successes in the Gulf War. Their capabilities and ease of acquisition or manufacture make them an ideal attack platform for rogue states, emerging nations, or non-state actors. Additionally, UAVs and RPVs have several salient characteristics that make them a much better delivery system for biological agents than any other.

Although biological agents have not been employed militarily in recent times, there are indications that they may well be the next of the three WMD (nuclear, chemical and biological) to be used. The wide availability of cruise missiles, UAVs and RPVs, along with breakthroughs in navigational and propulsion systems make them an ideal delivery system. Additional factors in the nature of sub-state conflict and emerging non-state actors and transnational terrorists only enhance the possibility that these two systems will be mated and employed against the United States.

Biological Weapons

The use of biological warfare to prevail in combat is not new. Early recorded uses include the hurling of plague-infested bodies over the walls of the besieged city of Kaffa (modern-day Feodosia in the Crimea) to subvert its defenders in the year 1346 AD. The tactic not only worked, but is suspected of having contributed to or possibly begun the bubonic plague epidemic that swept through medieval Europe during the 'dark ages' of the 1300's, killing an estimated 25 million people.[2] Often confused or lumped together with chemical weapons, biologicals are, in fact, easier to acquire and employ and can be many times more deadly. Labeled the 'poor man's atomic bomb' because of their relatively low cost and ease of manufacture, a report by the Congressional Office of Technology Assessment (OTA) estimated the cost of a large biological arsenal at as low as $10 million. Compared to a conservative estimate of the cost to develop a single nuclear weapon at $200 million, the BW option can look very cost effective to rogue states, emerging states, or non-state actors.[3] The United States unilaterally abandoned its offensive BW program by Presidential Order in 1969, and was fully disarmed of BW weapons by 1972. This led to wide acceptance by the world community of the Biological and Toxin Weapons Convention (BWC), which commits signatories to "…never in any circumstances develop, produce, stockpile, or otherwise acquire or retain any biological weapons."[4] While some key officials have disagreed as to the actual ease of manufacture and weaponization, evidence exists that several nations, notably Iraq, Iran, Libya, North Korea, Israel, Egypt, Cuba, Taiwan, China, Romania, Bulgaria, Pakistan, India, South Africa, Syria, as well as Russia, are either known or suspected of having pursued BW development and stockpiling efforts.[5]

Proliferation

The relative ease with which biological weapons can be acquired has been identified by multiple sources. A 1993 OTA report states:

"Biological warfare agents are easier to produce than either nuclear materials or chemical warfare agents because they require a much smaller and cheaper industrial infrastructure

and because the necessary technology and know how is widely available."[6]

More recently, in the Spring 1998 issue of the *Journal of Counterterrorism & Security International*, a former FBI Chief of Counter-Terrorism stated:

"Biological and chemical weapons are certainly available to sophisticated terrorist organizations, especially those, like many of the Middle East groups, that operate with the support of governments. These weapons are both relatively easy to acquire and lethal in their application."[7]

Those desiring to acquire a biological agent can do so via several routes. They could acquire it from a pharmaceutical supply house, steal it from a laboratory or, if sufficiently trained, skilled and equipped, they could grow the agent themselves. While this might prove difficult for most, it is not beyond the capability of any nation or group with access to a pharmaceutical laboratory.

It has been confirmed that several rogue states, notably Iraq, Iran, and Syria, as well as known terrorist groups such as the German Red Army Faction (RAF) and Aum Shinrikyo cult in Japan, have possessed biological warfare capabilities. Several other terrorist organizations have expressed interest in acquiring biological agents as far back as a reported attempt by the radical underground Weathermen organization in 1970.[8]

Post-Gulf War United Nations inspectors from 1991 to 1995 were able to identify a biological weapon production capability in Iraq, but they were never able to definitively link it to a biological warfare program. Iraq repeatedly denied any BW capabilities, and then suddenly recanted. In 1995, following the defection of Lt. Gen. Hussein Kamel Majeed, the Iraqi General who ran their WMD program, Iraqi officials admitted that they had a biological research and development program, but claimed that all biological weapons had been destroyed.[9]

Subsequent investigation revealed enormous production of biological agents. Iraq had produced 19,000 liters of botulinum toxin, 8,500 liters of anthrax and 2,400 liters of aflatoxin. They had also produced quantities of other less well-known but still deadly agents, and had conducted field trials employing anthrax and botulinum toxin together in aerial bombs.[10]

Clearly, Iraq had a well developed, aggressive program, but one which could not be detected or verified through outside means. It took a defector or Iraq's fear of what the defector would reveal for the world to have definitive evidence.

While it appears that the German RAF group never attempted to employ the clostridium botulinum they had acquired,[11] and the Aum Shinrikyo organization had difficulty with the potency and delivery methods of their biological assets, it was likely a matter only of time before the latter group solved their challenges had they not been stopped in 1995. Aum Shinrikyo was later found to have possessed both anthrax and clostridium botulinum. More disturbing is Aum's attempt to operationalize an anthrax capability—a biological agent with a near-100% fatality rate.[12] Their 1995 chemical attack on the subways of Tokyo using the nerve agent Sarin followed nine separate attempts to employ aerosolized bacteriological agents between 1990 and 1995, including one attack using botulinum toxin against the city of Yokohama and the U.S. Navy's Yokosuka Naval Base. While the biological attacks were unsuccessful, the subway chemical attack killed 12 people and injured over 5,500 others.[13]

Advances in medical technology, which have benefited mankind in many ways, have also complicated the BW environment. The same technologies have made the production of BW agents much simpler. A nation with a "modest pharmaceutical expertise can develop BW for terrorist or military use."[14] The Federation of American Scientists has reported that:

> *"Any country having pharmaceutical, cosmetic, or advanced food storage industries will have stabilization facilities similar to those that could be used for biological weapons. The ability to disseminate the biological agent over a wide area would be limited to those countries having cruise missiles or advanced aircraft. Even the smallest country or a terrorist group, however, has the capability to deliver small quantities of BW agent to a specific target."[15]*

Numerous nations have taken up the mantle. Open-source estimates indicate that between 10 and 20 countries have, want or are considering a BW capability.[16] Disturbing among these figures is that of seven countries identified by the U.S. Department of State as supporters of terrorism, five

(Iran, Iraq, Libya, North Korea, and Syria) were reported by the U.S. Arms Control and Disarmament Agency to possess biological warfare programs. The remaining two (Sudan and Cuba) are reported by other sources, including British Intelligence, to have biological warfare programs.[17] A U.S. intelligence source indicates the belief that Osama bin Laden funded a research institute for chemical and biological warfare for the Sudanese government. This led to the United States' conventional cruise missile strikes against a pharmaceutical facility in Khartoum, Sudan in August of 1998.[18] The prospect of a non-state actor such as Al-Qaeda acquiring a biological weapon is distinctly unsettling.

Weaponization

The actual weaponization of biological agents is undoubtedly the most challenging phase in the development of a biological weapon. Developing or growing a biological agent is only the first step, and is the relatively easiest part. However, weaponizing it, producing sufficient quantities, achieving the correct 'formulation' of the agent, milling it to properly sized spores of agent, and microencapsulizing it in the correct storage or transport medium or mixture is extremely complicated. Although a biological agent is potent once developed or grown, unless it is properly weaponized, it will not be useful as a weapon. Weaponization is necessary if it is to be able to incapacitate or kill on a large scale.

Formulation

Once produced, the biological microorganisms or toxins must be milled to between 1 and 5 microns in size, then stabilized and packaged until dispersed. Failure to achieve the correct formulation will cause the agent to lose its toxicity in storage, to clog sprayer nozzles during dispersal, or to fail to be absorbed properly into the human body. Agent spores smaller than 1 micron will not be easily absorbed into the lungs of the human target. Conversely, if larger than 5 microns they become too heavy to achieve a good aerosol cloud and tend to fall to the ground before they can be inhaled.[19] If not properly stabilized the microorganisms will deteriorate quickly in the atmosphere. Each microorganism will deteriorate at a different rate, making some more valuable in weapons. Reportedly, Q-fever agent will decay at a rate of 10 percent per minute;

yellow fever at approximately 30 percent per minute. Disturbingly, the decay rate for the plague and tularemia agents is only 2 percent per minute, and anthrax decays at only 0.1 percent per minute.[20] Although obviously highly technical, and requiring special milling equipment and refrigeration systems, the procedures and equipment to perform these tasks are the same that are required for commercial pharmaceutical manufacturing, and are easily within the reach of most states.

Dispersal

Dispersal of biological weapons via aerosolization of the agent using spray devices is the delivery method of choice. While the agent could also be sprayed from a motor vehicle or boat, such sprayers may not achieve the optimal downwind results or cover as wide an area.[21] On the other hand, a crop duster-type dispenser on an RPV or cruise missile/UAV carrying BW munitions, gravity bombs or spray attachments might be other methods of dispersal. Delivery using explosives is probably the least efficient of all options, since heat and blast effects may "inactivate the biological agent."[22] Also, delivery via ballistic missile may be ineffective since the speed and heat generated by the reentry vehicle or warhead could render biological weapons harmless. Effective use of ballistic missiles with BW warheads is a technical challenge difficult to engineer. Interestingly, Iraq reportedly experimented in December 1990 and January 1991 on an unmanned aircraft, which could deliver biological agent via spray nozzles, and with a biological weapons spray tank developed from an aircraft "drop tank." Iraqi officials claimed to United Nations inspectors that the experiment did not work; however, UN inspectors found evidence the Iraqis had subsequently modified and stored three additional drop tanks.[23] Under favorable weather conditions, with a properly sized aerosol dispersal system, an aircraft, cruise missile or UAV could deliver BW weapons and cause mass casualties in densely populated areas. For example, it has been calculated that 100kg of anthrax sprayed over a 300 square kilometer area, theoretically could cause up to 3 million deaths if the targeted population density is 3,000 to 10,000 per square kilometer.[24] The effects of each biological agent will be different, however, depending upon its resiliency to the environment. An additional consideration in the type of agent employed is persistency. While most biological agents are sensitive to heat, oxidation and desiccation, once stabilized through the freeze-drying process for effective weaponization, their persistency is increased dramatically. Notably, live anthrax can be persistent on the ground for up to 40 years.[25] Obviously, weaponization is entirely feasible.

Given that anthrax or a botulinum toxin is openly available, and the physical infrastructure needed to weaponize involves available "dual-use" technology also employed for legitimate pharmaceutical production, it is understandable that the proliferation and weaponization of biological agents is difficult to detect or halt. All that remains is a reliable means of delivery and the will to employ this means of creating mass casualties.

Cruise Missiles

Much attention has been given in the international and national press about the scourge of the proliferation of short and intermediate range ballistic missiles (BMs). However, in spite of the apparent capabilities and threat posed by ballistic missile proliferation, the greater threat to the United States, and specifically to USAF assets, may be the proliferation of cruise missiles (CMs).

The technological complexity, cost, challenges in development and complexity of employment of ballistic missiles make them harder to acquire and use. Conversely, the relative ease of acquisition, operation and employment of simple and even some relatively advanced cruise missiles makes a much more attractive option. Cruise missiles are essentially small, lightweight, unmanned aircraft. They are much less expensive and easier to acquire than ballistic missiles, either by purchase from another country, through independent development, or by acquiring and modifying an existing UAV or RPV.[26] Cruise missiles are much easier to weaponize, test, and employ. The successes and worldwide publicity of U.S. cruise missiles during the Gulf War (admittedly at the 'high end' of the cruise missile family) illustrated their capabilities and utility. Future opposing forces could well look to a cruise missile capability as a better way to challenge U.S. interests rather than the more costly, harder-to-produce, more-difficult-to-operate ballistic missiles.

Argument Against Ballistic Missiles

As the proliferation of ballistic missiles continues, several factors make the acquisition of ballistic missiles a significant challenge to developing nations and sub-state actors. Ballistic missiles, while capable, are increasingly difficult to buy outright due to the Missile Technology Control Regime (MTCR) efforts to limit their proliferation. They require an enormous effort to develop autonomously due to controls placed on the transfer of critical technology by the MTCR. Further, BMs require extensive testing to perfect the propulsion and guidance systems and can be difficult to weaponize due to the challenges involved in developing an effective warhead.

MTCR Restrictions

Established in 1987, the MTCR is not a formal treaty, but is a voluntary organization of 29 member states that prohibits the sale and export of certain missiles and missile technologies to other states. While the provisions of the MTCR apply to both ballistic and cruise missiles, the main emphasis of the Regime has been to restrict ballistic missile proliferation. The effect of the MTCR has been the significant reduction in export of ballistic missiles and critical ballistic missile technology. However, proliferation of missile technology continues. Both Russia and China continue to contribute technical assistance to some countries, and the Democratic People's Republic of Korea (North Korea) continues to market its missiles and related technologies.[27] Additionally, Iran (also not a member of the MTCR) is reported to have sold or transferred an undetermined number of Scud-B IRBM systems to the Democratic Republic of the Congo.[28]

Table 1. Ballistic Missile Categories

Type Missile	Maximum Range
Short-Range Ballistic Missile (SRBM)	<1,000 km (621 mi)
Medium-Range Ballistic Missile (MRBM)	1,000 – 3,000 km (621 – 1,864 mi)
Intermediate-Range Ballistic Missile (IRBM)	3,000 – 5,500 km (1,864 – 3,418 mi)
Intercontinental Ballistic Missile (ICBM)	>5,500 km (3,418 mi)
Submarine-Launched Ballistic Missile (SLBM)	Any ballistic missile launched from a submarine regardless of maximum range

Source: Federation of American Scientists, "Ballistic and Cruise Missile Threat National Air Intelligence Center NAIC-1031-0985-98," National Air Intelligence Center, 1998, n.p.; on-line, Internet, 5 October 1999, available from http://www.fas.org/irp/threat/missile/nie99msl.htm.

Challenges to Developmental Programs

In spite of challenges involved in purchasing or creating a ballistic missile program, the prestige involved in owning such a "high-tech" weapon system seems to be a continual lure to developing nations. Several are pursuing their own indigenous developmental programs. By limiting the ability to buy systems outright, the MTCR has forced nations desiring ballistic missiles to create their own developmental programs. These programs have multiple impacts themselves. First, they are expensive and technologically complex. In addition to the costs involved in developing an adequate rocket motor and airframe and guidance system, the ballistic missile is a challenge to weaponize. Developmental programs themselves tend to telegraph a nation's intent to those other nations who may be observing. Static (ground) test firing of a rocket motor to ensure its ability and reliability can be monitored by U.S. national technical intelligence means.[29] Satellites orbiting overhead can, for example, detect and measure the 'thermal bloom' or heat signature of the rocket test or of a test flight. Additional technical systems can intercept and monitor telemetry data from the test rocket. The effect of testing is to telegraph a nation's ballistic missile development intentions, giving the international community the warning and time to either persuade the developing country to curtail development or prepare to meet the challenge militarily.

Developing the reentry vehicle and warhead alone has been estimated by some experts as one of the major challenges to emerging ballistic missile programs, particularly when dealing with more exotic weaponization such as chemical or biological warheads. The payload or warhead must be stressed to survive the high 'G,' or force of gravity loading on launch, as well as survive the extremely high speeds and resultant heat caused by air friction during the warhead's flight. Additionally, the timing of detonation or agent release in order to achieve efficient agent dispersal is critical to a successful program.

Finally, once a nation develops or otherwise acquires a ballistic missile capability, the system may be vulnerable. Requiring fixed launch sites, or large trucks for mobility, the ballistic missiles of a nation will be targeted by an opponent's aircraft and special operations forces throughout a period of conflict. The Coalition Forces' 'Scud hunt' during the 1990-91 Gulf War is an example of such 'seek and destroy' operations which would increase the vulnerability of ballistic missile assets. On launch, a ballistic missile is visible to national technical intelligence, its flight can be predicted and warning can be provided to its intended target area, making it less effective through loss of surprise. Finally, the direction the ballistic missiles will come from is somewhat predictable, and as more effective tactical ballistic missile defensive systems, such as the Patriot PAC-3, have come on line the ballistic missile is increasingly vulnerable to in-flight interception.[30]

The Case for Cruise Missiles

Cruise missiles are defined as "an unmanned self-propelled guided vehicle that sustains flight through aerodynamic lift for most of its flight path and whose primary mission is to place an ordnance or special payload on a target." While most often associated with the jet-powered cruise weapons of Desert Storm fame, this definition also includes unmanned air vehicles (UAVs) and remotely piloted helicopters or aircraft (RPVs).[31]

Cruise missiles are generally categorized into three types: strategic cruise, anti-ship cruise and tactical land attack missiles based upon range capabilities.

Table 2. Cruise Missiles Categories

Mission	TYPE MISSILE	RANGE
Land Attack	Strategic Cruise	2,000-3,000km
Land Attack	Tactical Land Attack Missile (TLAM)	180-600km
Anti-Ship	Anti-Ship Cruise Missile (ASCM)	50-500km

Source: Tara Kartha, "The Rationale of Cruise Missiles-I," Institute for Defence Studies and Analyses, New Delhi, India, 1998, n.p.; on-line, Internet, 29 September 1999, available from http://www.idsa-india.org/an-aug8-9.html.

The National Air Intelligence Center (NAIC) refers specifically to two "types" of cruise missiles: anti-ship cruise and land attack, using their intended mission instead of their range or capabilities. For the purpose of this chapter we will acknowledge the "mission" categorization, with the land attack divided into strategic (range up to 3,000km) and tactical (maximum range of 180-600km). Strategic land attack missiles, in the Tomahawk (U.S.) class, are expensive and complicated for the developing world, employing larger, more complicated engines as well as more

155

complex guidance systems such as the U.S. terrain contour matching or TERCOM system. Anti-ship cruise missiles in general are shorter-range and normally carry a lighter payload than the land attack missiles. There is general agreement that the tactical land attack cruise missiles are the 'ones to watch out for' in the area of future proliferation. (Note: A TLAM could easily be used to strike a strategic target and a strategic land attack could be targeted against a tactical objective, hence the designators are purely reflective of their relative range capabilities.) While the TLAM is the apparent focus of research and development for both producers and aspirants alike, conversion and upgrade of anti-ship cruise missiles or UAV/RPV is entirely feasible.[32] The TLAM, if not purchased from an exporting country, may be an indigenous development item (difficult in the near term – 5-10 years), a modified anti-ship missile, or it may be a modified UAV or RPV. The NAIC, in a 1998 assessment reported that:

> "The majority of new LACMs will be very accurate, conventionally armed, and available for export. The high accuracy of many LACMs will allow them to inflict serious damage on important targets, even when the missiles are armed only with conventional warheads. U.S. defense systems could be severely stressed by low-flying stealthy cruise missiles that can simultaneously attack a target from several directions."[33]

There are reportedly some 130 cruise missile types in the world, spread among 75 different nations. Of those 75 nations possessing cruise missiles 19 were 'producers' and of those 19 only six (India, Japan, Taiwan, South Africa, Iran, and Syria) were non-exporters.[34] Lieutenant General Jay M. Garner, former commander of the U.S. Army Space and Strategic Defense Command, summed up the cruise missile proliferation problem when he stated:

> Interestingly enough, cruise missiles are cheaper to buy or produce than ballistic missiles. Improving cruise missiles' accuracy (e.g. by adding precision navigation devices) is not nearly as expensive or technologically challenging as improving ballistic missile accuracy.

> Visit any international air show to see how a number of nations aggressively market cruise missiles and UAVs. We are

convinced that our soldiers will face this very real threat in the near future.[35]

Purchase

While cruise missiles capable of carrying 500kg payloads to ranges of 300km or more are subject to MTCR restrictions, several nations are producing cruise missiles which fall just below the parameters and others have modified missiles to produce a 'less capable' variant of a proscribed missile.[36] In fact, the United States is one of the world's largest proliferators of cruise missiles, having sold the Harpoon ASCM to some 23 nations. The Harpoon has already been reverse-engineered by Taiwan and is reportedly for sale as the Hsiung Feng-2 or HF-2. Significantly, the Harpoon has a land-attack variant known as the SLAM, in service with the U.S. Navy.[37]

In an effort to circumvent MTCR restrictions, presumably to generate hard currency income, Russia, at the 1992 Moscow Air Show, offered a modified, shorter range version of their 3,000km-range AS-15 cruise missile for sale, advertising it as a 410kg payload with just over 500km range. Disturbingly, the missile reportedly was equipped with the Russian equivalent of the terrain contour matching (TERCOM) guidance system supplemented by the Russian Global Navigation Satellite System (GLONASS), an equivalent to the U.S. global positioning system (GPS).[38] While technically meeting the restrictions of the MTCR, the fact is that 'upgrading' a proven missile airframe to extend its range and payload is not considered an insurmountable or even major technical challenge. Virtually any country with an active aircraft production or major aircraft maintenance capability could accomplish the modifications.

The French also are marketing a disturbing product in the form of their *Apache* stealth cruise missile.[39] The *Apache* is being developed in several variants, some for export and some for domestic-only use. Displayed at the Paris Air Show in June 1993 and in Singapore in February 1994, the export variant *Apache* is reported to have terrain following millimeter wave radar for guidance, with a GPS option, and capable of a payload of 400-500kg and range of 150km.[40] The prospect of marketing the advanced stealth and guidance technology is of concern due to the high probability of follow-on reverse-engineering and further proliferation.

Figure 1. French *Apache – Storm Shadow variant*

Indigenous Development or Conversion

Alternatively, any nation with at least a fledgling aircraft manufacturing or enhanced maintenance capability can either build from scratch, or modify an existing UAV or RPV. In the past, availability of effective guidance systems and engines has stymied indigenous development of cruise missiles. However, with the current level of development and proliferation of the U.S. Global Positioning System and the Russian GLONASS equivalent, the navigation challenge is solvable. A significant impediment was the small, lightweight jet engine requirement, but this can be offset by acquiring the engine through normal aircraft manufacturing channels. Russia, China, France, and the U.K. all produce and market suitable turbojet engines, and the U.S. has sold turbofan engines to China for use in jet trainer aircraft.[41] Alternatively, an engine could be acquired by stripping it from an anti-ship missile or modifying an anti-ship missile for a land attack mission. Iraq appears, for example, to have used the Italian turbojet-powered *Mirach 600* RPV to develop its 450km-range *Ababil* land attack cruise missile, which reportedly possesses a 250kg payload capability.[42] The *Mirach 100,* also turbojet-powered, has been exported to Iraq, Libya, and Argentina, and is capable of transporting 70kg up to 900km. The United States has also contributed to the proliferation challenge, having sold the Teledyne Ryan *Scarab* RPV to Egypt. The *Scarab* boasts a turbojet capability of transporting a 100kg payload over 2500km.[43] Should this system, which includes an inertial navigation system and GPS capability, be further proliferated the potential adverse impact could be tremendous.

Critical capabilities that cruise missiles possess are that they are accurate, survivable, difficult to detect, and relatively inexpensive. The emergence of low-cost GPS systems in the 1980's has greatly improved cruise missile accuracy. With widely available satellite imagery and computer graphics, terrain mapping, previously reserved for 'high end' U.S. and Russian cruise missiles, is now available to the Third World. Cruise missiles can be launched from aircraft, from shipboard or from land with minimal ancillary equipment. Capable of being stored or transported in metal 'Sea-Land' type containers to both protect them from the elements and reduce their visibility, cruise missiles are highly mobile and thus very survivable. With their ability to fly a pre-determined circuitous route to target they are less predictable, can attack from any direction (unlike ballistic missiles) and their small size and low radar cross section make them a challenge to air defenses. Finally, their relatively low cost not only makes them affordable to an emerging nation, but for a given amount, that nation may be able to buy many more cruise than ballistic systems. The advantage is that even if detected by an air defense system they may be able to attack in numbers and so saturate defenses that at least some of them get through.[44]

The inherently stable, aircraft-like performance envelope of the cruise missile, with its relatively low g-loads (force of gravity), and low operating speeds (especially when compared to an SRBM or IRBM warhead) makes it an easier and cheaper delivery system for chemical and biological weapons.[45]

Employment Considerations

Biological weapons and cruise missiles have been around for several years now, therefore, why haven't they been employed together yet? What is constraining states that have this dual capability? And how long will these constraints last? How and when might these weapons be employed against U.S. military personnel, the U.S. homeland, and military expeditionary forces?

Constraints

Since Iraq possessed BW during the 1990-91 Gulf War, why did they not employ them? While the Coalition Forces feared and prepared for a chemical or biological attack by Saddam Hussein, none ever materialized. The Aum Shinrikyo cult obviously had no qualms about employing their BW capability—they failed only because of technical shortfalls. Given Iraq's significant stockpiles of biological weapons at the time, such weapons could have had a major impact on the course of the Gulf War, yet they were withheld.

Just prior to the Gulf War Saddam Hussein received two very similar and very stern warnings about the implications of employing BW should the pending crisis result in armed conflict. Secretary of Defense Dick Cheney, during a 23 December 1990 news conference, cautioned publicly that should Iraq employ weapons of mass destruction the "U.S. response would be absolutely overwhelming and it would be devastating." Not three weeks later, President George Bush reinforced Cheney's statement in a letter to Hussein, warning that the American people would "...demand the strongest possible response" and warning that Iraq would pay a "terrible price" if chemical or biological weapons were employed.[46] Presumably, this implied threat of a nuclear retaliation in exchange for Iraq's use of chemical or biological weapons kept Saddam Hussein from ordering their use in 1991. What happened in Operation Iraqi Freedom in 2003 is still an open question.

Jeffrey D. Simon, in a 1989 RAND report on "Terrorists and the Potential Use of Biological Weapons, A Discussion of Possibilities" put forward several plausible reasons which may help explain why no state actor has employed biological weapons. Mr. Simon submits that terrorists have had several reasons to defer using biological weapons:

- To avoid a backlash or loss of support from their supporters
- To avoid an overwhelming or devastating response from the target of the attack
- To avoid the personal risk inherent in biological weapons
- Due to reluctance to work with "unfamiliar" weapons
- Due to a belief that conventional attacks are meeting their needs.[47]

While each of these is a valid reason, he goes on to state in his paper that these constraints may be weakening as religion-based terrorism grows and as terrorist groups acquire support elements which may be able to justify to themselves the magnitude of the horror of biological warfare. He further warns that once there is a first-use, others will follow (the "copycat" phenomenon).[48]   Mr. Simon's report written presents an ominous prediction for the future, having had a terrorist "first-use" in 1995. With the current state of proliferation of biological weapons and the publicity surrounding Aum Shinrikyo's difficulties with their delivery systems, the inhibitions against using biological weapons may indeed be down. There are several scenarios where terrorist groups might use BW weapons. One is if a group felt that conventional attacks were not getting their message across. If they felt their supporters would accept the magnitude of the attack (or decided that the opinion of their supporters didn't matter). Also, they might act if they believed they could safely execute a biological attack and do so anonymously, so as to avoid retaliation. Might a group or state attempt a biological attack? Possibly only two things are deterring governments and non-state actors: the lack of an effective delivery system and plausible deniability.

Effective delivery systems are available now. We have already examined the huge proliferation of cruise missiles and their related UAV and RPV cousins that could be easily modified to deliver BW. Their low signature means that a nation or sub-state actor could be carrying out experimentation and proof of concept testing in some remote region of the world today and we might have no way of knowing, making clandestine attacks possible, coupled with plausible deniability.

Presuming a nation wanted to inflict major damage upon the United States or U.S. forces and escape a retaliatory attack, they would need to find a way to deliver the attack without leaving 'proof-positive' evidence of from whence it came. For while the threat has been made and is ever-present, it is very doubtful the United States could or would execute a retaliatory nuclear strike without 'smoking gun' evidence to present to the rest of the world community. However, some type of advanced retaliatory strike would no doubt be called for. The use of a nuclear weapon with its resultant collateral damage to infrastructure and noncombatants, even in response to a biological WMD strike against the United States or U.S. forces would bring a huge outcry of world opinion against the United States. In order to maintain influence in the community of nations, the United States would likely feel inhibited in the use of nuclear weapons, but undoubtedly a hue and cry would come from the American people, demanding justice against so heinous a sneak attack. The full conventional weight of the U.S. Armed Forces would no doubt be brought to bear. So the question is how to use BW weapons without being blamed for it!

Several terrorist groups have the funding, worldwide contacts and anti-American zealotry to take on the task. The Osama bin Laden organization has a following that appears to support all methods of attack against the United States. With a history of U.S. cruise missile attacks being used against his organization, the opportunity to reply in kind could seem very attractive.

Possible Employment Scenarios

Two possible employment scenarios present themselves: one against the United States homeland and the other against USAF expeditionary forces. The first objective would be for a hostile nation to locate a trans-national terrorist group, such as Osama bin Laden's organization, willing to carry out the attack. With a state sponsor to provide the delivery system (cruise missile, UAV/RPV), the biological weapon(s) and necessary training, all that would be needed would be the logistics support and training in use of the system.

One employment scenario could be to acquire three to four merchant freighters to transport containerized cruise missiles to waters off the U.S.

coastline. Freighters are often hijacked by pirates in the South China Sea and adjacent waters, and not located for months, if then. The ships with their containerized cargo of cruise missiles in the short range category—150 to 300km—could be sailed to within 50km or closer to the U.S. coastline, just off shore from major cities or desired military locations, such as Norfolk, VA. Released in the early evening and programmed to disperse their cargo while the sea breeze is blowing towards shore and the crowds are still out, with a persistent form of anthrax or other bio-toxin, these missiles could cause a major catastrophe. If flown at low-level to the target areas, and programmed to dispense the agent, then to turn back to sea, the missiles could conceivably disperse their agent without notice and cause a biohazard with no apparent explanation of its origin.

A second scenario would be a similar attack, but against an airfield and surrounding town or city designated to receive a deploying Air Expeditionary Force (AEF) in the event of an increase in regional tensions. Since the USAF AEFs routinely deploy to the same locations in Southwest Asia due to equipment prepositioning and good relations with host nations, anticipating which airfields to attack should not be difficult. By attacking the installation before tensions increase and the USAF AEF responds, the biological weapon would have time to incubate and breakout. While this could trigger supporter backlash because of collateral Islamic civilian casualties, an organization such as bin Laden's might feel the public relations storm worth weathering if the attack sufficiently halted United States deployment or degraded their ability to launch combat aircraft. If executed carefully, as in the continental United States attack scenario, identifying the responsible organization or nation could prove extremely difficult, thus avoiding both public and United States backlash. The idea of deploying troops from the United States into an airfield known to be contaminated with biological weapons could cause the U.S. National Command Authority to reconsider the value of the mission. At the very least, such an attack would massively complicate and slow the U.S. response.

The worrisome aspect of these scenarios is that biological agents and weapons are available now. The cruise missile/UAV/RPV technologies are available now. The hostile feelings and intent towards the United States and U.S. forces are there now. The only missing element is an organization or state willing to fuse and employ them.

Conclusions

It is a doctrine of war not to assume the enemy will not come, but rather to rely on one's readiness to meet him; not to presume that he will not attack, but rather to make one's self invincible.

--Sun Tzu

The information on cruise missile proliferation and capabilities is overwhelming. The Internet itself is almost a cookbook on what kind of missile to go shopping for, and what or whom one would need in their program to ensure it works. Likewise, the Internet is replete with information on the proliferation of biological weapons, their ease of manufacture and weaponization, and their enormous ability to take lives if surprise can be achieved.

Given that some terrorists will seek a "bigger bang" than the last event perpetrated, in order to maintain shock effect and adequate publicity, a cruise/biological attack may well be the next step up the ladder of escalation.

In light of all this however, several key people or agencies continue to acknowledge the threat is out there, but they "feel" it is not "probable." What is certain is that:

- Acquisition of cruise missiles is spreading, making standoff CM attack feasible for more nations and substate actors.
- Biological weapons are relatively inexpensive WMD and are within the technical capability of Third World States and possibly by sophisticated and well-funded sub-state groups.
- The potential for an attack employing a land attack cruise missile armed with biological weapons increases each year.

What has not been examined and discussed in this chapter, i.e., the next logical step, is to review current and planned capabilities to stop an inbound cruise missile at a safe distance. And failing that, it will be imperative to review preparedness to survive an attack on the air base—or the nation—by biological weapons.

If the USAF is to continue to project power forward it will need safe and secure operating locations, both abroad and in CONUS. The threats posed by cruise missiles armed with biological weapons must first be acknowledged as a present day threat. They are not a "sometime in the future" threat but are a current "clear and present danger." The threat posed by CMs carrying biological weapons needs to be dissected and analyzed country by country and group by group. Adequate defenses and/or recovery methods must be developed and promulgated. To do otherwise would be to expose the United States, its forces, and its allies to a terrible new threat without an adequate response.

Table 3. Cruise Missile Proliferation/Possession

The table below depicts the wide possession of cruise missiles among selected nations. It is not intended to be an all-inclusive list, but illustrates the wide variety of cruise missiles available from various nations, as well as domestic development programs.

Country/ System	Origin country	Type system	Launch method	Max range (km)	Payload (kg)	Status
ARGENTINA						
Exocet MM-38	France	AS	Gnd/ship	42	165	In service
Exocet AM-39	France	AS	Air	50	165	In service
Exocet SM-39	France	AS	Submarine	50	165	In service
Exocet MM-40	France	AS	Gnd/ship	70	165	In service
MQ-2 Figua	Domestic	Lnd Atk	Air/gnd	900	70	Development
CHINA						
SY-1/HY-1	Dom	AS	Gnd/ship	50	513	In service
HY-2 Silkworm	Dom	AS	Gnd/Ship	95	513	In service
HY-3/C-301	Dom	AS	Gnd/Ship	100	500	Development
HY-4/C-201	Dom	AS	A/G/S	150	500	In service
FL-1	Dom	AS	Gnd/ship	40	513	In service
FL-2/SY-2	Dom	AS	A/G/S	50	365	In service
C-101	Dom	AS	A/G/S	50	400	In service
C-601	Dom	AS	Air	95	500	In service
YJ-1/C-801	Dom	AS	A/G/S	40	165	In service
YJ-2/C-802	Dom	AS	A/G/S	95	165	In service
C-802 (modified)	Dom	AS/Lnd Atk	A/G/S	180	Unknown	Development

INDIA						
Exocet AM-39	France	AS	Air	50	165	In service
SS-N-2c Styx	Russia	AS	Air	85	513	In service
SS-N-2d Styx	Russia	AS	Air	100	513	In service
SS-N-7 Starbright	Russia	AS	Submarine	65	500	In service
SS-N-22 KORAL	Dom/ Russia	AS	Ship/ Submarine	110	500	Development
SEA EAGLE	United Kingdom	AS	Air/Ship	110	230	In service
LAKSHYA	Dom	Lnd Atk	Ground	500	200	In service
IRAN						
AS-11 KILTER	Russia	AS/Lnd Atk	Air	50	130	In service
AS-9 KYLE	Russia	AS/Lnd Atk	Air	90	200	In service
YJ-2/C-802	China	AS	A/G/S	95	165	In service
HY-2 SILKWORM	China	AS	Gnd/ship	95	513	In service
SS-N-22 SUNBURN	Ukraine	AS	Gnd/ship	110	500	In service
RGM-84A HARPOON	USA	AS	Ship	120	220	In service
HY-4/C201	China	AS	A/G/S	150	500	In service
SILKWORM (modified)	Dom/North Korea	AS	Gnd/Ship	450	500	Development
IRAQ						
YJ-1/C-801	China	AS	A/G/S	40	165	In service
AS-11 KILTER	Russia	Lnd Atk/AS	Air	50	130	In service
FAW 70	Domestic	AS	Gnd/Ship	70	500	In service
HY-2 SILKWORM	China	AS	Gnd/Ship	95	513	In service
C-601 (Nisan 28)	China	AS	Air	95	500	In service
FAW 150	Domestic	AS	Gnd/Ship	150	500	In service
FAW 200	Domestic	AS	Gnd/Ship	200	500	In service
AS-4 KITCHEN	Russia	Lnd Atk/AS	Air	400	1,000	In service
AS-5 KELT	Russia	Lnd Atk/AS	Air	400	1,000	In service
ABABIL	Domestic	Lnd Atk	Air	500	250	Development
ISRAEL						
GABRIEL II	Domestic	AS	Ship	36	100	In service
GABRIEL III	Domestic	AS	Air/Ship	36	150	In service
POPEYE	Domestic	Lnd Atk	Air	100	395	In service

AGM-84A HARPOON	USA	AS	Air	120	220	In service
RGM-84A HARPOON	USA	AS	Ship	120	220	In service
UGM-84A HARPOON	USA	AS	Submarine	120	220	In service
GABRIEL IV	Domestic	AS	Air/Ship	200	240	In service
DELILAH	Domestic	Drone	Air/Ground	400	54	In service
DELILAH (modified)	Domestic	Lnd Atk	Air/Ground	400	450	Development
JAPAN						
ASM-1	Domestic	AS	Air	50	150	In service
ASM-2	Domestic	AS	Air	150	150	Development
AGM-84A HARPOON	USA	AS	Air	120	220	In service
RGM-84A HARPOON	USA	AS	Ship	120	220	In service
UGM-84A HARPOON	USA	AS	Submarine	120	220	In service
SSM-1	Domestic	AS	Gnd/Ship/ Submarine	150	250	In service
NORTH KOREA						
S-N-2a STYX	Domestic	AS	Ship	43	513	In service
HY-1/SY-2 SILKWORM	Domestic	AS	Gnd/Ship	95	513	In service
SILKWORM (modified	Domestic	AS	Gnd/Ship	160+	Unknown	Development
SOUTH AFRICA						
SKORPIOEN	Domestic	AS	Ship	36	100	In service
EXOCET AM-39	France	AS	Air	50	165	In service
SKORPIOEN II	Domestic	AS	Ship	Unknown	Unknown	Development
SKUA	Domestic	Lnd Atk	Gnd/Ship	800	100	Development
TAIWAN						
HSUING-FENG1	Domestic	AS	Air	36	100	In service
HSUING-FENG 2	Domestic	Lnd Atk/AS	Air	170	75	In service
HSUING-FENG 3	Domestic	Lnd Atk/AS	Air/Ship	300	Unknown	Development

Source: Centre for Defense and International Security Studies (CDISS), "Capabilities & Suppliers," January 2000, n.p.; on-line, Internet, 2 January 2000, available from http://www.cdiss.org/tabanaly.htm

Notes

1. Ed Regis, *The Biology of Doom; The History of America's Secret Germ Warfare Project,* (New York, NY; Henry Holt and Company, 1999), 143, 144, 228.

2. Terry N. Meyer, Lt Col, "The Biological Weapon: A Poor Nation's Weapon of Mass Destruction," *Battlefield of the Future, 21st Century Warfare Issues,* edited by Barry R. Schneider and Lawrence E. Grinter, (Maxwell AFB, AL: Air University Press, Revised Edition No. 3, September 1998), 207.

3. Robert P. Kadlec, Lt Col, "Biological Weapons for Waging Economic Warfare," *Battlefield of the Future, 21st Century Warfare Issues*, edited by Barry R. Schneider and Lawrence E. Grinter, (Maxwell AFB, AL: Air University Press, Revised Edition No. 3, September 1998), 255.

4. Terry N. Meyer, Lt Col, Op. Cit., 208.

5. Ibid., 215.

6. U.S. Congress, Office of Technology Assessment (OTA), *Proliferation of Weapons of Mass Destruction: Assessing the Risks* (Washington, D.C.: GPO, 1993), 38.

7. W. Seth Carus. *Bioterrorism and Biocrimes, The Illicit Use of Biological Agents in the 20th Century,* (Washington, D.C.: Center for Counterproliferation Research, National Defense University, August 1998 [March 1999 Revision]), 30.

8. Ibid., 157, 161-168.

9. Schneider, Barry R., *Future War and Counterproliferation, U.S. Military Responses to NBC Proliferation Threats,* (Westport, Connecticut: Praeger Publishers, 1999), 14-15.

10. Ibid.

11. W. Seth Carus, *Bioterrorism and Biocrimes, The Illicit Use of Biological Agents in the 20th Century,* Op. Cit., 157.

12. U.S. Army Medical Research Institute of Infectious Diseases, *Medical Management of Biological Casualties Handbook, Third Edition,* (Fort Detrick, Frederick, Maryland, July 1998), 17.

13. W. Seth Carus, *Bioterrorism and Biocrimes, The Illicit Use of Biological Agents in the 20th Century,* Op. Cit., 56.

14. Robert P. Kadlec, Lt Col., Op. Cit., 227.

15. Federation of American Scientists (FAS), "Biological Weapons Delivery," September 1999, n.p.; on-line, Internet, 29 September 1999, available from http://www.fas.org/ nuke/intro/cm/index.html.

16. Terry N. Meyer, Lt Col, Op. Cit., 215.

17. W. Seth Carus, *Bioterrorism and Biocrimes, The Illicit Use of Biological Agents in the 20th Century* Op. Cit., 31-33.

18. Ibid., 163-164.

19. Raymond Zilinskas, "Assessing the Threat of Bioterrorism: Congressional Testimony by Raymond Zilinskas," Monterey Institute of International Studies, October 1999.

20. W. Seth Carus, "Biological Weapons: The Threat Posed by Terrorists," testimony at the Joint Hearing Before the Senate Select Committee on Intelligence and the Senate Judiciary Subcommittee on Technology, Terrorism and Government Information, 4 March 1998, n.p., on-line, Internet, 3 February 2000, available from http://www.senate.gov/~judiciary/wlterm4.htm.

21. U.S. Congress, Office of Technology Assessment, *Proliferation of Weapons of Mass Destruction: Assessing the Risks,* Op. Cit., 40.

22. FAS, "Biological Weapons Delivery," Op. Cit.

23. Kalpana Chittaranjan, "Iraq's BW Programme: UNSCOM Stays On," Institute for Defence Studies and Analyses, New Delhi, India, 1998, n.p.; on-line, Internet, 6 February 2000, available from http://www.idsa-india.org/an-jul8-9.html.

24. U.S. Congress, Office of Technology Assessment, *Proliferation of Weapons of Mass Destruction: Assessing the Risks*, Op. Cit., 54.

25. U.S. Army Medical Research Institute of Infectious Diseases, *Medical Management of Biological Casualties Handbook, Third Edition,* (Fort Detrick, Frederick, Maryland, July 1998), Appendix H.

26. Tara Kartha, "The Rationale of Cruise Missiles-I," Institute for Defence Studies and Analyses, New Delhi, India, 1998, n.p.; on-line, Internet, 29 September 1999, available from http://www.idsa-india.org/an-aug8-9.html.

27. Bob Walpole, "Foreign Missile Developments and the Ballistic Missile Threat to the United States through 2015," *National Intelligence Council Paper,* September 1999, n.p.; on-line, Internet, 1 December 1999, available from http://www.fas.org/irp/threat/missile/nie99msl.htm.

28. Bill Gertz, "Iran Sold Scud Missiles to Congolese," *The Washington Times,* November 1999.

29. K. Scott McMahon and Dennis M. Gormley, *Controlling the Spread of Land-Attack Cruise Missiles,* The AISC Papers, No. 7, (Marina del Rey, California: American Institute for Strategic Studies, January 1995), 59.

30. Ibid., 17.

31. Federation of American Scientists, "Cruise Missiles," September 1999, n.p.; on-line, Internet, 29 September 1999, available from http: //www. fas.org/ nuke/ intro/ cm/ index.html.

32. Tara Kartha, Op. Cit.

33. Federation of American Scientists, "Ballistic and Cruise Missile Threat National Air Intelligence Center NAIC-1031-0985-98," National Air Intelligence Center, 1998, n.p.; on-line, Internet, 5 October 1999. Available from http://www.fas.org/irp/threat/ missile/nie99msl.htm.

34. Tara Kartha, Op. Cit.

35. Robin Ranger, et al. "Cruise Missiles: New Threats, New Thinking," *Comparative Strategy*, Vol 14, 1995, 255-275.

36. Dennis M. Gormley, "Hedging Against the Cruise-Missile Threat," Carnegie Endowment for International Peace, Non-Proliferation, n.p. On-line Internet, 5 October 1999. Available from http://www.ceip.org/programs/npp/gormley%20survival.htm.

37. K. Scott McMahon and Dennis M. Gormley, Op.Cit., 12-13.

38. Dennis M. Gormley, Op. Cit.

39. K. Scott McMahon and Dennis M. Gormley, Op. Cit., 14.

40. K. Scott McMahon and Dennis M. Gormley, Op. Cit., 51.

41. Ibid., 18, 25.

42. Dennis M. Gormley, Op. Cit.

43. K. Scott McMahon and Dennis M. Gormley, Op. Cit., 48.

44. Ibid., 15-17.

45. U.S. Congress, Office of Technology Assessment (OTA), *Technologies Underlying Weapons of Mass Destruction*, (Washington, D.C.: GPO, 1993), 244.

46. Terry N. Meyer, Lt Col, Op. Cit., 214.

47. Jeffery D. Simon, *Terrorists and the Potential Use of Biological Weapons,* A RAND Report (Santa Monica, CA:The RAND Corporation, December 1989), 11.

48. Ibid., 20.

CHAPTER 7

Combat Effectiveness In MOPP 4:
Lessons from the U.S. Army CANE Exercises

Barry R. Schneider

From the early 1980s until the early 1990s, the U.S. Army ran a series of exercises to gauge the combat effectiveness of military forces engaged in combat when forced to wear protective gear to prevent casualties from chemical and nuclear attacks. These exercises were called CANE or Combined Arms in a Nuclear/Chemical Environment.

Those who have worn the cumbersome Mission Oriented Protective Posture (MOPP) 4 overgarments, gas masks, gloves and heavy boots that provide a measure of protection against different chemical and biological agents, know first hand that wearing such gear significantly degrades the efficiency and effectiveness of military personnel in combat operations. The longer our military is forced to wear such protective equipment, the worse the problem of conventional combat effectiveness becomes. Protection against one threat -- chemical weapons -- raises other risks to our forces and can hinder the accomplishment of their mission against opponents also waging conventional warfare.

The psychological and physical effects of prolonged wear of nuclear, biological, and chemical (NBC) protective gear can severely degrade command and control, communications, mobility, rates of fire, sortie rates, and defensive measures when compared to the unit's baseline performance in these areas when not forced into the protective posture against chemical and biological warfare (CBW) threats. One of the conclusions of virtually every CANE exercise for a decade is that combat effectiveness at all unit levels, large and small, is adversely affected and the effect is likely to be dangerously significant the longer MOPP gear is worn, the more extreme the temperatures, the more physically demanding the jobs to be performed, and the more complex the task at hand.

Since the CANE exercises, and the results of the Air Force equivalent exercise in SALTY DEMO, the U.S. armed services have made some equipment upgrades to reduce the weight and heat problems of the battle dress overgarments (BDOs).

Today, the Joint Service Light Weight Integrated Suit Technology (JS-LIST) suit has replaced the older heavier, bulkier, warmer protective garments. JS-LIST suits provide 45 days of wear versus 22 days for the BDOs. In addition, they can be washed up to six times without losing protective qualities. Thus, fewer suits are needed, provided soap and water are at hand in combat zones. New better fitting protective boots and improved masks are also coming on line. Nevertheless, most of the same problems remain for the fighter clothed in still-somewhat restrictive MOPP 3/4 gear, and combat efficiency will suffer compared to that of fighters not so encumbered.

The Exercises

The Combined Arms in a Nuclear/Chemical Environment (CANE) exercises were two-sided, force-on-force, real-time casualty assessment war games conducted with four types of units. CANE I tested how well U.S. Army mechanized infantry squadrons and platoons fare in performing their missions in extended operations where simulated nuclear and chemical weapons were employed. This set of exercises was completed by May 1983. CANE IIA tested the combat effectiveness of tank company teams in that same stressful environment and was completed by April 1985. CANE IIB tested an Army heavy armor battalion in the same mode and these exercises were completed by March 1988. Finally, the Army ran similar tests with close combat light infantry rifle companies and platoons, these exercises coming to an end in May 1991. Another such series was completed and run from March to May 1992.[1] Each engagement was performed on two tracks. First, Army units performed in normal battle array. Then, the exercise was repeated at another time in full MOPP 4 gear. Each engagement was performed at approximately the same time and on the same terrain in each of the exercises.

MOPP 4 Command and Control Implications

As one U.S. Army report concludes "command and control suffers significantly in the nuclear chemical environment due to exhaustion of leaders, leadership behavioral changes and increased periods when no one is in charge."[2] Prolonged wearing of masks and full overgarments can lead to stress, fatigue, disorientation, confusion, frustration, and irritability. Dehydration causes problems and in these exercises 17 percent of the soldiers involved were clinically dehydrated. The wearing of masks led to problems of recognizing who the leader was and whether the leader was still functioning. Even with special markings, there was delayed recognition of leaders on the simulated battlefields.

When U.S. Army platoon leaders were deemed killed in action during the exercises, the next senior man assumed command in only 23 percent of the cases when in full MOPP gear as compared to 100 percent in normal gear. As one report summarizes, "it takes a unit four times as long to realize they are leaderless when the leader is incapacitated."[3] Wearing cumbersome MOPP gear also makes the leaders less agile and more vulnerable to conventional fire. In CANE II exercises it was reported that "leaders are more active, sleep less, delegate less, and do not pace themselves. They get lost more easily, and find it difficult to reorient themselves." Disorientation, confusion, and frustration are common. Leaders become irritable, impatient with subordinates, and effectiveness declines rapidly after six hours in MOPP 4. Leaders especially can become seriously dehydrated, but do not know it. Dehydration causes further irritation and paranoia, compounding leadership dehydration. During these periods, battle casualties among leaders doubles.[4] In the Combined Arms in a Nuclear/Chemical Environment (CANE) there was registered a 34 percent increase in leaders being killed in action as compared to combat exercises where such gear was not worn.

These exercises of rifle platoons and companies showed that leaders operating behind masks, wearing protective overgarments and having to operate in heavy boots and gloves, continually tended to delegate less to subordinates, generally got more involved in direct battle command, and became both mentally and physically exhausted sooner than in normal conditions.[5] This led often to lack of focus and irritability.

Leaders often had a tendency to delegate less authority and to communicate less frequently and in less detail. As exhaustion set in leaders sometimes neglected critical tasks and coordination of the units and synchronization of movements with adjacent units suffered.

People operating in a highly stressful and tiring posture often performed less well when met with novel challenges that could not be met with standard operating procedures. As one study states, "Routine tasks which were reduced to SOP could be accomplished with little or no degradation. However, battlefield tasks involving cognitive skills, movement to contact, maneuver, and attack or defense over difficult terrain under varying weather conditions were rapidly degraded under nuclear and chemical conditions, greatly affecting command and control."[6]

In MOPP 4, leaders tended to cut corners, took easier routes, used roads and trails more often, and took unnecessary tactical risks.

One of the lessons from these field exercises in a simulated chemical and nuclear environment is that "leaders must pace themselves, delegate, and observe a strict work-rest regimen. Forced liquid intake, especially when operating in a nuclear and chemical environment, will minimize dehydration, stress and poor performance."[7]

Communications and MOPP 4

Communications in the CANE maneuvers were deemed only about half as effective in that environment as in a non-threatening one. In MOPP 4 conditions, "soldiers perceive radio communications to be garbled, even though recordings show the transmissions to be clear."[8] The length of radio transmissions increased by 47 percent and by 100 percent in battles. Even verbal face-to-face communications were only half as effective while each was trying to talk and hear through a mask. Obviously, non-verbal communications conveyed through facial expressions were eliminated. As a result, soldiers more readily communicated with each other by hand and arm signals where feasible.

Fire Support and MOPP 4

Platoons in full mask and overgarments were more reliant on supporting indirect fires from artillery and mortars and other sources. They also called on three times more supporting fire than in a non-nuclear, non-chemical environment. More firepower was asked for due to the longer attack times caused by wearing cumbersome gear and the fear within advancing platoons that they could not be as effective in accurately aiming direct fire weapons at the enemy. Units generally took twice as long to complete attacks in MOPP 4 as compared to normal clothing.

Units in MOPP gear did not engage the enemy force until they were at shorter ranges.[9] An after-action report stated that, "25 percent fewer soldiers fired their weapons and 45 percent fewer firers hit a target in the nuclear and chemical environment."[10] In this situation, all units fired their weapons from 25 to 60 percent less than in the non-contaminated battlefield exercise.[11] Overall, it was calculated that 73 percent fewer enemy targets were engaged when friendly rifle units were in full chemical protective gear because of the lower rate of fire and increased inaccuracy of fire.[12]

Light infantry platoons were slower to advance, called for more indirect fire support, and their supporting artillery and mortars were slower to respond when the forward and supporting unites were both in full protective postures.

The fire support system was slower to respond and both forward platoons and supporting units fired fewer rounds and were less accurate in MOPP 4 conditions because more mistakes were made in communicating coordinates of targets and, in the process of firing. Firing units moved more slowly, taking one-third more time to put guns into position after unit movements.[13]

As a result of operating in MOPP gear, Army rifle platoons took twice as long to complete attacks, firing rates declined from 20 to 40 percent, and twice as many soldiers were required to achieve objectives. As they advanced they were less effective in taking cover and concealing their locations. Also, soldiers in overgarments and masks had more difficulty in locating and identifying their targets.[14]

Casualty Rates in MOPP 4

During the CANE maneuvers, friendly forces burdened with wearing masks, protective overgarments, special gloves and boots, were able to inflict only half as many "deaths" on enemy forces as would have occurred in conventional combat where troops were not so equipped.

Casualties mounted, increasing by 75 percent when the enemy counterattacked. Friendly troops were more vulnerable in the nuclear-chemical battlefield simply because of the requirement to wear masks and overgarments and gloves. They made more noise and did not maintain good discipline about restricting lights from lamps, flashlights, fires, and other sources. They also moved slower and were less disciplined in their maneuvers, and this allowed the enemy to find them and target them more effectively. There was also more fratricide, as soldiers in full protective gear, confused by the mask and burdened by the protective gear, fired 20 percent of their rifle rounds at friendly forces as compared to 5 percent in conventional combat exercises.

Many other military tasks were under-performed once rifle platoons and companies donned full chemical protection gear. For example, some tasks were omitted to simplify life for those burdened by MOPP 4 masks and overgarments. Illustratively, these units cut camouflage actions by 15 percent the first day in such gear and 30 percent by the second day. By the third day, camouflaging was abandoned altogether in these exercises. Overstressed leaders did less supervision as time wore on and their personnel did less on their own.[15]

Discipline and Cohesion Decline in MOPP 4

As one U.S. Army study reports, "enforcement of tactical discipline declined, units became less cohesive, and the synchronization of plans, maneuver, and both direct- and indirect fire support . . . were significantly degraded. Units took longer to establish communications and had to ask for more radio transmissions to be repeated and clarified. In contrast, tasks which were routine in nature and practiced on a regular basis revealed little or no degradation."[16]

Difficult Engineering Tasks Harder in MOPP 4

Engineers, operating in full MOPP gear, also had a harder time and were less efficient. At times it took engineers three to four times longer to complete tasks when encumbered with protective gear. One report states "MOPP 4 caused greater fatigue and slowed completion of tasks involving physical labor . . . Protective gloves caused loss of manual dexterity while both emplacing obstacles and breeching wire . . . The M-1 protective mask created problems in seeing and communicating."[17] For example, "breeching of wire obstacles took over twice as long"[18] and such units' movement on the battlefield was degraded by 50 percent.[19]

According to another CANE report, "Engineering support was degraded in the nuclear-chemical environment. The rate of movement, engineer security, and coordination of obstacles were degraded by 36 percent, 37 percent, and 14 percent respectively."[20]

Conclusions and Recommendations

As one CANE summary evaluation report concludes about light infantry combat performance on the simulated nuclear-chemical battlefield, there were a number of battle implications for units adopting a MOPP 4 protective posture:[21]

- "Leaders took tactical risks by selecting easier tasks."

- "(Units) maintained direction of movement one-sixth less effectively."

- "(Units) synchronized plans about one-fourth less effectively."

- "(Units) rehearsed about one-tenth less."

- "One-fourth of leaders received inadequate information on the opposing forces."

- "(Units) required clarification/repetition of one-fourth more radio messages."

- "(Units) received one-sixth fewer reports from security elements."

- "(Units) suppressed opposing forces one-fourth less effectively."

- "(Units) maintained unit cohesiveness one-fifth less effectively."

The longer friendly forces were in full MOPP 4 protective gear, the more poorly they performed on the simulated chemical and nuclear battlefield. As one observer reported, "After six hours in MOPP 4, personnel tend to omit such tasks as camouflage and combat service support activities. The unit takes significantly longer to execute the same mission on the third day of extended operations compared to the first day."[22]

The U.S. Army's conclusion was that more of their forces needed extended NBC training to prepare to cope with this contaminated situation when units would have to operate in full protective modes. After-action evaluators concluded that the Army's participants were "marginally trained to operate in MOPP 4. If the units had come under actual chemical attack, they would have suffered needless casualties."[23]

While by most measures U.S. Army units performed very poorly in full protective gear compared to normal battle dress, not all Army activities were degraded as a result of wearing individual protective equipment. In some cases of planning and coordination there was an actual improvement as units prepared to enter the battle exercises in the chemical/nuclear scenarios because more care was given in advance to mission analysis, developing alternative courses of action, and making of tentative plans. The after action report concluded that, these units knowing they would be tested in the harder environment, paid more advance attention to solutions in planning and coordination.

Notes

1. Mr. Fraker, U.S. Army Information Paper, "Combined Arms in a Nuclear/Chemical Environment," October 4, 1991, 1.

2. U.S. Army Chemical School, "CANE: Summary Evaluation Report, Phase I," Ft. McClellan, Alabama, March 1986, 1-2. See also, Col. Knoop, "Information Paper,

CANE II, Force Development Test and Experimentation," U.S. Army Chemical School, Ft. McClellan, Alabama. These were supplied to the author by the U.S. Army Chemical School, Fort Leonard Wood, MO, undated, 2 pages.

3. Col Knopp, "Information Paper, CANE II, Force Development Test and Experimentation," U.S. Army Chemical School, Ft. McClellan, Alabama, 1.

4. Ibid.

5. U.S. Army Chemical School, "Close Combat Light (CCL) Lessons Learned: Combined Arms in a Nuclear/Chemical Environment (CANE), Force Development Test and Experimentation," Fort McClellan, Alabama, March 12, 1993, 1-1.

6. Ibid., 2-10.

7. U.S. Army Pamphlet, "Winning in a Nuclear/Chemical Environment," Undated.

8. Knoop, op. cit.

9. U.S. Army Chemical School, "Close Combat Light (CCL) Lessons Learned: Combined Arms in a Nuclear/Chemical Environment (CANE), Force Development Test and Experimentation," Fort McClellan, Alabama, March 12, 1993, 2-6.

10. Ibid.

11. Ibid.

12. Ibid.

13. CANE Summary Evaluation Report, Close Combat Light, op. cit., 1-3.

14. U.S. Army Pamphlet, "Winning in a Nuclear/Chemical Environment," Undated.

15. Ibid.

16. Ibid., 1-2.

17. Ibid., 2-12.

18. Ibid.

19. Ibid.

20. CANE Summary Evaluation Report, Close Combat Light, 2-11.

21. CANE Summary Evaluation Report, Close Combat Light, op. cit., 1-3.

22. Knoop, op. cit., 2.

23. <u>CANE Summary Evaluation Report, Close Combat Light</u>, op. cit., For example, it was reported that prior to their first CANE maneuvers, 18 percent of participating soldiers had never worn MOPP 4 protective gear, and 60 percent had done so for only 1-3 hours. 22 percent had never before performed skin decontamination. Only 42 percent of frontline soldiers and 30 percent of the entire infantry team, had received training in firing their weapons in MOPP 4. Only 30 percent of drivers had been trained to drive in MOPP 4. Only 34 percent had been trained to operate the M8A1 alarm.

CHAPTER 8

The Threat of Biological Weapons: Prophylaxis and Mitigation of Psychological and Social Consequences[*]

Harry C. Holloway, Ann E. Norwood, Carol S. Fullerton,
Charles C. Engel, Jr., Robert J. Ursano

The microbial world is mysterious, threatening, and frightening to most people. The stressors associated with a biological terrorist attack could create high numbers of acute and potentially chronic psychiatric casualties who must be recognized, diagnosed, and treated to facilitate triage and medical care. Media communications, planning for quarantine and decontamination, and the role of community leaders are important to the mitigation of psychological consequences. Physicians will need to accurately diagnose anxiety, depression, bereavement, and organic brain syndromes to provide treatment, reassurance, and the relief of pain.

Biological weapons have emerged as a significant threat in the 1990s.[1,2] Other reports in this issue have established the potential likelihood of the use of biological weapons and the nature of the biological and toxic threats. Herein, we discuss the psychophysiological and social implications of such agents and propose recommendations for developing primary interventions and treatment.

Psychosocial Responses Following A Biological Attack

The idea of infection caused by invisible agents is frightening. It touches a deep human concern about the risk of being destroyed by a powerful, evil, imperceptible force. These beliefs activate emotions that are extremely difficult to direct with the tools of reason. The response of specialists in medicine, epidemiology, infectious disease, molecular biology, nursing, and emergency medical services can bring some discipline and rationality to this situation. To be effective, the response must be well organized and communication must be made in terms that the public understands. Multiple organizations with conflicting and overlapping goals and responsibilities (eg, health care, law enforcement, and social welfare) may increase the confusion and anxiety for the individual and community. The novelty of biological weapons in combination with the activation of deeply rooted fears predict that strong psychological and physiological responses will occur.

The immediate stressors associated with a biological terrorist attack are the threat and the consequences of infection. The specific nature of these stressors will depend on the organism or toxin used. Characteristics such as the incubation period and the virulence and toxicity of the agent will contribute to the psychological impact. The process of seeking and receiving immunization or treatment is potentially stressful. Examples of common psychosocial responses are noted in Table 1.

Table 1. Psychological Responses Following a Biological Terrorist Attack

Horror
Anger
Panic
Magical thinking about microbes and viruses
Fear of invisible agents
Fear of contagion
Anger at terrorists, government, or both
Attribution of arousal symptoms to infection
Scapegoating
Paranoia
Social isolation
Demoralization
Loss of faith in social institutions

One can anticipate that there will be acute and chronic psychiatric casualties as in other disasters.[3][4][5][6] While the majority of people do not develop long-term psychiatric sequelae following disasters, certain groups are at higher risk (eg, the previously traumatized, those without social supports, and first-responders, such as police and emergency medical personnel). Biological agents may cause mental disorders due to toxins or infectious conditions such as viral encephalitis or bacterial meningitis. Illness and injury secondary to the attack increase the risk of the development of acute stress disorder and posttraumatic stress disorder, as well as depression and bereavement in survivors.[7][8] Psychiatric disability is a likely chronic outcome of biological attack. The incidence and prevalence of such problems remain a matter of speculation, although past occurrences can be used to anticipate consequences. Experiences with chemical weapons used by terrorists have demonstrated that psychiatric casualties are likely.[9]

The psychiatric sequelae will depend on the nature of and the response to the assault. In contrast to explosive or chemical weapons, biological weapons may not produce instantaneously horrifying results. (An exception to this might be the use of a biological toxin that kills quickly and with frightening manifestations, such as seizures or suffocation.)

As the attack is discovered and the media reports the news, exposed and unexposed individuals may experience acute autonomic arousal. Signs and symptoms of muscle tension, tachycardia, rapid breathing (perhaps hyperventilation), sweating, tremor, and a sense of foreboding are likely to generate health concerns. These signs and symptoms may be misattributed to infection or intoxication. The acutely stressed and symptomatic individuals will add complexity and additional patients for triage during the initial phase of the crisis. However, if initial triage and management are successful, the risk for the development of psychiatric problems can be minimized.

Forensic issues involved in the medical response influence psychological responses and treatment options. Preservation of evidence maximizes the possibility of the perpetrators' being punished. The perception that justice is ultimately served can have a very positive psychological impact on those exposed and society. Some survivors may be critical witnesses in future legal actions. This may have little consequence for immediate lifesaving care, but it might prompt the selection of psychotropic drugs that minimally interfere with recall or discourage the use of a technique, like hypnosis, that can potentially damage the future credibility of a witness report.

Acute Intervention Following A Biological Attack

Rapid, accurate triage and effective treatment (or immunization) will be the cornerstones of initial management (Table 2). Distinguishing symptoms of hyperarousal from those of intoxication and infectious disease prodromes will be crucial. The type of exposure and any lack of complete information about the agent will increase uncertainty and the risk of psychiatric morbidity. The risk for secondary psychological trauma will increase if actions by leaders or helpers fail to provide a quick, accurate diagnosis, a sensitive process for communicating the nature of the risk, and a supportive environment for those exposed and their families.

Table 2. Psychiatric Intervention

Prevention of group panic
Careful, rapid medical evaluation and treatment
Avoidance of emotion-based responses
    (eg, knee jerk quarantine)
Effective risk communication
Control of symptoms secondary to hyperarousal
    Reassurance
    Diazepamlike anxiolytics for acute relief, as indicated
Management of anger, fear, or both
Management of misattribution of somatic symptoms
Provision of respite as required
Restoration of an effective, useful social role
    (perhaps as worker at triage site)
Return to usual sources of social supports in the community

An attitude of expectation that those with hyperarousal or demoralization will soon return to normal activities should be conveyed.

Patients should be moved out of the patient role as quickly as possible. Diazepamlike anxiolytics may be helpful in reducing anxiety for patients who do not respond to reassurance. The assignment of simple work tasks that facilitate the care of other patients can help restore function to the psychological casualties. The recovery environment should be constructed to create a sense of safety and to counteract the helplessness induced by the terrorist act.[10]

A well-organized, effective medical response contributes to the creation of a supportive environment and accurate data for the at-risk population. Individuals can assess their risk and determine the actions that they can take to reduce the risk. Ideally, risk information should involve dialogue. Dialogue lets the at-risk population define the information that they need, and it enables the community leaders to assess their effectiveness in communicating the appropriate data. Failure to provide a public forum for information exchanges may actually increase anxiety and misunderstanding and amplify health concerns since individuals will tend to attribute autonomic symptoms to catastrophic illness. One consequence of appraisal error may be disabling somatic complaints offered in a setting where failure to find a medical or surgical disease is experienced as stigmatizing and sadistic by the patients. In this situation, the patient's life may become focused on an unending search for an "acceptable" diagnosis.[11 12 13]

Implications Of Psychological Reactions For The Medical System

Following a biological terrorist attack, physical injury, disruption of daily communal routine, and increased use of public health facilities could place overwhelming demands on the medical systems.[14] Feelings of helplessness and hopelessness could be increased if the rescue and postdisaster medical efforts appear to be failing.[15] Angry, intense competition for available but limited resources can generate even more societal disruption and casualties. The belief that treatment will be provided to some but not to others will contribute to the possibility of social disruptions such as riot or panic. Panic will be a particular risk when biological agents are used to threaten or to attack a sizable civilian population.[16] Demoralization can also be a response to the predicaments presented by a biological attack. Demoralized individuals often lose their sense of social and group responsibilities and roles. If major community institutions fail to provide protection, citizens can lose faith in the ideological metaphors that bind the community together. In this way, demoralization can increase isolation and feelings of hopelessness. In this complex setting, some are likely to manifest psychiatric symptoms. Given the stigma attached to psychiatric illness and the fact that the individuals who manifest them are more likely to have been injured and to have been exposed to multiple infectious, environmental, and toxicological risks, the diagnostic and therapeutic dilemmas will be quite difficult.[17][18]

Quarantine requires the development of a specialized environment that will limit exposure to secondary infections. The creation of such an environment may disrupt social supports that reduce the postexposure risk of stress-induced disorders. It can create a situation characterized by separation from friends and family, isolation, and a sense of stigmatization. Prior planning can ensure that modern communication technology (telephone, television, and computer Internet connection) can be used to mitigate these untoward effects by providing ongoing contact with families and others in the community outside quarantine. The maintenance of contact between parents and children is particularly important for the children. This may result in putting unexposed adult caregivers in quarantine.

Additional stressors may arise from the mundane logistical demands associated with managing mass contamination and infection. One of the difficulties in the Japanese sarin attack was undressing patients and disposing of their clothing.[9] Obtaining the necessary shower facilities for a large number of exposed survivors may be problematic. The provision of privacy and assurance of conventional modesty may have to be sacrificed. It should not be forgotten that privacy and modesty are important to maintaining an individual's sense of control and autonomy. The imposition of special requirements such as public bathing should be accompanied by an explanation that attributes this undesirable demand to the terrorist attacker.

Disaster responders and medical personnel also will have to contend with their own psychological reactions. One of the terrorist's goals is to provoke intense emotions that interfere with the capacity of caregivers to react in a thoughtful, organized fashion. A biological attack using a highly infectious and virulent organism (eg, anthrax), dispersed in a fine spray, poses special stressors. Medical responders may be required to work in protective clothing and masks ("moon suits"). This barrier protection will make the care of patients more difficult and increase the risk of heat, fatigue, and isolation stress for medical personnel.[19] [20] It will be important to establish work-rest schedules and to limit the exposure of medical and rescue personnel to the grotesque and the dead.

Planning And Preparation

Disaster plans for managing a biological attack must be developed and realistic training provided to ensure effective response to an actual terrorist event. These plans must assume that emotional and psychiatric problems will occur in the unexposed population as well as the exposed. The exercises should be carried out with sufficient realism, so that the process of disrobing and showering is practiced in real time. Medical responders will need training to recognize the symptoms of anxiety, depression, and dissociation. It is critical that psychological responses be managed in ways that facilitate the triage, diagnosis, and treatment of those exposed or infected.[21] Such plans need to include strategies for prevention and mitigation of stress for survivors as well as for those responding to the crisis and its consequences. Debriefing, commonly used by emergency personnel following trauma, has been used to mitigate the effects of severe stress and can be helpful in identifying individuals who may need further assistance. Results from controlled studies of debriefing are only now beginning to become available.[22] [23] These studies will help clarify the role of intervention in the alleviation of pain, prevention of disability, return to social involvement, and the prevention of disease. Ironically, should a highly infectious agent be used, bringing people together for a debriefing may be contraindicated. Perhaps "teledebriefing" (analogous to telemedicine) is a technology that could be developed for such situations.

Communicating Risk To The Public

The communication of the risk to individuals following a bacteriologic attack will critically affect how communities and individuals respond.[24][25][26][27][28] The media coverage and behavior of public officials can contribute to the stress and precipitate panic or demoralization, particularly if inaccurate, confusing, or contradictory information is provided to the public. Rumors must be anticipated, monitored, and corrected with accurate information.[17] Any damage to public trust at the beginning of the crisis ensures that distrust will continue throughout the crisis. There are psychological and physiological costs attendant to the loss of trust.

For example, the handling of information by officials and the media during the release of nuclear radiation at Three Mile Island became a major source of anxiety and stress for people living in the vicinity of the nuclear facility. At Three Mile Island, there were no casualties or severely injured individuals. The stress was fear and uncertainty about exposure to excess radioactivity, loss of faith in local authorities and those managing operations of the reactor, and financial uncertainties.[29] Baum followed individuals at the Three Mile Island site and at 3 control sites for 10 years.[29] He found evidence of chronic arousal as indicated by elevated norepinephrine and epinephrine in some individuals.

Conclusion

Governmental and private agencies should develop detailed strategies for responding to a biological terrorist attack that include consideration of the psychological and social impact of such an attack. Inattention to the phenomenon of terror and its consequences for individuals, institutions, and society jeopardize the efficacy of disaster mitigation efforts. Leaders, scientists, and the media should develop protocols covering a broad range of scenarios that communicate accurate information about risk and diminish rumors. These primary prevention efforts will be critical in preventing panic and demoralization in the attacked community. The possible forensic responsibilities of first responders should receive appropriate consideration when collecting data and preparing for future action that will determine responsibility for the attack.

Realistic training for biological attacks should include the probability of large numbers of psychological casualties. Training exercises should be designed to test cooperation and coordination between organizations as well as test first responders and hospital staff. Hospital accrediting bodies should encourage medical facilities to incorporate biological scenarios into their annual training.

Planning and preparation for biological attacks and their attendant psychological consequences can diminish the terrorists' ability to achieve their overall goal the induction of terror. Education of the public and institutional preparedness can mitigate the horror of terrorism. The media could play an active prevention role by realistically educating the public about the impact of terrorist attacks with biological weapons. Such preparation efforts should be given high priority.

Notes

1. US Congress, Office of Technology Assessment. *Technology Against Terrorism: The Federal Effort* Washington, DC: Government Printing Office; 1991. Publication OTA-ISC-481.

2. Flanagin A, Lederberg J. The threat of biological weapons: prophylaxis and mitigation: call for papers. *JAMA.* 1996;276:419-420.

3. Ursano RJ, Fullerton CS, Norwood AE. Psychiatric dimensions of disaster: patient care, community consultation, and preventive medicine. *Harv Rev Psychiatry.* 1995;3:196-200.

4. Ursano RJ, Rundell JR. Psychological problems of prisoners of war: the trauma of a toxic and contained environment. In: Ursano RJ, ed. *Individual Response to Disaster*. Bethesda, Md: Uniformed Services University of the Health Sciences; 1988: 79-112. Publication DTIC: A203310.

5. Ursano RJ, Fullerton CS, McCaughey BG. Trauma and disaster. In: Ursano RJ, McCaughey BG, Fullerton CS, eds. *Individual and Community Responses to Trauma and Disaster: The Structure of Human Chaos*. Cambridge, England: Cambridge University Press; 1994:3-27.

6. Weisaeth L. War-related psychopathology in Kuwait: an assessment of war-related mental health problems. In: Fullerton CS, Ursano RJ, eds. *Posttraumatic Stress Disorder: Acute and Long-Term Responses to Trauma and Disaster*. Washington, DC: American Psychiatric Press; 1997:91-122.

7. American Psychiatric Association. *Diagnostic and Statistical Manual of Mental Disorders, Fourth Edition*. Washington, DC: American Psychiatric Association; 1994.

8. Shalev A. Posttraumatic stress disorder among injured survivors of a terrorist attack: predictive value of early intrusion and avoidance symptoms. *J Nerv Ment Dis.* 1992;180:505-509

9. Okumura T, Takasu N, Ishimatsu S, et al. Report on the 640 victims of the Tokyo subway sarin attack. *Ann Emerg Med.* 1996;28:129-135.

10. Raphael B, Wilson J, Meldrum L, Mcfarlane AC. Acute preventive interventions. In: van der Kolk B, Mcfarlane AC, Weisaeth L, eds. *Traumatic Stress: The Effects of Overwhelming Experience on Mind, Body, and Society*. New York, NY: Guilford Press; 1996:463-479.

11. Kassirer JP. Our stubborn quest for diagnostic certainty. *N Engl J Med.* 1989;320:1489-1491.

12. Schwartz SP, White PE, Hughes RF. Environmental threats, communities, and hysteria. *J Public Health Policy.* 1985;6:58-77.

13. Blackwell B, De Morgan NP. The primary care of patients who have bodily concerns. *Arch Fam Med.* 1996;5:457-463.

14. Relationship of mustard agent and lewisite exposure to psychological dysfunction. In: Pechura CM, Rall DP, eds *Veterans at Risk*. Washington, DC: National Academy Press; 1993.

15. Ursano RJ, ed, Fullerton CS, ed. *Performance and Operations in Toxic Environments*. Bethesda, Md: Uniformed Services University of the Health Sciences; 1988. Publication DTIC: A203162.

16. Russell PK. Biologic terrorism: responding to the threat. *Emerg Infect Dis.* 1997;3. Accessed June 26, 1997. Available at: http://www.cdc.gov/ncidod/EID/eid.htm.

17. Ursano RJ, ed, Fullerton CS, ed. *Individual and Group Behavior in Toxic and Contained Environments*. Bethesda, Md: Uniformed Services University of the Health Sciences; 1988. Publication DTIC: A203267.

18. Fullerton CS, Ursano RJ. Behavioral and psychological responses to toxic

exposure. In: Ursano RJ, ed. *Individual Response to Disaster*. Bethesda, Md: Uniformed Services University of the Health Sciences; 1988: 113-128. Publication DTIC: A203310.

19. Fullerton CS, Ursano RJ. Health care delivery in the high-stress environment of chemical and biological warfare. *Mil Med.* 1994;159:524-528.

20. Fullerton CS, Ursano RJ, Kao T, Bhartiya V. The chemical and biological warfare environment psychological responses and social support in a high-stress environment. *J Appl Soc Psychol.* 1992;22:1608-1623.

21. Fullerton CS, Brandt GT, Ursano RJ. Chemical and biological weapons: silent agents of terror. In: Ursano RJ, Norwood AE, eds. *Emotional Aftermath of the Persian Gulf War: Veterans, Families, Communities, and Nations*. Washington, DC: American Psychiatric Press; 1996:111-142.

22. Kenardy JA, Webster RA, Lewin TJ, Carr VJ, Hazell PL, Carter GL. Stress debriefing and patterns of recovery following a natural disaster. *J Trauma Stress.* 1996;9:37-49.

23. Raphel B, Meldrum L, McFarlane AC. Does debriefing after psychological trauma work? *BMJ.* 1995;310:1479-1480.

24. National Research Council. *Health Risks of Radon and Other Internally Deposited Alpha-emitters (BEIR IV)*. Washington, DC: National Academy Press; 1988.

25. National Research Council. *Improving Risk Communication*. Washington, DC: National Academy Press; 1989.

26. National Research Council. *Risk Assessment in the Federal Government: Managing the Process*. Washington, DC: National Academy Press; 1983.

27. National Research Council. *Understanding Risk: Informing Decisions in a Democratic Society*. Washington, DC: National Academy Press; 1996.

28. Presidential Advisory Committee on Gulf War Veterans' Illness. *Presidential Advisory Committee on Gulf War Veterans' Illness: Final Report*. Washington, DC: US Government Printing Office; 1996.

29. Baum A. Stress, intrusive imagery, and chronic distress. *Health Psychol.* 1990;9:653-675.

CHAPTER 9

The Economic Impact of a Bioterrorist Attack: Are Prevention and Postattack Intervention Programs Justifiable?[*]

Arnold F. Kaufmann, Martin I. Meltzer, and George P. Schmid

Understanding and quantifying the impact of a bioterrorist attack are essential in developing public health preparedness for such an attack. We constructed a model that compares the impact of three classic agents of biologic warfare (*Bacillus anthracis*, *Brucella melitensis*, and *Francisella tularensis*) when released as aerosols in the suburb of a major city. The model shows that the economic impact of a bioterrorist attack can range from an estimated $477.7 million per 100,000 persons exposed (brucellosis scenario) to $26.2 billion per 100,000 persons exposed (anthrax scenario). Rapid implementation of a postattack prophylaxis program is the single most important means of reducing these losses. By using an insurance analogy, our model provides economic justification for preparedness measures.

Bioterrorism and its potential for mass destruction have been subjects of increasing international concern. Approximately 17 countries (including five implicated as sponsors of international terrorism) may have active research and development programs for biologic weapons.[1] Moreover, groups and individuals with grievances against the government or society have been known to use or plan to use biologic weapons to further personal causes.

Only modest microbiologic skills are needed to produce and effectively use biologic weapons. The greatest, but not insurmountable, hurdle in such an endeavor may be gaining access to a virulent strain of

[*] Originally published in *Emerging Infectious Diseases*, Volume 3, Number 2, April-June 1997. Centers for Disease Control and Prevention, Atlanta, Georgia, USA.

the desired agent. Production costs are low, and aerosol dispersal equipment from commercial sources can be adapted for biologic weapon dissemination. Bioterrorists operating in a civilian environment have relative freedom of movement, which could allow them to use freshly grown microbial suspensions (storage reduces viability and virulence). Moreover, bioterrorists may not be constrained by the need for precise targeting or predictable results.

The impact of a bioterrorist attack depends on the specific agent or toxin used, the method and efficiency of dispersal, the population exposed, the level of immunity in the population, the availability of effective postexposure and/or therapeutic regimens, and the potential for secondary transmission. Understanding and quantifying the impact of a bioterrorist attack are essential to developing an effective response. Therefore, we have analyzed the comparative impact of three classic biologic warfare agents (*Bacillus anthracis*, *Brucella melitensis*, and *Francisella tularensis*) when released as aerosols in the suburbs of a major city and compared the benefits of systematic intervention with the costs of increased disease incidence (from the economic point of view used in society).

Analytic Approach

Scenario Assumptions

We compared the impact of a theoretical bioterrorist attack on a suburb of a major city, with 100,000 population exposed in the target area. The attack was made by generating an aerosol of an agent (*B. anthracis* spores, *B. melitensis*, or *F. tularensis*) along a line across the direction of theprevailing wind. The meteorologic conditions (thermal stability, relative humidity, wind direction and speed) were assumed to be optimal[2], and the aerosol cloud passed over the target area within 2 hours. We projected impact on the basis of 10% and 100% of the target population being exposed to the aerosol cloud.

We assumed that, when inhaled, the infectious dose$_{50}$ (ID$_{50}$) was 20,000 spores for *B. anthracis* and 1,000 vegetative cells for *B. melitensis* and *F. tularensis*. The rate of physical decay for airborne particles 5 μm or less in diameter was estimated to be negligible during the 2-hour transit time. The rate of biologic decay of the particulate agents was estimated to be negligible for the *B. anthracis* spores and 2% per minute for the *B. melitensis* and *F. tularensis* vegetative cells. Viability and virulence did not dissociate. Persons who were exposed to the *B. anthracis* cloud at any point during the 2-hour transit time inhaled one ID_{50} dose, and persons who were exposed to either the *B. melitensis* or *F. tularensis* cloud inhaled one to 10 ID_{50} doses, depending on their proximity to the origination point of the aerosol cloud.

The epidemic curve for anthrax by days after exposure was assumed to be <1 day, 0% of cases; 1 day, 5%; 2 days, 20%; 3 days, 35%; 4 days, 20%; 5 days, 10%; 6 days, 5%; and 7 or more days, 5%.[3-5] Case-fatality rates were also assumed to vary by the day symptoms were first noted. The case-fatality rate was estimated as 85% for patients with symptoms on day 1; 80% for patients with symptoms on day 2; 70% for those with symptoms on day 3; 50% for those with symptoms on days 4, 5, and 6; and 70% for those with symptoms on and after day 7. The increased death rate in persons with an incubation period of 7 or more days is calculated on an assumption of delayed diagnosis, with resultant delayed therapy.

When estimating days in hospital and outpatient visits due to infection, we assumed that 95% of anthrax patients were hospitalized, with a mean stay of 7 days. Patients not admitted to a hospital had an average of seven outpatient visits, and surviving hospitalized patients had two outpatient visits after discharge from the hospital. Persons who received only outpatient care were treated for 28 days with either oral ciprofloxacin or doxycycline. No significant long-term sequelae resulted from the primary infection, and no relapses occurred.

The epidemic curve for brucellosis by days after exposure was assumed to be 0 to 7 days, 4% of cases; 8 to 14 days, 6%; 15 to 28 days, 14%; 29 to 56 days, 40%; 57 to 112 days, 26%, and 113 or more days, 10%.[4, 6-9] The case-fatality rate was estimated to be 0.5%. Fifty percent of patients were hospitalized, with an average stay of 7 days. Nonhospitalized patients had an average of 14 outpatient visits, and hospitalized patients had seven outpatient visits after discharge from the hospital. Outpatients received a combination of oral doxycycline for 42 days and parenteral gentamicin for the first 7 days of therapy. Five percent of patients had a relapse or long-term sequelae, and required 14 outpatient visits within 1 year.

The epidemic curve for tularemia by days after exposure was assumed to be: <1 day, 0% of cases; 1 day, 1%; 2 days, 15%; 3 days, 45%; 4 days, 25%; 5 days, 10%; 6 days, 3%; and 7 or more days, 1%.[4, 10-11] The estimated case-fatality rate was 7.5%; and 95% of patients were hospitalized, with an average stay of 10 days. Nonhospitalized patients had an average of 12 outpatient visits, and hospitalized patients who survived the acute illness had two outpatient visits after discharge from the hospital. Outpatients received oral doxycycline for 14 days and parenteral gentamicin for 7 days. Five percent of patients had a relapse or long-term sequelae and required an average of 12 outpatient visits.

The efficacy of intervention strategies is unknown; our projections are our best estimates based on published clinical and experimental data.[4, 12-14] For anthrax, the projected intervention program was either a 28-day course of oral ciprofloxacin or doxycycline (assumed to be 90% effective), or a 28-day course of oral ciprofloxacin or doxycycline plus three doses of the human anthrax vaccine (assumed to be 95% effective); for brucellosis, a 42-day course of oral doxycycline and rifampin (assumed to be 80% effective), or a 42-day course of oral doxycycline, plus 7 days of parenteral gentamicin (assumed to be 95% effective); for tularemia, the intervention program was a 14-day course of oral doxycycline (assumed to be 80% effective), or a 14-day course of oral doxycycline plus 7 days of parenteral gentamicin (assumed to be 95% effective). Only 90% of persons exposed in the target area were assumed to effectively participate in any intervention program. Because the target area cannot be precisely defined, we estimated that for every exposed person participating in the intervention program, an additional 5, 10, or 15 nonexposed persons would also participate.

Economic Analyses of Postattack Intervention

To analyze the economic factors involved in establishing an intervention program, we compared the costs to the potential savings from such an intervention. Following the recommendation of the Panel of Cost-Effectiveness in Health and Medicine (PCEHM), we used estimates of actual costs rather than financial charges or market prices, which usually incorporate profit.[15] We calculated the net savings (cost reductions) by using the following formula: Net savings = (number of deaths averted x present value of expected future earnings) + (number of days of hospitalization averted x cost of hospitalization) + (number of outpatient visits averted x cost of outpatient visits) - cost of intervention.

When we calculated the costs of hospitalization and outpatient visits, we assumed that only persons with symptoms (i.e., case-patients) would use medical facilities. The remainder of the exposed and potentially exposed populace would receive postexposure prophylaxis.

Present Value of Expected Future Earnings

The cost of a premature human death was nominally valued at the present value of expected future earnings and housekeeping services, weighted by the age and sex composition of the work force in the United States.[16] The undiscounted average of future earnings is $1,688,595. As recommended by PCEHM,[17] the stream of future earnings was discounted at 3% and 5%, to give values of $790,440 and $544,160, respectively. The present value of expected future earnings was estimated with 1990 dollars, adjusted for a 1% annual growth in productivity.[16] However, in constant terms (1982 dollars), the average hourly earnings in private industry fell from $7.52 in 1990 to $7.40 in 1994[18]; therefore, the estimate of future earnings was not adjusted upwards.

Cost of Hospitalization

In 1993, the average charge for a single day of hospitalization was $875.[19] To derive true cost, we multiplied the average charge by the cost-to-charge ratio of 0.635, (the April 1994 statewide average cost-to-charge ratio for urban hospitals in New York state).[16] On this basis, we estimated true hospitalization costs at $556/day (Table 1). Hospital costs included all professional services, drugs, x-rays, and laboratory tests. Lost productivity during hospital stay was valued at $65/day (the value of an "unspecified" day's earnings, weighted for age and sex composition of the U.S. work force).[16]

Table 1. Costs of hospitalization and outpatient visits (OPVs) following a bioterrorist attack

	Anthrax		Tularemia		Brucellosis	
	Base	Upper	Base	Upper	Base	Upper
Hospitalized patient						
Days in hospital	7	7	10	10	7	7
Cost per day ($)(a)	556	669	556	669	556	669
Lost productivity ($/day)	65	65	65	65	65	65
Follow-up OPVs (no.)	2	2	2	2	7	7
Cost 1st OPV ($)	28	44	28	44	28	44
Cost other OPVs, ea. ($)	13	24	13	24	13	24
OPV laboratory ($)(b,c)	87	174	87	174	131	261
OPV x-rays costs ($)(d)	66	66	0	0	0	0
Lost productivity ($/OPV)(e)	16	16	16	16	16	16
Total costs ($)	4,541	5,380	6,338	7,582	4,584	5,587
Avg. costs/day ($/day)	649	769	634	758	655	798
% increase: Base to upper estimate		*18*		*20*		*22*
Nonhospitalized patient						
Number of OPVs	7	7	12	12	14	14
Cost 1st OPV ($)	28	44	28	44	28	44
Cost other OPVs, ea. ($)	13	24	13	24	13	24
Lost productivity ($/OPV)(e)	16	16	16	16	16	16
Laboratory costs ($)(b,f)	131	174	261	522	261	522
X-ray costs ($)(d)	66	66	66	66	66	66
Drugs used(g)	D	C	D+G	D+G	D+R	D+R+G
Cost of drugs ($)	6	181	29	29	220	246
Total costs ($)	422	810	722	1,120	972	1,418
Avg. costs/day ($/day)	60	116	60	93	69	101
% increase: Base to upper estimate		*93*		*55*		*46*

Notes: All costs rounded to the nearest whole dollar.
(a) Hospital costs assumed to include all costs such as drugs, laboratory tests, and x-rays.
(b) Laboratory tests consists of general health panel (CPT code 80050) and an antigen or antibody test (modeled on the cost of a *Streptococcus* screen, CPT code 86588).
(c) Follow-up OPVs for hospitalized patients included two laboratory test sets for anthrax and tularemia patients and three laboratory test sets for brucellosis patients.
(d) X-ray costs (CPT code 71021), included two sets taken at different OPVs.
(e) Productivity lost due to an OPV was assumed to be one-quarter of an unspecified day's value.
(f) For OPVs of nonhospitalized patients, one set of laboratory tests is assumed for every two visits.
(g) Drugs used: D = doxycycline; C = ciprofloxacin; R = rifampin.
Sources: See text for explanation of sources of cost estimates.

Cost of Posthospitalization Outpatient Visits

After discharge from the hospital, a patient was assumed to have follow-up outpatient visits, the number of which varied by disease (Table 1). Outpatient visit costs were valued by using the Medicare National Average Allowance,[20] which was chosen to represent the equivalent of bulk purchase discounted costs (i.e., actual costs) (Table 1). The first visit has a Current Procedural Terminology (CPT) code of 99201, which is classified as a "level 1" visit, requiring a physician to spend an average of 10 minutes with a patient.[20] Subsequent level 1 visits, with the physician spending an average of 5 minutes with each patient, have a CPT code of 99211.[20] During outpatient visits, a general health panel test incorporating clinical chemistry tests and complete blood counts (CPT code 80050) and a single antigen or antibody detection test (e.g., CPT code 86558) were assumed to be ordered.[20] Although data on Medicare allowances for office visits and many other procedures were available, data on Medicare allowances for laboratory tests were not. Thus, to establish the costs of the tests, we arbitrarily divided the lowest allowable charge for each test in half. X-rays (CPT code 71021) were valued according to the Medicare National Average Allowance (Table 1). In terms of lost productivity, we assumed that each outpatient visit cost the equivalent of 2 hours, or one-quarter, of the value of an unspecified day.[16]

Cost of Outpatient Visits of Nonhospitalized Patients

For nonhospitalized outpatients, the cost of each visit, laboratory test, x-ray, and lost productivity was the same as an outpatient visit for discharged hospital patients and varied by disease (Table 1). We assumed that one set of laboratory tests would be ordered every other visit and that two sets of x-rays (CPT code 71021) would be ordered during the therapeutic course. Drug costs are discussed below.

Cost of an Intervention

The costs of an intervention can be expressed as follows: Cost of intervention = (cost of drugs used) x ([number of people exposed x multiplication factor] - number killed - number hospitalized - number of persons who require outpatient visits).

The intervention costs per person depend directly on the costs of the antimicrobial agents and vaccines used in a prophylaxis program (Table 2). We obtained drug prices from the 1996 Drug Topics Red Book and used the lowest cost available for each drug.[21] The cost of doxycycline ($0.22 per 200 mg total daily dose) was the Health Care Financing Administration cost, whereas the cost of gentamicin ($3.76 per 160 mg total daily dose), ciprofloxacin ($3.70 per 1,000 mg total daily dose), and rifampin ($5.01 per 900 mg total daily dose) were wholesale costs from pharmaceutical companies. The cost of anthrax vaccine was $3.70 per dose (Helen Miller-Scott, pers. comm., 1996). The cost of administering one vaccine dose or gentamicin injection was estimated at $10.00, on the basis of the 1992 cost of administering a vaccine in a clinical setting (Valerie Kokor, pers. comm., 1996). In estimating the cost of administering oral antimicrobial agents, we assumed weekly visits, during which the drug would be distributed and counseling would be given ($15.00 for the first visit and $10.00 for each subsequent visit).

Table 2. Costs of prophylaxis following a bioterrorist attack

Level of effectiveness	Anthrax	Tularemia	Brucellosis
Lower			
Effectiveness (%)	90	80	80
Drugs used(a)	D or C	D	D+R
Cost of drugs ($)(b)	6 or 181	3	220
No. of visits(c)	4	2	6
Total cost/ person ($)	51 or 226	28	285
Upper			
Effectiveness (%)	95	95	95
Drugs used(a)	D+V or C+V	D+G	D+G
Cost of drugs ($)(b)	17 or 193	29	36
No. of visits(c)	4	7	12
Total cost/ person ($)	62 or 238	104	161
Minimum No. participants(d)	451,912	418,094	423,440
Maximum No. participants(e)	1,492,750	1,488,037	1,488,037

Notes: All costs are rounded to the nearest whole dollar.

(a) Drugs used: D = doxycycline; C = ciprofloxacin; V = anthrax vaccine; G = gentamicin; R = rifampin.
(b) See text for explanation of drug costs.
(c) Cost of visit to drug-dispensing site: 1st visit = $15/person; follow-up visits = $10/person/visit.
(d) Estimate assumed that the prophylaxis program was initiated on postattack day 6 for anthrax and tularemia and postattack day 113 for brucellosis, that the prophylaxis program had the lower effectiveness level, and that the multiplication factor for unnecessary prophylaxis given to unexposed persons was 5.
(e) Estimate assumed that prophylaxis was initiated on postattack day 0 (day of release), that prophylaxis had the upper effectiveness level, and that the multiplication factor for unnecessary prophylaxis given to unexposed persons was 15.

We assumed that more people would receive prophylaxis than were actually exposed because of general anxiety and uncertainty about the boundaries of the attack, the timing of the attack, and the time it would take nonresidents to travel through the attack area. Three different multiplication factors[5,10, and 15] were used to construct alternative cost-of-intervention scenarios that take into account persons who were not at risk but participated in the prophylaxis program. Thus, if 1000,000 people were exposed, we assumed that the maximum number seeking prophylaxis was 500,000, 1,000,000, or 1,5000,000.

Economic Analysis of Preparedness: Insurance

The analyses outlined above consider only the economics of an intervention after an attack and include several assumptions: First, stockpiles of drugs, vaccines, and other medical supplies would be available and could be rapidly moved to points of need. Second, civil, military, and other organizations would be in place and have the capability to rapidly identify the agent, dispense drugs, treat patients, and keep order within the population. Finally, ongoing intelligence gathering would detect possible bioterrorist threats. The cost of these prerequisite activities can be calculated if they are seen as a form of insurance, the goal of which is to "purchase" the maximum net savings through preparedness to manage the consequences of an attack and reduce the probability of an attack. The "actuarially fair premium" for the "insurance" can be defined as follows[22]: Actuarially fair premium = reduction of loss probability x value of avoidable loss.

The term "reduction of loss probability" indicates that, although increased surveillance and related activities can reduce the odds of an attack, they cannot guarantee absolute protection. The term "avoidable loss" refers to the fact that, even if a postexposure prophylaxis program were implemented on the day of release (day zero), some deaths, hospitalizations, and outpatient visits would be unavoidable.

Various reductions of attack probability illustrated the impact of these estimates on the calculation of actuarially fair premiums. Such reductions included reducing the probability from 1 in 100 years (0.01) to 1 in 1,000 years (0.001), a reduction of 0.009, and reducing a probability from 1 in a 100 years (0.01) to 1 in 10,000 years (0.0001), and from 1 in 100 years (0.01) to 1 in 100,000 years (0.00001). The attack probability of 0.01 in the absence of enhanced preventive actions was selected for illustrative purposes and does not represent an official estimate.

A range of minimum and maximum values of avoidable loss was derived from the net savings calculations. The values reflect differences in effectiveness of the various prophylaxis regimens, the reduced impact of delayed prophylaxis on illness and death, and the two discount rates used to calculate the present value of earnings lost because of death.

Sensitivity Analyses

In addition to the scenarios discussed above, three sensitivity analyses were conducted. First, the impact of increasing the cost of hospitalization and outpatient visits was assessed by using a set of upper estimates (Table 1). The cost of a hospital day was increased to $669 by increasing the cost-to-charge ratio from 0.634 to 0.764 (the ratio for Maryland).[16] The costs of outpatient visits (first and follow-up) were increased by assuming each visit was a "level 2" visit, doubling the average time a physician spends with each patient. The costs of laboratory tests were increased to the full amount of the allowable charge.[20]

The second sensitivity analysis considered a reduced impact, in which only 10% of the original 100,000 target population were considered exposed. All other estimates were held constant. The third sensitivity analysis considered the threshold cost of an intervention, given differences due to the effectiveness of various drug regimens, and discount rates used to calculate the present value of expected lifetime earnings lost to a death. The threshold cost occurs when net savings equal $0. Thus, the threshold value represents the maximum that could be spent per person on an intervention without having the intervention cost more than the loss from no intervention.

Findings

Postattack Illness and Death

In our model, all three biologic agents would cause high rates of illness and death. In the absence of an intervention program for the 100,000 persons exposed, the *B. anthracis* cloud would result in 50,000 cases of inhalation anthrax, with 32,875 deaths; the *F. tularensis* cloud in 82,500 cases of pneumonic or typhoidal tularemia, with 6,188 deaths; and the *B. melitensis* cloud in 82,500 cases of brucellosis requiring extended therapy, with 413 deaths.

The speed with which a postattack intervention program can be effectively implemented is critical to its success (Figure 1). For diseases with short incubation periods such as anthrax and tularemia, a prophylaxis program must be instituted within 72 hours of exposure to prevent the maximum number of deaths, hospital days, and outpatient visits (Figure 1). Some benefit, however, can be obtained even if prophylaxis is begun as late as day 6 after exposure. The relative clinical efficacy of the intervention regimen has a lesser but definite impact on observed illness and death rates (Figure 1).

A disease with a long incubation period such as brucellosis has a similar pattern (Figure 1); an important difference is the time available to implement an intervention program. Having more time available to implement an intervention program can make a marked difference in its effectiveness. However, the prolonged incubation period creates a greater potential for panic in potentially exposed persons because of the uncertainty about their health status.

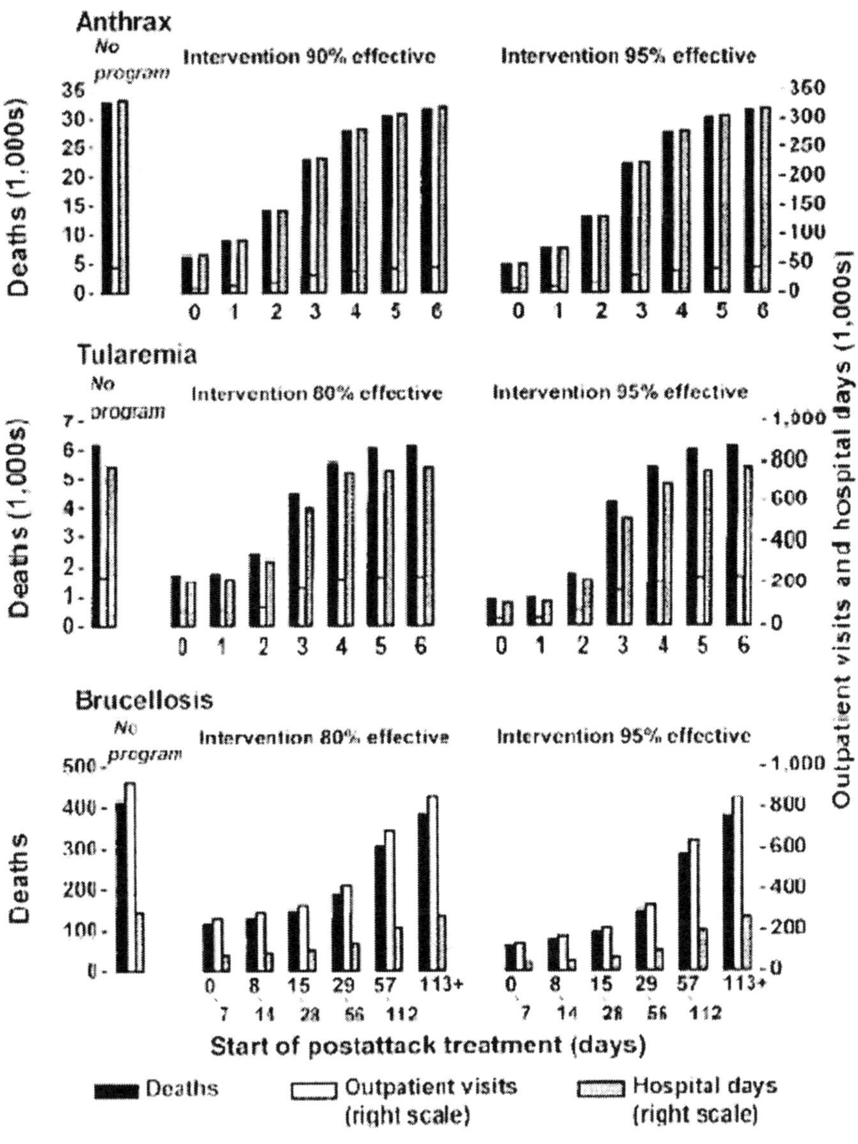

Figure 1

Total deaths, hospital days, and outpatient visits associated with aerosol releases of B. anthracis, B. melitensis, and F. tularensis by the postattack day of prophylaxis initiation and level of prophylaxis effectiveness.

Economic Analyses of Postattack Intervention: No Program

Without a postexposure prophylaxis program, an attack with *B. anthracis* is far costlier than attacks with *F. tularensis* or *B. melitensis* (Table 3). The differences between agents in medical costs as a percentage of total estimated costs are due to the large differences in death rates attributed to each agent (Figure 1).

Table 3. Costs(a)($ millions) of a bioterrorist attack with no postexposure prophylaxis program

	Anthrax	Tularemia	Brucellosis
Direct costs			
Medical: Base Estimates (b)			
Hospital	194.1	445.8	170.3
OPV(c)	2.0	10.5	48.9
Medical: Upper estimates (d)			
Hospital	237.1	543.3	211.7
OPV(c)	4.4	18.5	78.3
Lost productivity			
Illness(e)			
Hospital	21.6	50.9	18.8
OPV(c)	0.7	3.9	15.0
Death			
3% discount(f)	25,985.7	4,891.2	326.5
5% discount(f)	17,889.3	3,367.3	224.7
Total costs			
Base estimates			
3% discount(f)	26,204.1	5,402.4	579.4
5% discount(f)	18,107.7	3,878.4	477.7
Upper estimates			
3% discount(f)	26,249.7	5,507.9	650.1
5% discount(f)	18,153.1	3,983.9	548.4

(a) Assuming 100,000 exposed.
(b) Medical costs are the costs of hospitalization (which include follow-up outpatient visits) and outpatient visits (Table 1).
(c) OPV = outpatient visits.
(d) Upper estimates calculated with data in Table 1.
(e) Lost productivity due to illness is the value of time spent in hospital and during OPVs (Table 1).
(f) Discount rate applied to calculate the present value of expected future earnings and housekeeping services, weighted by age and sex composition of the United States workforce,[16] lost due to premature death.

Net Savings Due to a Postexposure Prophylaxis Program

If the postexposure prophylaxis program is initiated early, it reduces the economic impact of all three diseases, especially anthrax (Figure 2). Regardless of drug costs, the largest cost reductions are obtained through a combination of the most effective prophylaxis regimen (i.e., 95% effective, Table 2), the smallest multiplication factor to adjust for persons who unnecessarily receive prophylaxis, and a 3% discount rate to calculate the present value of the expected value of lifetime earnings.

In the case of anthrax, either doxycycline or ciprofloxacin could be used in the intervention program (Table 2), but the use of doxycycline generated the largest savings. The largest difference in net savings between the two drugs was approximately $261.6 million. This difference occurred when it was assumed that the program began on day zero (day of release), each drug was used in combination with the anthrax vaccine, a 3% discount rate was used, and a multiplication factor of 15 for unnecessary prophylaxis was used. This amount is equal to approximately 1.2% of the maximum total net savings generated by using a regimen of doxycycline plus the anthrax vaccine.

Some scenarios, particularly those in which prophylaxis programs were started late, generated negative net savings (i.e., net losses). In the case of tularemia, at a 5% discount rate, net losses of $10.7 to $115.1 million occurred when a post-exposure program was delayed until day 6 after exposure, and a prophylaxis regimen of doxycycline and gentamicin (estimated 95% efficacy) was used. For the same scenario, but with a 3% discount, a net savings of $1,513.3 million was observed when a multiplication factor of five for unnecessary prophylaxis was used. However, multiplication factors of 10 and 15 generated net losses of $49.8 and $102.0 million, respectively. With the same drug combination, beginning the program 1 day earlier (day 5 after exposure) resulted in net savings in all scenarios except when a multiplication factor of 15 and a discount rate of 5% were used. Under the latter two assumptions, net savings result only for prophylaxis initiated by day 4 after exposure.

In the case of brucellosis, the use of a doxycycline-rifampin regimen (estimated 80% efficacy), a multiplication factor of 15 for unnecessary prophylaxis, and a discount rate of either 3% or 5% generated net losses regardless of when intervention began (Figure 2). The doxycycline-gentamicin regimen (estimated 95% efficacy) generated net losses only when it was assumed that the start of a program was delayed until 113 or more days after exposure.

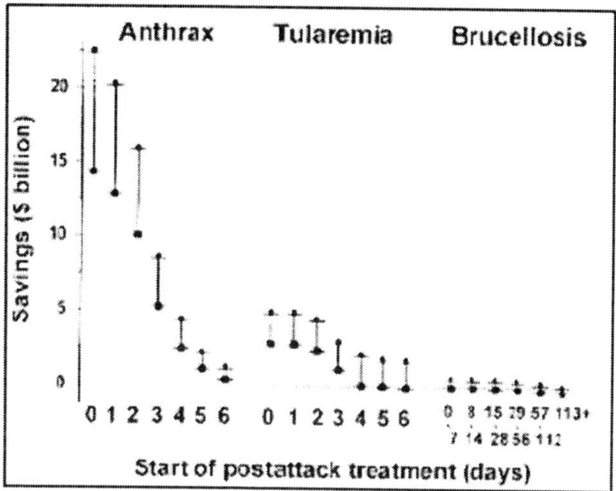

Figure 2

Ranges (a) of net savings due to postattack prophylaxis by disease and day of prophylaxis program initiation.

a) Maximum savings (l) were calculated by assuming a 95% effectiveness prophylaxis regimen and a 3% discount rate in determining the present value of expected lifetime earnings lost due to premature death[16] and a multiplication factor of 5 to adjust for unnecessary prophylaxis. Minimum savings (n) were calculated by assuming an 80% to 90% effectiveness regimen and a 5% discount rate and a multiplication factor of 15. In tularemia prophylaxis programs initiated on days 4-7 postattack, the minimum savings were calculated by assuming a 95% prophylaxis regimen effectiveness rather than an effectiveness of 80% to 90%.

Preparedness: Insurance

The annual actuarially fair premium that can be justifiably spent on intelligence gathering and other attack prevention measures increases with the probability that a bioterrorist attack can be decreased by such measures (Table 4). However, the potential net savings attributed to reduced probability are minor compared with the potential net savings from implementing a prophylaxis program. Depending on the level of protection that can be achieved, the annual actuarially fair premium in an anthrax scenario would be $3.2 million to $223.5 million (Table 4). The lower premium would be justifiable for measures that could reduce the risk for an attack from 0.01 to 0.001 and provide the ability to mount an intervention program within 6 days of the attack. The higher premium would be justifiable for measures that could reduce the risk from 0.01 to 0.00001 and allow immediate intervention if an attack occurred.

Table 4. The maximum annual actuarially fair premium(a) by reduction in probability of event and size of avoided loss: Anthrax

Days Post-attack(b)	Preventable Loss ($millions)	Actuarially fair annual premium ($ millions)		
		0.01 to 0.001	0.01 to 0.0001	0.01 to 0.00001
Maximum loss estimate(c)				
0	22,370.5	201.3	221.5	223.5
1	20,129.4	181.2	199.3	201.1
2	15,881.5	142.9	157.2	158.7
3	8,448.0	76.0	83.6	84.4
4	4,200.1	37.8	41.6	42.0
5	2,076.1	18.7	20.6	20.7
6	1,013.8	9.1	10.0	10.1
Minimum loss estimate(d)				
0	14,372.4	128.9	141.8	143.1
1	12,820.1	115.4	126.9	128.1
2	10,049.1	90.4	99.5	100.4
3	5,200.1	46.8	51.5	51.9
4	2,429.7	21.9	24.1	24.3
5	1,004.2	9.4	10.3	10.4
6	351.2	3.2	3.5	3.5

(a) See text for definition.
(b) No. of days from attack to effective initiation of prophylaxis.
(c) Maximum loss preventable (potential net savings) occurs with the doxycycline-anthrax vaccine prophylaxis regimen, a multiplication factor of 5 for unnecessary prophylaxis, and a discount rate of 3% (Table 2).
(d) Minimum loss preventable (potential net savings) occurs with the ciprofloxacin prophylaxis regimen, a multiplication factor of 15 for unnecessary prophylaxis, and a discount rate of 5% (Table 2).

Sensitivity Analyses

The upper estimates of the cost of hospitalization increased average costs per day by 18% to 22%, and upper estimates of the cost of outpatient visits increased average costs per day by 46% to 93% (Table 1). However, the upper estimates only increased medical costs by 1% to 6% of the total medical costs associated with a bioterrorist attack (Table 3). The largest increase was for brucellosis, for which upper estimates increased medical costs from 38% to 44% of total costs (Table 3).

When the number of persons infected during an attack was reduced tenfold, the patient-related costs were reduced proportionately (Table 3). In most cases, however, the net savings in total costs are less than 10% of the net savings when 100% of the target population was presumed infected. The shortfall in savings is caused by an increase in the number of unexposed persons receiving prophylaxis. In the case of anthrax, when intervention programs are initiated within 3 days of exposure, savings are 4.1% to 10% of those in the original scenario (Figure 2). Delaying initiation of prophylaxis until days 4, 5, or 6 after exposure, however, results in net losses of $13.4 to $283.1 million. Losses occur regardless of prophylaxis regimen, discount rate, or multiplication factor used to adjust for unnecessary prophylaxis by unexposed persons.

In scenarios in which a multiplication factor of 15 was used to adjust for unnecessary prophylaxis, the threshold value of intervention was always above the prophylaxis cost for anthrax but not above the prophylaxis costs for tularemia and brucellosis (Table 5). For tularemia, the threshold intervention costs exceeded disease costs up to day 5 in the scenario with 95% effectiveness and a 5% discount, and for brucellosis, at all levels in the scenarios with 80% effectiveness and up to day 56 in the scenarios with 95% effectiveness. This is consistent with the lower range of estimated net savings (net losses) given in Figure 2. Reducing the number of unexposed persons receiving prophylaxis increases the cost thresholds, making the program cost beneficial. For example, changing the multiplication factors for unnecessary prophylaxis to 5 and 10 increases the cost thresholds to $659 and $319, respectively, for a brucellosis prophylaxis program initiated 15 to 28 days after exposure, with a 5% discount rate. If a discount rate of 3% is used instead of 5%, the cost thresholds increase to $799 and $387. All these cost thresholds are above the estimated prophylaxis cost of $285 per person for the doxycycline-rifampin regimen and $161 per person for the doxycycline-gentamicin regimen (Table 2).

Table 5. Cost thresholds(a) of interventions ($/person) by day of intervention initiation, prophylaxis effectiveness, and discount rates.

Threshold costs for intervention ($/person, multiplication factor of 15(b))								
Anthrax			Tularemia			Brucellosis		
Post-Attack Day (d)	Disc.rate (c)		Post-Attack Day	Disc.rate		Post-Attack Day	Disc.rate	
	5%	3%		5%	3%		5%	3%
90% effectiveness(e)			*80% effectiveness(e)*			*80% effectiveness(e)*		
0	9,838	14,238	0	1,891	2,633	0-7	233*	282*
1	8,851	12,809	1	1,873	2,609	8-14	224*	272*
2	7,022	10,162	2	1,599	2,227	15-28	211*	255*
3	3,775	5,463	3	756	1,053	29-56	179*	217*
4	1,893	2,739	4	258	366	57-112	86*	104*
5	944	1,366	5	79	110	113+	24*	30*
6	468	677	6	20*	28			
Prophylaxis cost(c)	*$226*				*$28*			*$285*
95% effectiveness(e)			*95% effectiveness(e)*			*95% effectiveness(e)*		
0	10,370	15,007	0	2,229	3,104	0-7	274	333
1	9,359	13,544	1	2,207	3,074	8-14	264	320
2	7,427	10,948	2	1,898	2,644	15-28	248	301
3	3,995	5,782	3	898	1,251	29-56	211	256
4	2,004	2,900	4	328	457	57-112	102*	124*
5	1,000	1,447	5	93*	131	113+	29*	35*
6	496	718	6	23*	32*			
Prophylaxis cost(e)	*$238*				*$104*			*$161*

*Threshold value is below estimated cost of prophylaxis.
(a) Cost threshold is the point where cost of intervention and net savings due to the intervention are equal.
(b) Multiplication factor to adjust for persons who participated in the prophylaxis program but were unexposed.
(c) Applied to present value of expected future earnings and housekeeping services (weighted average for age and sex).
(d) Postattack day on which prophylaxis was effecively implemented.
(e) See Table 2 for prophylaxis regimens assumed to give the stated levels of effectiveness and cost/person of prophylaxis.

Conclusions

The economic impact of a bioterrorist attack can range from $477.7 million per 100,000 persons exposed in the brucellosis scenario to $26.2 billion per 100,000 persons exposed in the anthrax scenario (Table 3). These are minimum estimates. In our analyses, we consistently used low estimates for all factors directly affecting costs. The ID_{50} estimates for the three agents are twofold to 50-fold higher than previously published estimates,[5,6,10,11] resulting in a possible understatement of attack rates. Also, in our analyses we did not include a number of other factors (e.g., long-term human illness or animal illnesses) (Table 6) whose cumulative effect would likely increase the economic impact of an attack.

Our model shows that early implementation of a prophylaxis program after an attack is essential. Although the savings achieved by initiating a prophylaxis program on any given day after exposure has a wide range, a clear trend of markedly reduced savings is associated with delay in starting prophylaxis (Figure 2). This trend was found in the analysis of all three agents studied.

Table 6. Potential factors affecting the economic impact of a bioterrorist attack

Factor	Potential impact on net savings	Relative magnitude of impact
Higher than projected case-fatality rate	Increase	++++
Long term illness (physical and psychological)	Increase	++
Decontamination and disposal of biohazardous waste	Increase	++
Disruptions in commerce (local, national, and international)	Increase	++
Animal illness and death	Increase	+
Lower than projected effectiveness of prophylaxis	Decrease	- - -
Adverse drug reactions due to prophylaxis	Decrease	-
Postattack prophylaxis distribution costs, including crowd control and security	Decrease	-
Training and other skill maintenance costs	Decrease	-
Procurement and storage of antimicrobial drugs and vaccines before attack	Decrease	-
Criminal investigations and court costs	Variable	+/-

Delay in starting a prophylaxis program is the single most important factor for increased losses (reduced net savings). This observation was supported by the actuarially fair premium for preparedness analysis (Table 4). Reductions in preventable loss due to early intervention had significantly greater impact on the amount of an actuarially fair premium than reductions in probability of an attack through intelligence gathering and related activities.

Although implemented at different times in a threat-attack continuum, both attack prevention measures and prophylaxis programs are forms of preventive medicine. Attack prevention measures seek to prevent infection, while prophylaxis programs prevent disease after infection has occurred.

Using an actuarially fair premium analogy in which cost and benefit are required to be equal, we find that the incremental rate of increasing prevention effectiveness (the marginal increase) declines rapidly as probability reduction targets go from 0.001 to 0.0001 to 0.00001. Because the loss probability is decreasing on a logarithmic scale, the potential increment in marginal benefit drops comparably, resulting in ever smaller increments in the protection above the preceding base level.

Conversely, delaying a prophylaxis program for anthrax, a disease with a short incubation period and a high death rate, increases the risk for loss in a manner akin to a semilogarithmic scale. Arithmetic increases in response time buy disproportionate increases in benefit (prevented losses.) The potential for reducing loss is great because an attack is assumed, thus increasing the actuarially fair premium available to prepare for and implement a rapid response.

Large differences between prophylaxis costs and the threshold costs for most scenarios, particularly if prophylaxis is early (Table 5), suggest that the estimates of savings from prophylaxis programs are robust. Even with large increases in prophylaxis cost, net savings would still be achieved.

The ability to rapidly identify persons at risk would also have significant impact on costs. For example, the threshold costs for brucellosis prophylaxis are often lower than intervention costs when the ratio of unexposed to exposed persons in the prophylaxis program is 15:1 (Table 5). This finding provides an economic rationale for preparedness to rapidly and accurately identify the population at risk and reduce unnecessary prophylaxis costs.

The maximum amount of the annual actuarially fair premium varies directly with the level of risk reduction and the rapidity of postattack response (Table 4). The calculated amount of actuarially fair premiums, however, should be considered a lower bound estimate. A higher estimate (called the certainty equivalent) can also be calculated; however, this requires the determination of a social welfare function (22), and such complexity is beyond the scope of this study.

Our model provides an economic rationale for preparedness measures to both reduce the probability of an attack and increase the capability to rapidly respond in the event of an attack. The larger portion of this preparedness budget (insurance premium) should be allocated to measures that enhance rapid response to an attack. These measures would include developing and maintaining laboratory capabilities for both clinical diagnostic testing and environmental sampling, developing and maintaining drug stockpiles, and developing and practicing response plans at the local level. These measures should be developed with a value-added approach. For example, the laboratory capability could be used for other public health activities in addition to preparedness, and drugs nearing their potency expiration date could be used in government-funded health care programs. However, these secondary uses should not undermine the preparedness program's effectiveness.

Notes

1. Cole LA. The specter of biological weapons. Sci Am 1996;275:60-5.

2. Gochenour WS. Aerobiology. Mil Med 1963;128:86-9.

3. Abramova FAN, Grinberg LM, Yampolskaya OV, Walker DH. Pathology of inhalational anthrax in 42 cases from the Sverdlovsk outbreak of 1979. Proc Natl Acad Sci 1993;90:2291-4.

4. Benenson AS, editor. Control of communicable diseases manual. 16th ed. Washington (DC): American Public Health Association, 1995.

5. Messelson M, Guillemin J, Hugh-Jones M, Langmuir A, Popova I, Shelokov A, et al. The Sverdlosvsk anthrax outbreak of 1979. Science 1994;266:1202-8.

6. Kaufmann AF, Fox MD, Boyce JM, Anderson DC, Potter ME, Martone WJ, et al. Airborne spread of brucellosis. Ann NY Acad Sci 1980;335:105-14.

7. Olle-Goig JE, Canela-Soler J. An outbreak of *Brucella melitensis* infection by airborne transmission among laboratory workers. Am J Public Health 1987;77:335-8.

8. Staszkiewicz J, Lewis CM, Colville J, Zervos M, Band J. Outbreak of *Brucella melitensis* among microbiology laboratory workers in a community hospital. J Clin Microbiol 1991;29:287-90.

9. Trever RW, Cluff LE, Peeler RN, Bennett IL. Brucellosis I. laboratory-acquired acute infection. Arch Intern Med 1959;103:381-97.

10. McCrumb FR. Aerosol infection of man with *Pasteurella tularensis*. Bacteriolical Reviews 1961;25:262-7.

11. Saslaw S, Eigelsbach HT, Wilson HR, Prior JA, Carhart S. Tularemia vaccine study II. respiratory challenge. Arch Intern Med 1961;107:689-701.

12. Friedlander AM, Welkos SL, Pitt MLM, Ezzell JW, Worsham PL, Rose, KJ, et al. Postexposure prophylaxis against experimental inhalation anthrax. J Infect Dis 1993;167:1239-42.

13. Sawyer WD, Dangerfield HG, Hogge AL, Crozier D. Antibiotic prophylaxis and therapy of airborne tularemia. Bacteriolical Reviews 1966;30:542-8.

14. Solera J, Rodriguez-Zapata M, Geijo P, Largo J, Paulino J, Saez L, et al. Doxycycline-rifampin versus doxycycline-streptomycin in treatment of human brucellosis due to *Brucella melitensis*. Antimicrob Agents Chemother 1995;39:2061-7.

15. Luce BR, Manning WG, Siegel JE, Lipscomb J. Estimating costs in cost-effectiveness analysis. In: Gold MR, Siegel JE, Russell LB, Weinstein MC, editors. Cost-effectiveness in health and medicine. New York: Oxford University Press, 1966:176-213.

16. Haddix AC, Teutsch SM, Shaffer PA, Dunet DO, editors. Prevention effectiveness: a guide to decision analysis and economic evaluation. New York: Oxford University Press, 1996.

17. Lipscomb J, Weinstein MC, Torrance GW. Time preference. In: Gold MR, Siegel JE, Russell LB, Weinstein MC, editors. Cost-effectiveness in health and medicine. New York: Oxford University Press, 1966:214-35.

18. U.S. Bureau of the Census. Statistical abstract of the United States: 1995. 115th ed. Washington (DC): U.S. Government Printing Office, 1996.

19. National Center for Health Statistics. Health, United States, 1995. Hyattsville (MD):U.S. Department of Health and Human Services, Public Health Service, 1996.

20. HealthCare Consultants of America, Inc. HealthCare Consultants' 1996 physicians fee and coding guide. 6th ed. Augusta (GA): HealthCare Consultants of America, Inc. 1996.

21. Cardinale V, editor. 1996 Drug Topics Red Book. Montvale (NJ): Medical Economics Company, Inc., 1996.

22. Robison LJ, Barry PJ. The competitive firm's response to risk. New York: Macmillan, 1987.

CHAPTER 10

Needed Now:
The 85 Percent Solution to the CBW Threat

Jim A. Davis and Bruce W. Bennett

Introduction

Some new proposals are presented to provide an "85% Quick Fix," including implementation of a Bio-Threatcon level, building preparation, providing off the shelf 1/2 mask respirators and more.

The search for the "best solution" for bio-defense is proving to be an obstacle to finding the more immediate "good solution." In the day when Americans have grown used to fast food, instant access to the Internet, and minimal United States' casualties during war, many have come to expect a "silver bullet solution" for almost any problem. The military, like the rest of America, is often in quest for the 100% solution to its challenges. For example, the military, now awakened to the biological warfare/biological terrorism (BW/BT) threat, is in search of the perfect solution to the problem posed by biological weapons. The pursuit of the 100% solution often diverts efforts from potential quick (though incomplete) fixes for such tough problems that could provide valuable protection. Some new proposals are presented to provide an "85% Quick Fix,"[1] including implementation of a Bio-Threatcon level, building preparation, providing off the shelf 1/2 mask respirators and more. While the technical information in this paper needs further study, it is hoped this chapter will provoke discussion and stimulate the development of new ideas for immediate solutions (albeit partial solutions) rather than waiting on the 100% solution.

In April 1990, two U.S. naval bases, Yokosuka and Yokohama, were attacked with botulinum toxin, and although they failed, the scenario could have turned out much different. A home-grown Japanese terrorist organization, Aum Shinrikyo, had amassed over a billion dollars in net worth and had developed a clandestine biological warfare program. This group became famous for its nerve agent attack in the Tokyo subways in March 1995 that killed 12 and injured 5,500. Fortunately, in 1990, technology and scientific know-how were not as accessible as they are today, and as a result, the Aum Shinrikyo cult had not perfected its program.[2] To our knowledge, no U.S. forces became ill from this attack. But if this attack occurred today when technological capabilities and the proliferation of information are rampant, it seems far more likely they would have been successful, leading to thousands of U.S. forces casualties.

Likewise, consider the Gulf War in 1991 when the U.S. had 320,000 military personnel massed in a 50 by 150 mile rectangular area southeast of Iraq. The Office of the Secretary of Defense estimated if an anthrax attack had occurred on our troops, 76,300 individuals would have died if they were not vaccinated. On the other hand, if all were vaccinated, it was estimated that only 122 would have died. Conversely, what if the attack had been tularemia, Q-fever, or a host of other biological agents for which we do not have a vaccine? Thousands would have died or become ill because we did not have even a partial protection from such agents. Yet, if an "85% Quick Fix" was put into place, hundreds or possibly thousands of lives could be saved, allowing the military mission to continue.

Since there is no mechanism in place today to provide even partial protection from a biological warfare attack at most military installations, both the Aum Shinrikyo and the Gulf War scenarios have grave implications. U.S. military forces could suffer death tolls higher than the tragic events of September 11, 2001, unless some interim efforts for partial protection occur prior to finding the 100% solution. With the "85% Quick Fix," it is hypothesized 85% of the affected soldiers would be protected.

Indeed, there is an obligation to protect our forces completely from threats when practical. We owe that protection to U.S. military personnel, to their families, and to our nation. Yet, the complexities of this threat make it difficult to field comprehensive defensive measures in the near-term — and BW/BT threats exist today. The weapons of this threat are bacteria, viruses, other microorganisms, and toxins. Unlike TNT, chemicals, and radioactive material, biological organisms are alive and can adapt to new challenges in the quest for survival. These invisible weapons are much different from other threats. They can be released to travel difficult terrain silently and effortlessly over long distances, creating sickness and death in their wake.

Sometime in the 21st century we may be able to provide 100% protection against all the dozens of pathogens that might be used as weapons. However, unless we adopt a group of partial fixes now, our military forces will be left grossly vulnerable to the BW/BT threat while we search for a more comprehensive breakthrough in vaccines, sensors, and other counters. We have much ground to make up in biodefense. Until very recently, senior DoD leaders were unable to grasp the urgency in protecting military forces and were unwilling to obligate large investments necessary to counter an unlikely event. Hopefully that has changed.

The anthrax attacks in the United States during the Fall of 2001 have helped convert many such doubters, but further complicating a solution is the fact that some within DoD have seen this problem as "too hard to do." Not knowing just what to do and not sure the threat was real, they did little. Also, one of the difficulties in preparing for this threat is the military's fixation on technological answers more than procedural solutions. That finally may be changing, because a few in the military are beginning to ask, "Is there an inexpensive, quick fix that can provide partial protection for our forces while we look for the 100% solution?"[3] Our frustrating quest for such items like the "detect to protect"[4] technology provided by biological detectors or highly reliable vaccines for a myriad of pathogens has led many to despair. Others have realized that for immediate protection, new technology innovations may not be the major portion of the immediate solution.

Today, more than a dozen countries are suspected of having some level of a biological warfare program. It is also true that terrorist organizations such as Al-Qaeda have shown a keen interest in obtaining these weapons. Since Al-Qaeda says it is their God-ordained responsibility to kill Americans and most of the countries with BW/BT programs are not our best of friends, it is important we get to the immediate business of what might be termed the "85% Quick Fix"– some simple, effective, and immediate counters to today's biological weapons threat. Effective interim and partial protection might be accomplished with several simple procedural changes and by minor applications of current technology at modest expense.

The quest for the perfect answer can be the enemy of the "good solution," and <u>no one would credibly argue that 100% of personnel left unprotected in the near term is better</u> than <u>protecting 85% of personnel immediately</u> through quick-fix procedures.

Defining the BW/BT Threat

The biological threat can be quantified by integrating three distinct variables:[5]

- An adversary's *intent* to use biological weapons

- An adversary's *capability* to use biological weapons

- Our own *vulnerability* to biological weapons

Enemy *Intent* + Enemy *Capability* + U.S./Allied *Vulnerability* = Threat

It is beyond the scope of this chapter to thoroughly analyze the possible intent of various rogue states/adversaries or to fully describe the myriad of biological weapon agents that may be used in an attack. Likewise, it is important to understand that to appropriately defeat BW/BT a full range of activities should be pursued, including: arms control, export controls, diplomatic and economic sanctions, deterrence, counterforce, active defense, passive defense and consequence management. However, this analysis will look at how a few simple and immediate steps can be taken to mitigate the hazards from biological weapons in the areas of passive defense, intelligence and warning, consequence management, and active defense/offensive options.

Understanding BW Agents

Threats like biological warfare/biological terrorism can be serious when the United States and/or its allies are vulnerable, and this is generally the case for every BW agent. This vulnerability is in turn a function of the characteristics of the BW agents and their various delivery systems. Nevertheless, the details of U.S. vulnerability are critical to determining the potential impacts of a BW attack.

Many sources suggest that BW threats can be overwhelming. The actual area in which people would be affected by BW would vary depending upon the means of delivery (aerosol delivery is generally expected to be the most serious),[6] the quantity and positioning of the BW source, time of day, weather conditions, where people are located, what they are doing when exposed, and various other factors. For example, the Congressional Office of Technology Assessment indicated that 100 kilograms of anthrax could cover 46 to 300 square kilometers with lethal effects, depending upon weather conditions,[7] while other sources suggest potentially larger areas.[8] Another source suggests that spray from "… a single airplane could be expected to infect a high percentage of individuals within an area of at least 10,000 km^2" with equine encephalitis (VEE, EEE, or WEE).[9] These large areas suggest that even Special Forces carrying a kilogram or so of BW, could affect large parts of a city, airfield, port, ground force base, or command/control or logistics facility. An aircraft or missile carrying tens of kilograms of BW agents could thoroughly overwhelm most military targets and cover much of the surrounding areas.

There are a significant number of biological agents that have different characteristics, as shown in Table 1. These weapons vary in their potency (ECt$_{50}$),[10] their lethality, their survivability in air and other media, their period of incubation and duration of effects, whether they are contagious between people, the degree to which they can be prevented (e.g., by vaccines) or treated (e.g., by antibiotics), and their potential resistance to various forms of treatment (e.g., in antibiotic resistance). For example, a toxin like Staphylococcal Enterotoxin B (SEB) could rapidly affect a military population (starting within 2 hours or so), would have serious effects for perhaps a day or so, have residual effects for as long as weeks, should cause few fatalities, and could be treated only by supportive treatment. Alternatively, some bacterial weapons like anthrax and plague take longer to incubate, are highly lethal, but can generally be countered by certain antibiotics if these are taken in a timely manner and the BW agent has not been engineered to resist the antibiotic.

Table 1

Characteristics of Some BW Agents

Agent	ECt_{50}* (μg)-min/m^3	Nighttime Decay (%/min)	Untreated Mortality(%)	Incubation (Days)	Contagious	Treatment	Vacc.
Bacteria							
Anthrax	0.01	0-0.1	100	1-6	No	Antibiotic	Yes
Plague	0.01	10	100	2-3	Yes	Antibiotic	No**
Tularemia	0.0001	5	5-60	2-10	No	Antibiotic	IND
Q Fever	0.00002	0-0.1	0-1	10-40	Rare	Antibiotic	IND
Toxins							
Bot Tox	0.1	5	5	1-5	No	Antitoxin*	IND
Ricin	200*	?	High*	18-24 hr*	No*	Support*	No*
SEB	0.03*	1	1	3-12 hr	No	Support*	No
Viruses							
VEE	?	?	Low*	2-6*	Low*	Support*	IND*
Ebola	?	?	50-90*	4-21*	Moderate*	Support*	No*
Smallpox	0.1	0.5	15-40	7-17	Yes	Support*	Yes

* ECt_{50}- Exposure Concentration Time 50%; Vacc. – Vaccine; SEB-Staphylococcal Enterotoxin B; VEE - Venezuelan Equine Encephalitis; IND – Investigational New Drug

Source: Brian G. Chow, et. al., *Air Force Operations in a Chemical and Biological Environment*, RAND, DB-189/1-AF. 1998, 29. Values with a "*" come from USAMRIID, *Medical Management of Biological Casualties Handbook*, February 2001, 64 and Appendices C, D, and I. The vaccine for plague "**" (actually for bubonic as opposed to pneumonic plague) is no longer being produced per Thomas V. Inglesby, et. al., "Plague as a Biological Weapon," *JAMA*, May 3, 2000, 2285.[11]

The impact of the different potency and decay rate values is illustrated in Figure 1, based on a series of biological weapons exposure curves produced by the Hazard Prediction and Assessment Capability (HPAC) model for a one-kilogram BW agent release of one-kilometer width. The model also assumes a temperature inversion and a wind speed of approximately 10 mph. Even in daylight (8:00 a.m.), the model shows that the concentration of viable anthrax stays above the median infective dose for an hour or so after the release (reflecting its relative resistance to

UV degradation). This is enough time to cover most fixed military targets as long as there is a temperature inversion, the wind was properly forecast, and the original release was sufficiently wide. At night (8:00 p.m.), the anthrax concentration stays above the median infective dose for several hours, sufficient to cover large military assembly areas with a favorable breeze. In contrast, the greater potency (determined by the reduced number of microorganisms required to induce infection) of tularemia starts with far higher infective dose levels, but the infective dose declines much more rapidly because of the decay rate of tularemia in air. Still, the dosage for tularemia is well above the median infective dose for almost two hours, giving reasonable time to cover most fixed targets. Indeed, even modest amounts (a kilogram or so) of both anthrax and tularemia should carry well beyond an intended military target and could affect large civilian areas under ideal conditions. With anthrax, doses well less than the median infective dose may still cause some lethal exposures many hours after the release, well downwind of the target.[12]

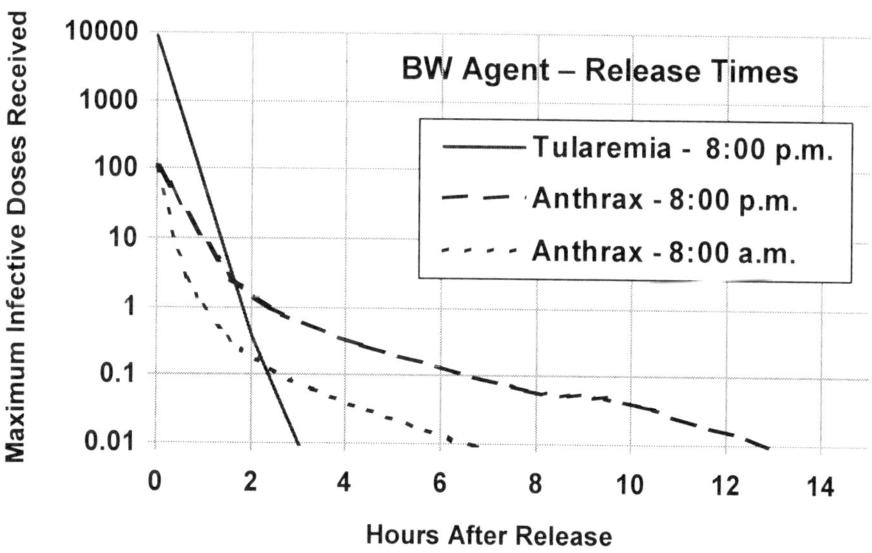

Figure 1 - Maximum Infective Dose Received at the Front of a BW Cloud traveling at approximately 10 mph.
(Decreased dose over time is primarily due to degradation from ultraviolet light and dispersion of the agent in the air. This figure is based on a one kilogram released over a distance of one kilometer.)[13]

Antibiotics against bacterial weapons can often be effective, whether used for treatment[14] or for post-exposure prophylaxis.[15] Nevertheless, use of antibiotics could still lead to some debilitating side effects[16] that could impact both civilian and military operations. While antibiotics fight bacteria, many toxins and viruses lack a direct means of treatment (as shown in Table 1), meaning that victims will be sick and many will be incapacitated for some period of time.

The Soviets, recognizing the potential for antibiotics to defeat many biological agents, developed genetic variations of BW agents (such as plague, anthrax, and tularemia), that were resistant to various antibiotics. One of the Soviets' former leading bio-weaponeers stated:

"There was a task force to develop a new strain of weapon with a resistance to ten antibiotics. These antibiotics were first released in the United States and some European countries just to treat infections. In 1989 it was very difficult to have strains of plague resistant to antibiotics. But one of our facilities developed a new approach. They developed two different strains resistant to five antibiotics each. And they cultivated them together and they have a mutual relationship, one with another. That was about ten, twelve, fifteen years ago. Recently, Russian scientists have proclaimed success in developing a *Bacillus anthracis* strain resistant to most antibiotics."[17]

Mitigating U.S./Allied Vulnerability Against Bio-Weapons

The U.S. military has studied the BW threat and concluded that the military's goal of full-dimensional protection, enshrined in *Joint Vision 2020*,[18] cannot be achieved against BW today (no 100% solution). Each element of a potential response to BW use is limited in its ability to resolve the threat. Therefore, no individual element can mitigate the BW threat. Yet, the "85% Quick Fix" could be realized if the following four areas are addressed: passive defense, intelligence and warning, consequence management, and active defense/offensive options.

Passive Defense Quick Fixes

Passive defenses seek to prevent the infection of people by a BW attack. Passive defenses include several elements:

Vaccines - A vaccine is an antigen that is introduced into the body to stimulate the immune system to build defenses against that antigen. An effective vaccine will neutralize a specific virus, bacteria, toxin, or rickettsiae - the four categories of BW agents. In the future it is hoped one vaccine will be developed that boosts the immune system against all or many diseases. But for now, vaccines are disease-specific. Relatively few vaccines are FDA approved for use against BW agents, and all of those, specifically the anthrax and smallpox vaccines, are controversial. Nevertheless, vaccines are one of the most effective ways to reduce BW vulnerability, especially against the most serious BW agents like anthrax and smallpox. This is probably the greatest payoff area for protecting military forces long term and DoD should fund this at much higher levels.

Individual protective equipment (IPE) - includes various kinds of masks and suits; it keeps BW agents away from people and thereby prevents infection. The quandary with IPE is that its use reduces operational effectiveness, and in many weather conditions, it can only be used for a limited period of time (it causes heat casualties and other effects after a period of minutes to hours). The most devastating BW threats come from aerosol delivery; a commercial half mask respirator will significantly reduce biological agent inhalation providing protection factors of 50 to 500 or more against BW stimulants—a level of protection often adequate to prevent infection, without the operational degradation and heat burden of traditional chemical masks.[19]

Collective protection systems (CPS) - are facilities that provide a BW-free area by filtering incoming air. These are places where people can eat and sleep, change clothes, and perform other operations without being vulnerable to BW agents or having to wear the hot and cumbersome protective boots, gloves, masks and over garments. Many facilities could provide much protection from BW agents, albeit not 100% protection, with minimal upgrades as outlined later.

Biological decontamination - includes solutions and delivery devices to neutralize BW agents in the air, ground, water, or on people or their clothing. Advances are being made technologically in this field and will help us move toward the 100% solution.

<u>Avoidance and Operations</u> - With chemical weapons, rapid detection of an attack allows commanders to direct personnel to avoid exposure, for example by moving in-doors and turning off heating, ventilation, and air conditioning (HVAC) systems that would otherwise draw the agent into the building. Because biological weapon detection is so slow, such procedures generally will not be implemented quickly enough after detection to help; indeed, by the time BW detection occurs, the air outside will likely be clear of contamination while the air inside buildings may be contaminated because of HVAC operations.[20] Therefore, if the HVAC was shut off shortly after an attack the levels of BW agent might linger in a building long after the outside air has cleared.

Dissimilarly, the sensitivity and rapid response of chemical detectors allows users to fairly quickly identify the area of contamination and mark it so that people can be directed to stay out. But with BW, most detectors, due to sensitivity and specificity shortfalls, may not identify some contaminated areas and may not be sufficiently sensitive to identify some potentially infectious dosages. As a result, an extremely conservative view is often taken whereby detection of any BW agent usually becomes the basis for complete isolation of that and surrounding areas; this will probably help people to avoid contamination but often restricts the use of more areas than necessary, while missing some areas that may be contaminated.

One concept of military operations when potentially facing chemical or biological weapon threats is similar to the concept when facing nuclear threats: forces should disperse to operate at low density to reduce the damage that can be done by any given attack. Currently most concepts of operations are designed to build tent cities that force all the personnel in a small area. It is not clear, however, that military units are prepared to execute dispersion of personnel on a base. While this would be beneficial for a point release close to the base, this concept would not be as helpful for a line source release that would disperse BW agent over a large area. Nevertheless, an effort to disperse people on a base if there is a potential BW attack might lessen the likelihood of some individuals being exposed once an attack occurs.

Operational procedures can also help when combined with knowledge of the limits of various biological weapons. Most biological agents degrade rapidly with ultraviolet (UV) light. For instance, *Francisella tularensis* dies at a rate of 50% every 20 minutes on a bright sunny day. There are only two biological agents that are generally considered "UV resistant" and those are *Bacillus anthracis* (anthrax) and *Coxiella burnetii* (Q Fever). Even though their degradation is refractory to UV light, they still decay at a rate of approximately or less than 0.1% per minute in sunlight.[21] Based on this understanding, it is far more productive and, therefore, likely for an adversary who wants <u>mass casualties</u> to launch a BW/BT attack when there is no sunlight, since such an attack has a much greater potential for delivering higher concentrations of virulent organisms.

Although biological agents can be delivered by several mechanisms, biological agents that are aerosolized would be dependent on the wind to move them. If it is a day with less than 3 mph of wind and an attacker is outside the fence of a military installation spraying a biological agent, the germ cloud will not move very far and probably will not pose a major threat to personnel on base. Conversely, if the wind is too strong, perhaps at speeds greater than 23 to 25 mph, the cloud of agent is thought to become so unstable and diffuse so rapidly that it is unlikely to deliver enough concentration to infect many individuals and cause a mass casualty event. Of course, distance from the point of dissemination is also important here. If an individual or group was very close to the release point, whether there was slow or fast wind speeds, concentrations may still be high enough to infect large numbers of people.[22]

In order for a biological weapons attack to be <u>optimally successful</u>, the wind needs to be blowing at certain velocities and no UV light should be present. Additionally, biological agents will not infect anyone unless they are close to the ground in the human breathing zone, 3 to 7 feet above the surface. This means a temperature inversion would be necessary to keep large concentrations of the BW agent close to the ground. Temperature inversions, where cold air overlays and pins warmer air against the ground, may occur at various times of the day but usually occur at dawn, dusk, or night. Also, certain seasons of the year are more likely to have temperature inversions than others, helping forecasters to predict their occurrence. Additionally, it may seem counterintuitive, but Bill Patrick, an expert in offensive biological warfare, has stated that light to moderate rain or snow will not appreciably affect the delivery of aerosolized BW agents. In other words, light to moderate rainstorms do not wash the skies clean of BW particles.[23]

<u>Building Preparation Before the Attack</u> - All buildings, including homes, where persons might be present during dawn, dusk or night should be inspected and made as airtight as possible. Simple efforts such as caulking, painting, taping, or sealing around doors or windows might greatly reduce the airflow through a building.[24]

Inexpensive small particle air filters are now available at hardware stores that can be installed in most existing air conditioning or heating units. This is not as good as creating positive pressure throughout a building to keep air flowing into it, nor does it provide as good a filtration as provided by a High Efficiency Particulate (HEPA) filter, but it is something that can be done now with minimal expense.

Although there are many manufacturers of these types of filters, here are two examples of filters that can be purchased at local hardware stores. Web Products from Kansas City, Kansas has a filter called *The Web Plus* that is marketed as "trapping 91% of the pollen, dust, and dander sized particles from 0.245 to 85 microns" and the fourteen by twenty inch version was priced at $8.40 per filter.

3M Construction and Home Improvement Markets Division from St. Paul, Minnesota has a filter called *Filtrete: Ultra Allergen filter* that is marketed as "90% effective at capturing large allergens like mold spores and pet dander ... captures bacteria and particles that can carry viruses" and in calling their toll free number, one of the authors was told that it is "90% efficient at removing particles from 0.1 to 10 microns." The 3M filter was $15.97 per filter for the sixteen by twenty inch size. The idea of using these higher efficiency filters is to get a quick improvement in filtering BW/BT agents without requiring new blowers or other expensive, time consuming modifications to be made to existing ventilation systems.

Since buildings with larger concentrations of people might elevate the risk of mass casualties if they became contaminated, some extra precautions might be reasonable for them. Buildings that would likely house over, perhaps, 50 people at dawn, dusk, or night could be equipped with counter-bactericidal UV lights in the ventilation systems. Rather than turning them on during higher Bio-Threatcon levels, it would probably be easiest to have them lit whenever the ventilation system is running. The lights would need to be arranged in ventilation ducts to provide maximum contact with BW agents. Although these may not affect *Bacillus anthracis*, *Coxiella burnetii*, or smallpox appreciably, the lights, if properly arranged, would likely have significant effect on many other bacterial agents.

Stand-alone room filtering devices are now available as commercial off-the-shelf items. These small freestanding units re-circulate the air in rooms through the unit's filter thereby trapping particles. If biological agents get into the building, these devices might greatly reduce the level of concentrations that people would breathe. This would be effective as long as the filter captured particle sizes in the 1 to 10 micron diameter range, the size that tends to lodge in the lungs of those exposed. A side benefit filters like this might offer is that if a BW attack did occur they could be sent to a diagnostic lab for confirmation of the particular agent that had been in the air.

Intelligence and Warning

The greatest problem in defending against BW attacks is the limited amount of intelligence and warning we will likely have. In contrast to chemical weapon attacks, where there are a multitude of detectors that can provide tactical warning of attacks, there are BW detectors at very few bases today (though the number of bases is expanding), and in general, they take too long to provide adequate attack warning.

For example, the Portal Shield system deployed at a number of U.S. military bases takes roughly half an hour to process an air sample and determine that it potentially contains a BW threat. By that time, an aerosolized BW cloud has usually passed through a military base being attacked, exposing almost everyone before protection can be applied in response to warning. This type of warning is usually referred to as "detect to treat" rather than "detect to protect," the preferred approach. Detect to treat allows the base to promptly begin treatment for BW exposure, which could significantly reduce or eliminate casualties in the case of most bacterial and some other biological weapons.

A preferred solution for warning would involve rapid standoff detection: the ability to see BW agents in an approaching cloud and quickly identify them. If this can be achieved, then personnel would have time to don protective clothing or move into protected buildings before arrival of a BW cloud, and thereby, not be infected. Work is ongoing to develop such detectors, but they appear to be still several years away from production and deployment.

In places where there are no BW detectors or as a back-up to BW detectors, discovery of a BW attack can be achieved by disease surveillance at hospitals and other medical facilities. Recognition of a BW attack may not happen until symptoms develop, which, according to the incubation periods in Table 1, will normally be days after the attack. Still, aggressive disease surveillance is an important part of the "85% Quick Fix" and should receive major attention and resourcing at installations.

However, when the initial detection of a BW attack has happened, it is then necessary to confirm that the suspected biological agent is indeed what it appears to be, and also to determine if it has been mixed with other biological agents (especially contagious ones) which have not yet been detected. This process is pursued through advanced medical laboratory capabilities. Once such a confirmation is accomplished, medical officers have a stronger basis for taking actions to treat for the identified BW agent.

While the military has labs capable of such confirmation in a few locations overseas, it needs to deploy more labs and enhance the capabilities of these facilities (giving them the ability to identify more types of BW agents)—an important part of the "85% Quick Fix." Although each year technology greatly improves the ability to detect and identify particular BW agents, appropriate resourcing with today's technology would provide a large and immediate improvement. The ongoing cost will be that the Department of Defense will need to be willing to switch out old systems as new technologies for bio-detection are developed, much like it does as it continually updates its computer and software systems.

Bio-Threatcon Levels - To reduce U.S. forces, Allied Forces, and civilian *vulnerability* to BW/BT attacks, military installations should develop and issue warnings of the daily Bio-Threat condition (Bio-Threatcon) level, reflecting the <u>likelihood of a successful aerosol BW attack that could inflict massive numbers of casualties</u>. Then decision guidelines can be established to help commanders make reasonable and logical force protection decisions.

The Bio-Threatcon level would be determined by two pieces of information – the first, "<u>BW/BT Intel Threat (BIT)</u>" levels, is designed to help predict the likelihood of a BW attack. The intelligence officer at each installation could fuse at least four and perhaps more types of information to assign a BIT level: (1) the current overall force protection level (alpha, bravo, charlie, delta), (2) current intelligence assessments of the BW/BT *capability* of an adversary, (3) assessments of the predicted *intent* of the adversary, and (4) assessments of adversary movement of SOF or activity with other potential BW delivery systems.

This data, some objective and some subjective, would be amalgamated to come up with a BIT level (ranging from 1 to 4). "One" would indicate that an adversary is very unlikely to use BW on the given military installation, whereas, "Four" would indicate a BW attack was very likely. Two and three would be interim ranges between one and four.

The BIT level would be integrated with another variable, the "Bio-Attack Climatology Effectiveness" (BACE) level, which would be made up of meteorological factors such as wind speed, ultraviolet light levels, and the probability of a temperature inversion. A meteorological computer model could be developed without great difficulty to integrate these three variables, as a minimum, giving current and projected <u>BACE levels that would predict the likelihood of specific meteorological conditions for successfully delivering enough biological agents to cover an airfield or other military facility to cause mass causalities</u>. Note, though, that depending upon the size of the target to be affected and other factors, a successful BW attack might still be carried out in conditions that are not climatologically ideal.

The BACE levels would be assigned so that BACE-1 means the climatogical conditions are extremely adverse toward a successful biological attack, whereas a BACE-4 rating would indicate the existence of optimal climatic conditions for a successful enemy biological attack.

For BIT level 2 and above (heightened likelihood of an attack), the BACE computer model should be run continuously. At these heightened threat levels the "Bio-Attack Climatology Effectiveness" levels should be available instantly to the Intelligence Officer and the Command Staff because BACE is meaningless unless it is combined with the "BW/BT Intelligence Threat" level. At the BIT level 1, "Bio-Attack Climatology Effectiveness" levels would only be calculated intermittently to indicate the conditions that would be climatologically ideal for a mass casualty attack using a BW agent.

After the "BW/BT Intel Threat"(BIT) level and "Bio-Attack Climatology Effectiveness"(BACE) levels are determined, it would be easy for a commander to see where their axes intersect and determine an overall Bio-Threatcon level (**BIT + BACE = Bio-Threatcon Level**). This intersection would be assigned a designator of alpha, bravo, charlie, or delta. Similar to other threatcon levels that the military are accustomed to, the alpha is the lower threat level while the delta is the highest threat level. The model (Table 2) shows alpha where the threat is so low that a commander would not need to implement protection procedures. But a delta would mean the highest level of threat for a successful biological attack that might cause mass casualties has been achieved, and all personnel on the installation are at great risk. Obviously, bravo and charlie are in between areas where there is a heightened threat of exposure but are less likely than delta.

A notification system for base personnel at military facilities also would need to be designed. Some options available are the installation "Giant Voice," audio and visual alarms, individually carried beepers, and/or television broadcast warnings. Base personnel should exercise these notification procedures during dawn/dusk hours or the times a given base is most likely to be vulnerable. The entire base populace, even civilians and dependents, will need to become familiar with these procedures because any large number of people that become casualties would affect the mission regardless of who they are.

Currently, most installation meteorologists, bioenvironmental engineers, epidemiologists and intelligence officers at the installation level do not have adequate training in biological warfare issues. To properly manage the Bio-Threatcon levels and be a valuable consultant to the commander, these individuals would require scientific training dealing with aerodynamics of BW agents, signatures of BW facilities, etc.

The idea of including a biological warfare threatcon level into the more well known "Force Protection Condition Level" (FPCON) is attractive to help simplify the number of indices a commander would have to keep track of to protect his forces, but it would undermine the awareness needed. Just as there is an "Information Threat Condition Level" (INFOCON) that is distinct from FPCON, Bio-Threatcon levels should also be distinct.[25]

Several unique aspects of BW/BT make it appropriate that the Bio-Threatcon level be separate from FPCON. Some examples of these unique aspects include: (1) silent weapons that can be delivered many miles from the base, (2) some adversaries are known to already possess BW/BT capability, (3) some adversaries are thought to be very <u>unlikely</u> to use BW/BT, (4) the intent of certain adversaries may be clearly toward civilian rather than military targets, (5) detection of an ongoing attack is not very likely because of the level of sophistication of today's detection systems, or, (6) unlike conventional weapons, aerosol delivered biological weapons can be greatly affected by meteorology.

Table 2

<u>Commander's Decision Matrix</u> to <u>Avoid Mass BW/BT Casualties</u>
Bio-Threatcon Levels[26]

'BIT-4: Attack most likely)	BIT-4	*Bravo*	*Charlie*	*Delta*	*Delta*
	BIT-3	*Alpha*	*Bravo*	*Charlie*	*Charlie*
	BIT-2	*Alpha*	*Bravo*	*Bravo*	*Bravo*
	BIT-1	*Alpha*	*Alpha*	*Alpha*	*Alpha*
'BIT-1: Attack least likely)					

<u>BW/BT Intel Threat</u> **<u>(BIT) level</u>**	BACE-1	BACE-2	BACE-3	BACE-4
	(Low effectiveness)			*(High effectiveness)*
(BIT level is derived from at least four components of information)	**<u>Bio-Attack Climatology Effectiveness (BACE)</u>**			
1. FPCON level 2. Capability of adversary 3. Intent of adversary 4. Adversary's movement of BW/BT delivery systems	*(UV light, Wind Speed,* *Probability of Temperature Inversion)*			

<u>Bio-Threatcon</u> **<u>Levels:</u>**	*Alpha* = Minimal Threat	*Charlie* = Partially Effective BW/BT attack possible with elevated risk
	Bravo = Partially Effective BW/BT attack is possible	*Delta* = Effective BW/BT attack is likely

Below are some thoughts on how a commander could respond at the different Bio-Threatcon Levels:

1. A (*Alpha*) - No precautions needed.

2. B (*Bravo*) -

   • All outside personnel on duty must wear lightweight half mask[27] respirators that cover nose and mouth, which can be purchased inexpensively using commercial off the shelf (COTS) technology.

   • All other personnel are encouraged to stay indoors or, if they must go outside, to wear the half mask respirator.

   • Outside personnel are educated to stand with their back to the wind as much as is possible when outside as long as it does not affect completion of the mission.[28]

   • Building ventilation systems should be turned off unless special filters are installed. (Discussed in section titled "Building preparation before the attack.")

   • Keep all windows and doors shut.

   • Assigned installation personnel should increase air-sampling procedures.

   • The medical staffs in hospitals/clinics are notified of the Bio-Threatcon level to give a heightened awareness of a biological threat and exhibit greater vigilance in disease surveillance.

   • Inside buildings and shelters, personnel must turn on room airflow filter units (Discussed in section titled "Building preparation before the attack.")

3. C (*Charlie*) -

   • All outside personnel on duty must wear lightweight half mask respirators that cover nose and mouth, which can be purchased inexpensively using commercial off the shelf (COTS) technology.

   • Only in an emergency situation should dependents or other personnel exit a building. In that case they should wear their half face respirator.

• Outside personnel are educated to stand with their back to the wind as much as is possible when outside as long as it does not affect completion of the mission.

• Building ventilation systems should be turned off unless special filters are installed. (Discussed in section titled "Building preparation before the attack.")

• Keep all windows and doors shut.

• Assigned installation personnel would increase air-sampling procedures.

• The medical staffs in hospitals/clinics are notified of the Bio-Threatcon level to give a heightened awareness of a biological threat and exhibit greater vigilance in disease surveillance.

• Inside buildings and shelters, personnel must turn on room airflow filter units (Discussed in section titled "Building preparation before the attack.")

• Personnel must have sleeves rolled down.

• Upon detection of BW agents in the area, prophylaxis must begin immediately.

4. D (*Delta*)-

• All outside personnel on duty should wear a <u>full-face</u> military protective mask and hood.

• Only in an emergency situation should dependents or other personnel exit a building. In that case, they should wear their half face respirator.

• Turn off ventilation units unless unbearable temperature demands they run; even then, let operate only if they have a special filter installed. (Discussed in section titled "Building preparation before the attack.")

• Keep all windows and doors shut.

• Assigned installation personnel would increase air-sampling procedures.

- The medical staffs in hospitals/clinics are notified of the Bio-Threatcon level to give a heightened awareness of a biological threat and exhibit greater vigilance in disease surveillance.

- Inside buildings and shelters, personnel must turn on room airflow filter units (Discussed in section titled "Building preparation before the attack.")

- Personnel must have sleeves rolled down.

- Upon detection of BW agents in the area, prophylaxis must begin immediately.

Consequence Management Suggestions

Once a BW attack has occurred, military efforts can be organized to manage the consequences of those attacks. A major aspect of consequence management involves medical treatment with antibiotics, serums, and other appropriate therapies designed to prevent, mitigate, and cure various diseases caused by BW agents. Sufficient medical care personnel will be required to handle casualties, and plans should be made for how to handle mass casualties. Likewise sufficient medications and supplies can be stockpiled in advance in specified locations.

Greater care needs to be taken after a contagious biological weapons attack to prevent further spread of the disease. Quarantine procedures need to be put in place to handle such situations, and police and other security personnel will need to be mobilized to enforce such quarantines. Unfortunately, it is often impossible to know whether a person is infected with a contagious disease until they show symptoms. Therefore, once it appears that a biological weapon has been used, it may be necessary to impose a local quarantine until medical authorities can explicitly rule out the possibility that contagious diseases were not included in the attack.

Note that this may impair the most likely approach to handling mass casualties: moving casualties to other medical facilities. It will often be necessary to solve the mass casualty problem in the area of the initial outbreak until the incubation period has passed for potential contagious diseases (as long as a couple of weeks) or until other actions can be taken to prevent the disease in those not yet symptomatic. This approach will be a serious problem for the U.S. military, which normally plans to stabilize and then evacuate all casualties. Instead, they may be forced to bring in medical care personnel, supplies, and equipment, and thereby potentially disrupt the force flow into a combat region. By resolving these quarantine, manpower, and supply issues in advance, the "85% Quick Fix" will help enhance protection immediately at other locations.

It may also be necessary to impose some travel restrictions after a biological warfare attack, even when it was clearly not contagious. For example, if a military service member were exposed in Country A, but was transported to Country B and then developed symptoms there, the military may not be able to prove whether this person was exposed in Country A or in Country B, potentially causing hysteria to spread to Country B unnecessarily. All travel should likely be restricted from the area where a BW attack occurred until enough time has passed to definitively diagnose the disease as non-contagious. Note that whether quarantine or travel restrictions are imposed, these will likely disrupt noncombatant evacuation and even conventional casualty evacuation from the area attacked.

With BW attacks, it will not be uncommon for psychological reactions to occur in greater numbers than actual BW/BT casualties. Masses of people, including many with little chance of having been in the infected area, will insist upon receiving medical treatment, potentially exhausting medical supplies in that area. Some will even develop psychosomatic symptoms, making them difficult to differentiate from actual casualties until laboratory work can be accomplished (and thus heightening the laboratory workload.) Many will also try to flee the area of infection, potentially seeking to break quarantine or travel restrictions.

Every effort needs to be made to prevent and then later treat psychological reactions. Efforts to understand the "panic phenomena" and the "worried well" in a BW event should be a priority but often remain under-funded. Aggressive efforts in planning and executing public relations and public information before an attack will probably be one of the commander's most valuable investments to ensure mission completion and prevent chaos. This will usually be best done with an active public information campaign to explain to people what has happened and what they should do about it. The public information effort can be vastly aided if authorities can accurately determine the time and area of the attack, thereby excluding many people from fear. But the capabilities to do so today are inadequate, and efforts to make such projections may only undermine the effectiveness of the public information as mistakes are made.

Every military facility should have public information packages for various BW agents and various scenarios detailing the types of information that should be released to the public or military forces and when they should be released. The Israeli Home Front Command has had hands on experience with many threats to their population over the last decade. As a result, they have a comprehensive system of communicating with the entire country through television, radio, faxes to key personnel, etc. Additionally, they have prepared thousands of information messages ready to be disseminated depending on the type of event. Their appreciation for minimizing panic and minimizing the numbers of "worried well" has helped them to come up with these valuable mitigation procedures.[29]

Active Defense and Offensive Options

Some BW threats may be best countered using active defenses or offensive options. Active defenses seek to intercept and destroy the means of WMD delivery before they reach the target area. U.S. and allied forces are normally very effective in intercepting opposing aircraft threats, though they would likely be less effective at intercepting ballistic and cruise missiles or terrorists/special forces. Since SOF-delivered BW is perhaps the largest BW threat, active defenses need to be augmented in the form of a more robust security system that is capable of patrolling and monitoring upwind of an installation.

Another way to defeat biological weapons use is to destroy BW through attack operations (counterforce) before the BW can be used. To do so, one must be able to locate the biological weapons storage and production sites and have the proper agent defeat type munitions available to destroy the BW in these sites. As noted earlier, it is difficult at best to locate these sites using current methods. These actions need to be taken before the adversary can disperse its BW agents.

Perhaps one of the strongest defenses against biological weapons use is the ability to inflict unacceptable levels of damage on countries that use such weapons. Such a retaliatory capability may deter BW attacks if the U.S. leadership possesses both the tools and the will to strike back. Nevertheless, even if he fears capture, a terrorist may not be deterred by retaliatory threats because the terrorist may lack a home location or some other valued item that he would not want damaged by retaliation.

Conclusions

The quest for the "perfect" long-term protection against biological warfare or terrorist attacks must not become the enemy of the "good" solution today. Partial measures can provide significant levels of protection against biological threats at U.S. and allied military bases and facilities.

First, a new Bio-Threat condition alerting system needs to be created, and personnel need to be trained in its use.

Second, each military base must make upgrades to its facilities and acquire commercial off-the-shelf technologies to provide protection to building occupants.

Third, inexpensive masks must be purchased and personnel, including civilians and dependents, should be trained in their use.

In addition, we must deploy biological agent detectors more broadly, enhance disease surveillance systems, enhance stocks of medical supplies needed to treat casualties of biological attacks, design realistic plans to handle mass bio-casualties, develop procedures for quarantine and travel restrictions, and prepare to manage the psychological effects that are expected in the wake of biological weapons attacks.

These are some of the effective quick fixes available to United States now to counter mass casualty bio-events. We need to bolster protection today via the "85% Quick Fix" while working on longer-term, more perfect countermeasures to protect against emerging biological warfare and terrorist threats.

Notes

1. The 85% number here is notional. We believe that a large percentage of potential BW casualties can be averted through a series of quick fixes, but the actual percentage will vary by type of BW and other issues. We cannot say with precision what the actual

improvement will be with detailed scientific studies. Nevertheless, the basis for the 85% number is derived from a scientific understanding of Biological Warfare.

2. David E. Kaplan and Andrew Marshall, *The Cult at the End of the World* (New York: Crown Publishers, 1996), 92, 251, 294.

3. An example of one effort is the U.S. Air Force's *Biological Defense Task Force*, which was a 120-day project in the summer and fall of 2002. This was an effort directed by the Chief of Staff of the USAF through HQ USAF/XONP to assist in developing a concept of operations for military installations in the event it was faced with biological warfare.

4. "Detect to protect" means that a biological attack can be detected before people are infected, giving them time to protect themselves from infection before it arrives.

5. Lt Col Don Noah, USAF, "Medical Intelligence with a Weapon Focus on Biological Warfare." Presentation was at the USAF Counterproliferation Center, Maxwell AFB, on 11 Jan 2000 to an Air War College elective class. He stated that U.S. national threat assessments often uses the formula of: intent + capability + vulnerability = threat. Lt Col Noah was the primary author of the National Medical Intelligence Threat Assessment for the United States, published in January 2000.

6. "Biological weapons can be deployed in three [primary] ways: by contaminating food or water supplies; releasing infected vectors, such as mosquitoes or fleas; or creating an aerosol cloud to be inhaled by the victims. By far, the most effective mode for applying biological weapons [to produce mass casualties] is an aerosol cloud. Such a cloud is made up of microscopic particles and is therefore invisible." Ken Alibek, Testimony to the House Armed Services Committee Oversight Panel on Terrorism, May 23, 2000.

7. *Proliferation of Weapons of Mass Destruction: Assessing the Risks*, U.S. Congress Office of Technology Assessment, August 1993, 53-54.

8. See Steve Fetter, "Ballistic Missiles and Weapons of Mass Destruction," *International Security*, Summer 1991. Computer models like Hazard Predication and Assessment Capability (HPAC) show areas where varying fractions of those present will become anthrax fatalities. Dr. Bruce Bennett did four HPAC runs assuming the use of five kilograms of anthrax, the results of which provide a useful comparison. For an untreated and non-vaccinated population the 90 and 50 percent lethality areas range from 2 to 26 square kilometers (90 percent lethality) and from 31 to 2,600 square kilometers (50 percent lethality). The 20 percent lethality areas run from 500 to 15,000 square kilometers, and the 2 percent fatality areas run from 6,000 to 32,000 square kilometers.

9. Jonathan F. Smith, et. al., "Viral Encephalitides," in *Medical Aspects of Chemical and Biological Warfare*, eds. Frederick R. Sidell, Ernest T. Takafuji, and David R. Franz,

(Washington, D.C.: Office of the Surgeon General, U.S. Army, 1997). (VEE is Venezuelan Equine Encephalitis; EEE is Eastern Equine Encephalitis; and WEE is Western Equine Encephalitis.

10. ECt_{50} is Effect Concentration Time 50%. The ECt_{50} is a measure of the dose at which 50 percent of the population experiences the agent's primary effect. "For a vapour cloud or aerosol presenting a respiratory hazard, the exposure can be conveniently expressed as the product of the agent concentration (C) and the exposure time (t), which is known as the 'Haber Product', or 'Ct' exposure, with units of milligrams minutes per metres cubed (mg.min.m-3). (33) Since the susceptibility to CW agents varies from human to human, it is not possible to specify an exact minimum effective dosage or lethal dose for each agent. As a result, scientists can only define the dosage that has a specified probability of producing a particular effect. It is possible to define the term 'Effect Ct_{50}' (ECt_{50}) which indicates the Ct exposure that has a 50% probability of producing some kind of an effect." Found at British Ministry of Defence site: http://www.mod.uk/issues/gulfwar/info/ukchemical/annexa.htm on 17 January 2003; Also see Brian G. Chow, et. al., *Air Force Operations in a Chemical and Biological Environment*, RAND, DB-189/1-AF. 1998, 29.

11. This table is a modification of the unclassified table at: Brian G. Chow, et. al., *Air Force Operations in a Chemical and Biological Environment*, RAND, DB-189/1-AF. 1998, 29. On-line. Internet, 9 September 2002. Available from http://www.rand.org/publications/DB/DB189.1/DB189.1.pdf/DB189.1.sec2.pdf. Values with a "*" come from USAMRIID, *Medical Management of Biological Casualties Handbook*, February 2001, 64 and Appendices C, D, and I. The vaccine for plague "**" (actually for bubonic as opposed to pneumonic plague) is no longer being produced per Thomas V. Inglesby, et. al., "Plague as a Biological Weapon," *JAMA*, May 3, 2000, 2285.

12. In the aftermath of the anthrax letters, the threshold dose required for some level of anthrax lethality was widely debated. A recent article indicated that even a few spores (about 0.0003 median lethal dose) might cause lethality in a small percent of those exposed, well below the 0.01 levels shown in this chart. See C.J. Peters and D.M. Hartley, "Anthrax Inhalation and Lethal Human Infection," *The Lancet*, February 23, 2002, 710.

13. Dr. Bruce Bennett employed a series of eight HPAC forecasts to estimate these curves; the results showed some variability for other factors, with these curves reflecting roughly median values.

14. For example, 6 of the 11 victims of inhalation anthrax from the 2001 anthrax letters survived based upon antibiotic treatment that started after the development of symptoms. Indeed, in all cases where antibiotic treatment was started during the initial phase of the illness (post-symptoms), the victims survived. See John A. Jernigan, et. al., "Bioterrorism-Related Inhalation Anthrax: The First Ten Cases Reported in the United States," *Emerging Infectious Diseases*, November-December, 2001, 933-944.

15. After potential anthrax exposure, antibiotic use (referred to as prophylaxis) can prevent the disease from developing. See Thomas V. Inglesby, et. al., "Anthrax as a Biological Weapon, 2002," *Journal of the American Medical Association*, May 1, 2002, 2244-2248.

16. See CDC, "Update: Adverse Events Associated with Anthrax Prophylaxis Among Postal Employees – New Jersey, New York City, and the District of Columbia Metropolitan Area, 2001," *Morbidity and Mortality Weekly Report*, November 30, 2001, 1051-1054.

17. Alibek Interview, *Op. cit.*

18. *Joint Vision 2020* is the vision document from the Chairman of the Joint Chief of Staff.

19. "Protection Factor (PF) and Saturation Testing of Commercial Negative Pressure Half-Mask Respirators," Edgewood Chemical & Biological Center (ECBC) Interim Technical Memorandum; Soldier and Biological Chemical Command (AMSSB-REN), Aberdeen Proving Ground, MD, November 9, 2001.

20. "Once the outdoor concentration has diminished to safe levels (as determined by emergency response teams), evacuate the building and flush it with outdoor air. After the contaminated plume passes, the concentration of contamination will actually be higher inside the building than outside, because the building will tend to retain contamination that managed to enter" Phillip N Price, Michael D Sohn, Ashok J Gadgil, et.al., *Protecting Buildings From a Biological or Chemical Attack: actions to take before or during a release., LBNL/PUB-5195.* (Berkeley, California: Lawrence Berkeley National Laboratory, January 10, 2003), 11.

21. Bill Patrick, Biological Warfare Consultant, "The United States Offensive Biological Program (1940-1972)." Presentation was at the USAF Counterproliferation Center, Maxwell AFB, on 19 Feb 1999 to an Air War College elective class.

22. Bill Patrick, Biological Warfare Consultant, "Fundamentals of Biological Warfare." Presentation was for the USAF Counterproliferation Center at USAMRIID, Ft Detrick, Maryland, on 13 Sept 2002 to an Air War College elective class.

23. This can be understood by realizing that only a small portion of each cubic foot of air will have water passing through it during a light or moderate rain or snow. This allows most BW agents to escape being washed to the ground by the water particles passing through it. Bill Patrick, Biological Warfare Consultant, "The United States Offensive Biological Program (1940-1972)." Presentation was at the USAF Counterproliferation Center, Maxwell AFB, on 19 Feb 1999 to an Air War College elective class.

24. Phillip N Price, Michael D Sohn, Ashok J Gadgil, et. al., *Protecting Buildings From a Biological or Chemical Attack: actions to take before or during a release, LBNL/PUB-5195.* (Berkeley, California: Lawrence Berkeley National Laboratory, January 10, 2003), page 30; Centers for Disease Control and Prevention, "Guidance for Protecting Building Environments from Airborne Chemical, Biological, or Radiological Attacks, " May 2002, 19; and on-line, Internet, 10 November 2002, available from http://www.cdc.gov/niosh/bldvent/2002-139.html.

25. There may be some who will complain that BIT, BACE, INFOCON, FPCON and the nation's new homeland security threat levels are all a bit too much for commanders to remember. Yet, the high consequence of an effective BW/BT attack necessitate it receive a separate threat condition from the FPCON. By commingling it with the existing FPCON, this will reinforce in commander's minds that BW/BT is like the chemical threat or other threats. Over time, this will ultimately diminish the commander's understanding of this threat and hence, decrease the proper emphasis that should be placed against this potentially catastrophic and unique danger.

26. The complex nature of command requires commanders to make assessment of risk and deal with those risks while completing the military mission. Dr. Jim Davis developed this table as one concept that could be used to help commanders make simple, yet critically important decisions. A table like this could be applied across the spectrum of all military installations. For instance, an installation in the continental U.S. would hopefully never reach a BIT-2 and would therefore never reach a Bio-Threatcon level of Bravo. Likewise, an installation located in South Korea might frequently be at BIT-2 necessitating its Bio-Threatcon level to change with as climatology (BACE) changes.

27. Two inexpensive respirators were bought randomly from a local hardware to show the accessibility of protective gear. Mine Safety Appliances (MSA) Company had two respirators priced reasonably: *Dust Respirator with odor filter for Harmful Dust* ($4.93) and *Dust Respirator with exhalation valve for Harmful Dust* ($6.97). Both respirators were rated N95. According to a manufacturer representative this means the filters in these masks can filter 95% of the particles down to 0.3 microns. The main concern for human infectivity of BW/BT agents is the 1 to 10 micron range.

28. Bill Patrick related through personal anecdotal experience that by having his back to the wind with even crude respiratory protection reduced the concentration of deposited BW agent simulate around his face. Bill Patrick, Biological Warfare Consultant, "Fundamentals of Biological Warfare." Presentation was for the USAF Counterproliferation Center at USAMRIID, Ft Detrick, Maryland, on 13 Sept 2002 to an Air War College elective class.

29. Col Gilad Shenhar, Head of Doctrine & Development Dept., Israeli Defense Force Home Front Command, "Home Front Command Overview with Emphasis on Chemical and Biological Warfare Issues. " Presentation was given at Home Front

246

Command Headquarters, Israel on 30 Oct 2002 to a delegation of USAF officers (one of the authors was part of the delegation) supporting the Office of the Secretary of Defense's Bilateral Counterproliferation Working Group.

Contributors

Dr. Bruce W. Bennett is the research leader for strategy, force planning, and counterproliferation within RAND's International Security and Defense Policy Center. His work focuses on the future of warfare and military analysis, especially in light of new technologies, operational concepts, and threats. He is examining the operational and strategic implications of possible chemical, biological, and nuclear threats that could be posed in Korea and the Persian Gulf, and the character of the U.S. strategy required in response, with a focus on deterrence. He facilitated the Coral Breeze seminars on CBW for CINC Combined Forces Command (Korea), the Desert Breeze seminars on CBW for USCENTCOM, and parts of USCENTCOM's Eagle Resolve exercises with the Gulf States. He has worked on defenses against chemical and biological weapons in the CASPOD ACTD (Contamination Avoidance at Sea Ports of Debarkation), the RestOps ACTD (Restoration of Operations at airfields after CBW attack), and the subsequent USPACOM Counter-BW research effort. He has also worked on deterrence-based strategy, future force planning procedures, peacetime force requirements, and future threats and the military forces required to counter them.

Dr. Bennett received a Ph.D. in policy analysis from the RAND Graduate School and a B.S. in economics from the California Institute of Technology. He has served as an Adjunct Professor at the U.S. National War College, as an Adjunct Lecturer in the School of Public Health at the University of California at Los Angeles, and is a Professor of Policy Analysis in the RAND Graduate School.

Dr. Stephen F. Burgess is Deputy Chair of the Department of Strategy and International Security, Assistant Professor of International Security, Air War College, and an Associate of the USAF Counterproliferation Center (CPC). Previously, he was a faculty member at the University of Zambia, Vanderbilt University, and Hofstra University. Dr. Burgess completed his Ph.D. at Michigan State University, was a Fulbright-Hays fellow, and a Research Associate at the University of Zimbabwe. His two books are *Smallholders and Political Voice Zimbabwe*, University Press of America, 1997, and *The United Nations Under Boutros Boutros-Ghali, 1992-97*, Scarecrow Press, 2002. Dr. Burgess and Dr. Helen Purkitt collaborated on a monograph, *The Rollback of the South African Chemical* *and Biological Warfare Program* for the CPC and the Institute of National Security Studies (INSS), U.S. Air Force Academy. They are writing a book, *South Africa and Weapons of Mass Destruction*, which will be published by Indiana University Press in 2004. Recently, Dr. Burgess completed research on "Arms Control and Missile Defense in South Asia" and "India's Emerging Security Strategy and Defense Capabilities" for CPC and INSS.

Lieutenant Colonel Harry W. Conley is Chief of the Force Analysis Branch at Headquarters Air Combat Command (ACC), Langley Air Force Base, Virginia. He is responsible to the ACC commander for analytic studies that evaluate the effectiveness and efficiency of current and future Combat Air Force weapon systems. He is currently investigating the effectiveness of Air Force precision-guided weapons used in Operation Iraqi Freedom. Lt Col Conley is a graduate of the U.S Air Force's Air War College, and holds a M.S. in Operations Research from the Georgia Institute of Technology, and a B.S. from the U.S. Air Force Academy. He won second place in the 2001 Chairman of the Joint Chiefs of Staff Strategy Essay contest for his paper entitled "Not With Impunity: Assessing U.S. Policy for Retaliating to a Chemical or Biological Attack." His publications include: "Air Force 2025 Operational Analysis," in *Military Operations Research*, Vol. 3, No. 4, 1997, and "Foundations 2025: A Value Model for Evaluating Future Air and Space Forces," in *Management Science*, Vol. 44, No. 10, October, 1998.

Colonel Jim A. Davis is the Deputy Director of the USAF Counterproliferation Center. Previously, Colonel Davis was the Deputy Chair to the Department of Future Conflict Studies at Air War College and the AF Surgeon General's Chair to Air University. He also served as the Commander, 48th Aerospace Medicine Squadron at RAF Lakenheath, UK where he was responsible for the largest Aerospace Medicine Squadron in USAFE, which oversees flight medicine, optometry, preventive medicine, health promotion, public health, industrial hygiene, and bioenvironmental engineering. He provided support to USAFE fighters, European Tanker Task Force, and MOOTW in Europe, Africa, and the Middle East. He also served as UK Medical Intelligence Officer and USAFE Consultant for Public Health. Colonel Davis served 4 years in the U.S. Army Veterinary Corps, 6 years in private veterinary medicine, and has been in the Air Force since 1987. His areas of special interest include CBW, bioterrorism, and occupational epidemiology. Colonel Davis has several academic degrees including a Doctorate of Veterinary Medicine from Texas A&M and a Doctorate of Public Health from the University of Texas. He is board certified with the American College of Veterinary Medicine and through his experience at Plum Island, New York, has become a Foreign Animal Disease Diagnostician.

Lieutenant Colonel Michael E. Dickey is the Deputy Commander, 99th Security Forces Group (ACC), Nellis Air Force Base Nevada. He is responsible for training, arming and equipping the 650+ person security group comprised of two operational security squadrons and one training squadron providing security, antiterrorism and force protection to Nellis AFB and the Air Warfare Center. Colonel Dickey enlisted in the USAF as a security specialist in 1973, and participated in the evacuations of Saigon, RVN, Phnom Phen Cambodia, and recovery of the SS Mayaguez before becoming an instructor at the USAF Security Police Academy. A 1979 distinguished graduate of Officer Training School, he has held a variety of leadership positions, from security shift commander through expeditionary support group commander. He has commanded four security forces squadrons; one training squadron, served as Deputy Commander, 820th Security Forces Group and as Commander, 366th Expeditionary Support Group during Operation ENDURING FREEDOM.

Charles C. Engel, Jr., MD, MPH, Lieutenant Colonel, Medical Corps, U.S. Army, is an Associate Professor & Assistant Chair (Research) of the Department of Psychiatry at the Uniformed Services University and the Director of the Department of Defense (DoD) Deployment Health Clinical Center at Walter Reed Army Medical Center. He is a psychiatrist-epidemiologist and an expert on population-based health care and clinical aspects of environmental risk communication for people with idiopathic symptom syndromes after war, terrorism, and disasters. Dr. Engel is a respected researcher who has coauthored over 60 scholarly articles including articles in JAMA, American Journal of Psychiatry, and Controlled Clinical Trials. He has served as co-PI on four nation-wide multicenter clinical trials testing the impact of various health care improvements for military and VA health care beneficiaries. The Deployment Health Clinical Center's mission is to improve post-deployment health care, and Dr. Engel is the DOD team leader for three DOD-VA clinical practice guidelines including post-deployment health evaluation and management, medically unexplained symptoms, and major depressive disorder.

Carol S. Fullerton, Ph.D., is a Research Associate Professor and the Science Director, Center for the Study of Traumatic Stress, Department of Psychiatry, USUHS. Dr. Fullerton did her undergraduate work in Psychology at Alfred University, NY and her graduate training at the Institute for Child Study, University of Maryland. Dr. Fullerton was the Research Psychologist for the Adolescent & Child Division at Chestnut Lodge Hospital, Rockville, MD from its inception (1974) until 1986. She helped establish the research program and served as coordinator of research for the Adolescent and Child Division, Chestnut Lodge. Dr. Fullerton joined the faculty of the Department of Psychiatry at USUHS as a Postdoctoral Fellow in 1986.

Dr. Fullerton has published in the areas of posttraumatic stress response, the role of social support following trauma, and the stress on spouses of disaster workers. She has examined adolescents and families in long-term psychodynamic psychotherapy. She serves as consultant to disasters and is currently examining the acute and long-term responses to disaster and trauma. Her funding sources include: National Institute of Mental Health, the U.S. Army, the U.S. Air Force and USUHS. Dr. Fullerton was the recipient of the Meritorious Service Medal in 1990 for her consultation and research to the Sioux City, Iowa plane crash of 1989 and the recipient of the USUHS Exceptional Service Award. She is a Fellow of the American Orthopsychiatric Association, and a member and journal reviewer for the American Psychological Association and the International Society for Traumatic Stress Studies. Her research focuses on the role of social support in responses to trauma.

Harry C. Holloway, M.D. a 1958 graduate of the University of Oklahoma School of Medicine, spent 30 years in the U.S. Army Medical Corps. During this time, he was Chief of Neuropsychiatry at SEATO Medical Research Laboratory in Bangkok, Thailand; Director of Neuropsychiatry at Walter Reed Army Institute of Research; and Chairman of the Department of Psychiatry at Uniformed Services University of the Health Sciences (USUHS). He remained Psychiatry Chairman until 1990 when he became Deputy Dean and Acting Dean of the School of Medicine at USUHS. From August of 1992 until March of 1993 he served as Deputy Dean. Dr. Holloway was awarded the honorary degree of Doctor of Military Medicine by USUHS in 1992. He has received the Legion of Merit and Defense Superior Service Medal.

Dr. Holloway has served as Chairman of the National Aeronautics and Space Administration (NASA) Aerospace Medicine Advisory Committee. Dr. Holloway served as the first Associate Administrator for the Office of Life and Microgravity Sciences and Applications at NASA from 1993 to 1996 and as Co-Director of the NASA Enterprise for the Human Exploration and Development of Space (HEDS). During his tenure, his office supported the integration of thirteen shuttle missions (including the first missions to Mir) and the development of the science facilities for the International Space Station. He has received three decorations from NASA: the NASA Medals for Leadership, Distinguished Public Service, and Distinguished Service.

Dr. Holloway is presently at the F. Edward Hébert School of Medicine where he serves as Professor of Psychiatry and Professor of Neuroscience and Assistant Chairman for Research in the Department of Psychiatry. He currently serves on the Gulf War Illness Advisory Committee of the Veterans Administration. Dr. Holloway is the author of over forty publications. He is Life Fellow of the American Psychiatric Association (APA) and has received the APA's Distinguished Psychiatrist Award.

Arnold Kaufmann, D.V.M., M.S., D.A.C.V.P., CAPT, USPHS (Ret), is currently a Senior Service Fellow with the Division of Emergency and Environmental Health Services, National Center for Environmental Health, Centers for Disease Control and Prevention (CDC), Atlanta, GA. Dr. Kaufmann is an infectious disease epidemiologist who has been associated with the CDC since 1963. His career has focused on the study of the epidemiology, pathology, clinical presentation, treatment and prevention of zoonotic diseases such as anthrax, brucellosis, tularemia, and plague in man and animals. These studies have been reported in more than 100 scientific and medical journal articles. Since 1995, Dr. Kaufmann has been involved in preparedness issues related to terrorism, such as the development of casualty projection models and training exercises. He was part of the team that documented the attempted use of *Bacillus anthracis* as a biological weapon by the Aum Shinrikyo.

Dr. Martin I. Meltzer is the Senior Health Economist, Office of Surveillance, Office of the Director, National Center for Infectious Diseases, Centers for Disease Control and Prevention (CDC) in Atlanta, GA.

He received a BSc Agric (Hons) from the University of Zimbabwe in 1982, and Masters and a Doctorate in Applied Economics from Cornell University, NY, in 1987 and 1990, respectively. His research interests include examining the cost-benefit and cost-effectiveness of various health interventions, and developing strategic plans and formulating policy guidelines and recommendations for the use of health technologies, such as vaccines. Much of his work is multi-disciplinary in nature and his research emphasizes "interfacing" between the biological and the social sciences. Examples of his more recent research include the modeling of potential responses to smallpox as a bioterrorist weapon, examining the economics of vaccinating restaurant foodhandlers against hepatitis A, evaluating the cost-effectiveness of Lyme disease vaccination, assessing the economic impact of pandemic influenza, modeling the economics of controlling raccoon rabies using an oral vaccine, assessing the global economic impact of dengue, and evaluating the economics of a planning and preparing for a bioterrorist attack.

Dr. Meltzer has published more than 100 publications, including approximately 60 articles in peer-reviewed journals, two U.S. patents and seven book chapters. He also led two teams, each of which produced software to help state and local public health officials plan and prepare of catastrophic infectious disease events. One program, FluAid, helps estimate the potential impact of the next influenza pandemic, and another, MaxiVac, helps officials plan a large-scale smallpox vaccination clinic. Among the honors accorded to him, Dr. Meltzer has been nominated four times for CDC's Charles C. Shepard award, winning it in 2001, and has been awarded the James H. Nakano citation four times. He is an associate editor for Emerging Infectious Diseases, and has been a guest editor and a member of the editorial board for Agriculture and Human Values. For The Lancet, he helps co-ordinate reviews of manuscripts on health economics and has refereed manuscripts for 15 different journals. He also supervises a number of post-doctoral health economists at CDC.

Ann E. Norwood, LTC(P), MC, USA, received her A.B. (1976) in Psychobiology from Vassar College, and M.D. (1981) from the Uniformed Services University of the Health Sciences. She completed her residency in Psychiatry (1985) at Letterman Army Medical Center, San Francisco. She was the Chief of Psychiatry at Darnall Army Community Hospital, Ft. Hood, TX before coming to the University in 1988. Dr. Norwood currently serves as Associate Professor of Clinical Psychiatry and

Associate Chairman for the Department of Psychiatry. Her excellence in teaching has been recognized through the Nancy C.A. Roeske Award for Outstanding Medical Student Education given by the American Psychiatric Association. She is also the recipient of the William C. Porter Award given by the Association of the Military Surgeons of the United States for outstanding contributions to military psychiatry. Dr. Norwood's major research interest is in the area of psychiatric responses to trauma and disaster with a special focus on stressors affecting women in the military. An extension of traumatic stress, family violence, is also an active area of research.

Dr. Helen E. Purkitt obtained her Ph.D. in International Relations from the University of Southern California. She is a Professor of Political Science at the U.S. Naval Academy. Her research and teaching interests include African politics, environmental politics, international relations theory, and political decision-making. Past INSS/NARC sponsored research includes developing a system to monitor environmental threats in African regions (1997) and "The Politics of Denuclearization: The Case of South Africa" (1995). She is currently completing an on-line introductory Political Psychology textbook and a book-length manuscript on South Africa's past, present, and future defense policies. Recent publications include, "A Problem Centered Approach for Understanding Foreign Policy: Some Examples from U.S. Foreign Policy toward Southern Africa" in S. Nagel (Ed.) *Handbook of Global International Policy* (New York: Marcel Dekker, 2000), Editor, *Annual Editions: World Poltics 00/01* (Dushkin/McGraw Hill, 2000); "Bridging Gaps: The Experiences of Two Members of the First Generation of Civilian Women Professors at USNA," in F. D'Amico and L. Weinstein (Eds.) *INSIDE/OUTSIDE: Women & the U.S. Military* (New York University Press, 1998); and, "Problem Representations and Political Expertise: Evidence from 'Think Aloud Protocols of South African Elites," in D. Sylvan and J.F. Voss (Eds.), *Problem Representation in International Relations* (Cambridge University Press, 1998).

George Schmid, M.D., M.Sc., CAPT, USPHS (Ret.), is an infectious diseases epidemiologist with the HIV/AIDS Department of the World Health Organization, Geneva, Switzerland. After receiving an M.D. degree from Northwestern University School of Medicine and subsequent training in family medicine, internal medicine, and infectious diseases, he joined the Centers for Disease Control and Prevention (CDC) in 1979, working initially with bacterial zoonoses, followed by 18 years' experience in the field of sexually transmitted infections. Although maintaining an interest in zoonotic diseases, he is most actively working in the fields of reproductive tract infections, HIV infection, health economics, and evidence-based medicine.

Dr. Barry R. Schneider is the Director of the USAF Counterproliferation Center (CPC) at Maxwell AFB, and is also a Professor of International Relations at the Air War College. Dr. Schneider specializes in WMD counterproliferation and nonproliferation issues. He is the author of *Future War and Counterproliferation: U.S. Military Responses to NBC Proliferation Threats* (Praeger, 1999); Editor, *Middle East Security Issues, In the Shadow of Weapons of Mass Destruction Proliferation* (CPC, 1999); and contributor to and co-editor of *Know Thy Enemy: Profiles of Adversary Leaders and Their Strategic Cultures* (CPC, 2003), *The Gathering Biological Warfare Storm* (CPC, 2002), *Pulling back from the Nuclear Brink: Reducing and Countering Nuclear Threats* (Frank Cass Ltd., 1998), *Battlefield of the Future: 21st Century Warfare Issues* (Air University Press, 1998), *Missiles for the Nineties: ICBMs and Strategic Policy* (Westview, 1984), and *Current Issues in U.S. Defense Policy* (Praeger, 1976). He has served as a Foreign Affairs Officer (GS-14) and Public Affairs Officer (GS-15) at the U.S. Arms Control and Disarmament Agency, as a Congressional staffer on arms control and defense issues, and was a Senior Defense Analyst at The Harris Group and the National Institute for Public Policy. He has taught at the Air War College since 1993. As a faculty member he has taught Air War College core courses of instruction and elective courses such as International Rivals, Homeland Security Issues, International Flashpoints, Counterproliferation Issues, 21st Century Warfare Issues, and CBW Issues for the USAF. He has taught at six other colleges and universities, and has a Ph.D. in Political Science from Columbia University.

Robert J. Ursano, M.D., Col, USAF, MC, FS (Ret.), Professor of Psychiatry and Director, Center for the Study of Traumatic Stress, Uniformed Services University of the Health Sciences Bethesda, MD. Educated at the University of Notre Dame and Yale University School of Medicine, Dr. Ursano did his psychiatric training at Wilford Hall USAF Medical Center and Yale University. He is a retired Colonel in the United

States Air Force. He graduated from the Washington Psychoanalytic Institute and is on the teaching faculty of the Institute. In addition to serving on many advisory mental health committees, he is listed in Who's Who in America and Who's Who in Medicine and Health Care. He was the first Chairman of the American Psychiatric Association's Committee on Psychiatric Dimensions of Disaster. He has been the recipient of many prestigious awards and was an invited participant to the White House Mental Health conference in 1999. He has received the Department of Defense Humanitarian Service Award and the highest award of the International Society for Traumatic Stress Studies, the Lifetime Achievement Award, for outstanding and fundamental contributions to understanding traumatic stress. He also serves on mental health advisory boards of the University of Oklahoma, University of Oslo and Hadassah University dealing with terrorism and bioterrorism.

He has published over 200 articles in the areas of Post-Traumatic Stress Disorder and the psychological effects of terrorism, bioterrorism, traumatic events and disasters and combat. He and his team have completed studies on numerous disasters, disaster rescue workers, motor vehicle accident victims, family violence and Viet Nam, Desert Storm and Gulf War veterans. He was a national consultant for planning clinical care responses and research programs following the September 11th terrorist attacks and a member of the National Academy of Sciences, Institute of Medicine Committee on Psychological Consequences of Terrorism.

The Honorable R. James Woolsey, joined Booz Allen Hamilton in July, 2002, as a Vice President and officer in the firm's Global Assurance practice located in McLean, Virginia. Previously Mr. Woolsey was a partner at the law firm of Shea & Gardner in Washington, D.C., where he practiced for twenty-two years, on four occasions, beginning in1973; his practice was in the fields of civil litigation and alternative dispute resolution. During the twelve years he has served in the U.S. Government, Mr. Woolsey held Presidential appointments in two Democratic and two Republican administrations. He was Director of Central Intelligence in 1993-95. He also served as: Ambassador to the Negotiation on Conventional Armed Forces in Europe (CFE), Vienna, 1989-1991; Under Secretary of the Navy, 1977-1979; and General Counsel to the U.S. Senate Committee on Armed Services, 1970-73. He was appointed by the President as Delegate at Large to the U.S.-Soviet Strategic Arms Reduction Talks (START) and Nuclear and Space Arms Talks (NST), and served in that capacity on a part-time basis in Geneva, 1983-1986. As an officer in the U.S. Army he was an adviser on the U.S. Delegation to the Strategic Arms Limitation Talks (SALT I), Helsinki and Vienna, 1969-1970. Mr. Woolsey is currently: the Chairman of the Board of Freedom House, the Chairman of the Advisory Boards of the Clean Fuels Foundation and the New Uses Council, and a Trustee of the Center for Strategic & International Studies. Mr. Woolsey is presently a principal in the Homeland Security Fund of Paladin Capital Group and a member of the Board of Directors of four privately held companies, generally in fields related to infrastructure protection and resilience. Mr. Woolsey is a frequent contributor of articles to major publications, and from time to time gives public speeches and media interviews, on the subjects of foreign affairs, defense, energy, critical infrastructure protection and resilience, and intelligence.

257

266